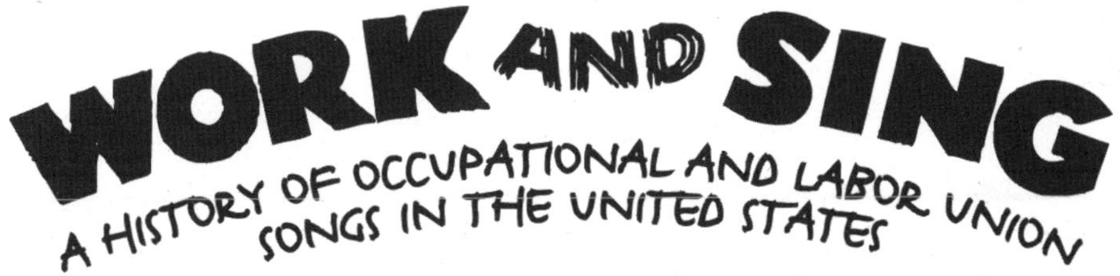

By RONALD D. COHEN

First Printing 2010

ISBN 987-0-974412-48-1

LCCN: 2009928855

Design by: Design Action, Oakland CA 94609
Copyeditor: Deborah Heinzmann

To order additional copies of this book please contact:

Carquinez Press
PO Box 571
Crockett, CA 94525
www.carquinezpress.com

Dedicated to

Archie

My Friend and Inspiration

(June 29, 1917 - March 22, 2009)

Table of Contents

Introduction

Labor songs have long pervaded workers' culture in the United States, beginning in the colonial period and running into the twenty-first century. Occupational songs—that is, songs about work and work experiences, often written and originally performed by those doing the work—date from the eighteenth century, proliferated through the nineteenth century and into the early decades of the twentieth century, only to wane by the 1940s. Labor unions published songbooks, labor schools encouraged singing, and radical organizations used songs about unions in political organizing, while scholars collected and published numerous books about work songs old and new.

Part of my focus is heavily on the collectors and their collections, but I avoid any critical analysis of their methods, biases, and selections. For such an approach, please consult D. K. Wilgus's exhaustive *Anglo-American Folksong Scholarship Since 1898*. Instead, I document the publication and collecting of occupational and labor union songs, and attempt to understand their use by workers and their supporters. As Pete Seeger explains, "There's as many different kinds of folk music as there are folk. There's Irish lumberjack folksongs, there's French Canadian lumberjack folksongs, Spanish American, Hispanic American cowboy songs, western songs, and Slovakian steelworkers songs." His emphasis on work songs is not incidental to his understanding of the complex history of folk music. Moreover, there were many intersections between the written word and labor organizing/workers' culture and society, although to what extent is difficult to document. Much of the recent literature (including my own) on the history of folk music in the twentieth century has focused on the post-World War II period, but I will demonstrate that there was a great deal of interest in collecting and publishing vernacular songs beginning early in the twentieth century. This is where the story should commence.[1]

Part of my interest is in narrating a history of a singing labor movement, drawing upon the publications of a variety of organizations, including unions, labor schools, radical organizations, university and commercial presses, and others. The structure is roughly chronological, for many nineteenth century songs were not published in their time, but lived on through an oral tradition. Additionally, much of my focus relates to earlier songs that only achieved recognition years later, particularly in the 1920s and after. Moreover, it is not clear how many songs were actually sung at rallies and on picket lines, or while at work, and by how many; but the fact of their being recorded in print or sound indicates some sort of popularity, however brief or limited. Workers from certain regional and ethnic groups had more of a musical tradition than others—black and white southerners more than some northern whites, for example. Some labor unions, particularly those with left-wing political connections, such as the Industrial Workers of the World

(IWW), published songbooks and encouraged singing at rallies and on the picket line, while others, such as the Teamsters, apparently had little or no unique musical heritage. In 1920 the sheet music for "A Little Child's Heart" listed numerous unions on the covers, including the American Federation of Musicians, Georgia State Federation of Labor, Chicago Federation of Labor, Glass Bottle Blowers Association, United Mine Workers of America District No. 12, Metal Trades Dept. of the A.F. of L. in Wilkes Barre and Vicinity, and dozens of others. This was indeed an unusual item, and it referred not to workers issues, but to a grieving child as the father was sentenced to prison. Most unions never published a songbook, but many, including labor colleges, did.[2]

Labor songs generally related to blue-collar occupations, including those of white, black, Asian, and Hispanic workers. Socialist and Communist political organizations used songs to promote labor consciousness and radical messages decrying capitalism. Not all workers' songs had a political message, and not all political songs championed workers and unions, but there was often some overlapping. Although similar conditions existed in Canada, Great Britain, Germany, and other industrializing countries, my interest is the United States. I draw mostly from printed sources, although I use recordings of labor songs, which proliferated after the Depression. And while I will be including songs of miners, railroaders, lumbermen, and other conventionally recognized occupational groups, I am also dealing with cowboys, sailors, and others sometimes left out of labor songs discussions, including hoboes. I have included as many foreign-language sources as possible, although there are certainly more to be discovered. Recent decades have been more difficult to capture and summarize, with much less documentation to rely upon, but I have tried my best to be fair and inclusive. Much more research is certainly warranted.

I have incorporated almost no song lyrics, since I have chosen not to pursue copyright permissions. But all of the songs mentioned can be found in the various songbooks I have cited in the bibliography. I have borrowed my title and cover art from Elie Siegmeister's *Work and Sing*, published in 1944, while Jonathan Strauss has wonderfully adapted the illustration. My intent is not to have an exhaustive history of songs connected with work, some written and/or sung by workers, others of a more commercial nature, but only to offer an introductory essay, and hope that others will follow with considerably more detail and critical exploration.

I want to thank, in particular, Bob Riesman, who has been my most careful and critical reader, as well as Clark "Bucky" Halker, Archie Green, Rob Weir, Gail Malmgreen, Marianne Robinson, Dan Leab, David Dunaway, Ted Gioia, Antonino D'Ambrosio, David Hajdu, and so many others for their assistance and encouragement. Archie has been my mentor, model, and staunch supporter, and no matter how much we might disagree on the details, this has never gotten in the way of his warm friendship. This book is dedicated to Archie! And Archie led me to John Robinson and Carquinez Press, so I am even more in his debt. Thanks John for a wonderful book! And thanks to Nancy, my longtime companion, who is always ready to listen to my folk music stories, no matter how redundant.

Ronald D. Cohen

April 2009

(Endnotes)

1 "Interview: Pete Seeger, San Francisco, 1989, with William R. Ferris and Michael K. Honey," *Southern Cultures*, vol. 13, no. 3 (Fall 2007), 12; D. K. Wilgus, *Anglo-American Folksong Scholarship Since 1898* (New Brunswick: Rutgers University Press, 1959). In my approach I have been partially guided by the scope of Ted Gioia's *Work Songs* (Durham: Duke University Press, 2006).

2 "*A Little Child's Heart*" (Wilkes Barre, PA: Billy Jones, 1920).

MECHANICS SONG.

Ye merry Mechanics' come join in my song,
And let the brisk chorus go bounding along,
Though some may be poor, and some rich there may be,
Yet all are contented and happy and free.

Ye Tailors ; of ancient and noble renown,
Who clothe all the people in country and town
Remember that Adam your father and head,
The Lord of the world was a tailor by trade.

Ye Masons ; who work in the stone mortar and brick
And lay the foundation deep solid and thick,
Though hard be your labour yet lasting your fame
Both Egypt and China your wonders proclaim,

Ye Smiths ; who forge tools for all trades here below,
You have nothing to fear while you smith and you blow,
All things you may conquer, so happy your lot,
If you're careful to strike while your iron is hot.

Ye Shoemakers ; noble from ages long past,
Have defended your rights with your awl to the last,
And Coblers, all merry, not only stop holes,
But work night and day for the good of our souls.

Ye Cabinet makers ; brave workers in wood,
As you work for the ladies your work must be good,
And Joiners, and Carpenters, far off and near,
Stick close to your trades and you have nothing to fear.

Ye Hatters ; who oft with hands not very fair,
Fix hats on a block for a blockhead to wear,
Though charity covers a sin now and then,
You cover the heads and the sins of all men

Ye Coach makers, must not by tax be controlled,
But ship off your coaches and fetch us home gold,
The roll of your coach made copernicus reel,
And fancy the world to turn round like a wheel.

And Carvers, and Spiners, and Weavers attend,
And take the advice of poor Richard your friend,
Stick close to your looms, your wheel and your card,
And you never need fear of the times being hard.

Ye Printers ; who give us our learning and news,
And impartially print, for Turks, Christians and Jews,
Let your favorite toasts ever sound in the streets,
The freedom of speech and a volume in sheets.

Ye Coopers; who rattle with driver and adze
And lecture each day upon hoops and on heads,
The famous old ballad of love in a tub,
You may sing to the tune of your rub a dub dub.

Ye Ship builders, Rigers and makers of Sails,
Already the new constitution prevails,
And soon you shall see o'er the proud swelling tide
The ships of columbia triumphantly ride.

Each Tradesman turn out with his tools in his hand,
To cherish the arts and keep peace through the land,
Each Apprentice and Journeyman join in my song,
And let the brisk chorus go bounding along.

Printed and sold at No. 42 North Main street (nearly opposite the museum.) where are kept for sale a great variety of popularsongs and ballads, by the hundred, dozen, or single.

"Mechanics Song", Broadside, *ca*, 1820

chapter one

The Early Decades

BACKGROUND

Before the late eighteenth century, skilled craftsmen, clustered mostly in the urban centers of New York, Boston, Philadelphia, Baltimore, Providence, and Charleston, often developed group solidarity that could be expressed through songs. They expressed their feelings about onerous work, oppression, poverty, and opposition to tyranny, both foreign and domestic. The political turmoil during the Revolutionary War was a particularly fruitful musical time. "Either through the Sons of Liberty or their benevolent societies . . . the colonial workers announced their determination to 'fight up to their knees in blood' rather than be ruled by tyrants," Philip Foner wrote. "They paraded to public meetings in military formation, with liberty tree medals suspended from their necks, and at singing festivals they raised their voices in revolutionary songs." Following independence, artisan clubs continued to use songs to express their grievances and worker solidarity.[1]

"In Colonial times, workers parodied both the British and their bosses," Robert Weir summarized. "Journeymen used music to protest against master craftsmen before and after the American Revolution, and organized labor's song tradition developed in earnest when journeymen's organizations became full-fledged trade unions in the 1820s." Celebrating work was common, as in the "Mechanics Song" of the 1820s: "Ye merry Mechanics come join in my song / And let the brisk chorus go bounding along / though some may be poor and some rich there may be / Yet all are contented and happy and free." As workers' collective security, through union and political organizing, increased in the 1830s, so did the amount of songs. Female textile workers in Lowell, Massachusetts, sang "The Lowell Factory Girl," as well as "I Will Not Be a Slave" during their 1836 strike. Immigrant songwriters (heavily Irish and German) were prolific. "The Tarriers' Song" became quite popular, as did one by Mike Walsh, written in prison in 1845, which began "Arise! Degraded sons of toil! Too long you've foully bent the knee."[2]

Blacks, free and slave, also produced many songs (while minstrel shows parodied such musical efforts). It is impossible to overstate the richness and vitality of the African American musical tradition, and songs relating to work, slavery in particular, were an integral element of this legacy. There was, for example, "Escape From Slavery of Henry Box Brown" from around 1848. While much of the music later collected and published focused on spirituals, there also existed numerous secular types, expressing all aspects of life and work. "As a group, the most musical black folk of the antebellum period may well have been the men working on the waters and waterfronts of the United States—on the eastern seaboard, the Gulf Coast, the Mississippi River and its two big tributaries, the Missouri and the Ohio," Eileen Southern remarks. "Stevedores always sang as they worked. . . . Black watermen carried their special worksongs, along with other kinds of Negro folksongs, up and down the rivers." There were various kinds of rowing songs, while each plantation had its own varieties of worksongs. "The term 'corn song' was used throughout the South to refer to the songs sung at corn-shucking frolics," Southern continues. Dena Epstein has supplied a more detailed account of the songs African Americans sang about their labors. "After 1800, descriptions of work-songs became more numerous," she has related, "associated with a variety of different occupations ranging from field labor through domestic chores such as flailing rice, grinding hominy, spinning, and making baskets, to more industrial employments such as loading cargo, processing hemp or tobacco, and firing engines."[2] There were also antebellum street cries and field hollers, although few were noted or collected at the time. Following the Civil War, as the black population began to scatter throughout the country, there were also numerous railroad, levee, and cowboy songs.[3]

"Though it cannot be said that the employment of music to lighten and quicken work and increase its efficiency was peculiar to the slave life of America," Henry Edward Krehbiel argued in *Afro-American Folksongs* in 1914, "it is nevertheless worth noting that this use, like some of the idioms of the music itself, was a relic of the life of the negroes in their aboriginal home." Such a connection between Africa and the New World, and the various benefits of music on the plantations, would be explored by numerous scholars. Roger Abrahams, for one, has explained that the "songs collected in connection with the corn shucking bespeak the Afro-Americans' excitement in working, competing, eating, and dancing together. They also continually comment upon the world the slaves saw around them, poked fun at the actions and attitudes of certain planters and other powerful whites, and expressed their shared anger at the agony they found in being 'sold off to Georgia,' and other inequities." Serving various functions, slave songs continued after emancipation, as working and living conditions remained onerous. William Francis Allen, Charles Pickard Ware, and Lucy McKim Garrison published their groundbreaking *Slave Songs of the United States* in 1867. While virtually all of their songs seemingly had a religious message, the editors admitted that they had not collected secular songs. They quoted from one source who noted, "Some of the best pure negro songs I have ever heard were those that used to be sung by the black stevedores, or perhaps the crews themselves, of the West Indian vessels, loading and unloading at the wharves in Philadelphia and Baltimore."[4]

By mid-century, working-class songs were common, and they would soon proliferate. Songwriters became increasingly productive by the 1870s, when strikes, economic depressions, and political organizing became more vigorous, controversial, and widespread. While scholars of occupational and union songs have focused on the twentieth century, many of their examples derived from a previous time. Songs were distributed through newspapers, broadsides, and the occasional songbook. James and Emily Tallmadge published twenty-nine *Labor Songs Dedicated to the Knights of Labor* in Chicago by the 1880s. Their version of "Hold the Fort," entitled "Our Battle Song," soon spread to England and Australia, then back to the United States where "Hold the Fort" became a labor staple.

In 1938, the folklorist Herbert Halpert described occupational songs as "the songs that sailors, cowboys, miners, lumberjacks, plantation workers sing. In the days before radio, all workers sang for amusement just as any isolated group did. And they had no particular respect for what we now call folk song; they sang any song they knew, no matter what its source. But in their singing they sometimes used songs that sprang out of the conditions of their work and expressed their attitude towards those conditions." More recently, Ted Gioia has furthered our understanding in *Work Songs*. "The simpler purposes that work songs had embraced in the past—to make the hours of toil more tolerable; to express the deeply felt emotions of a worker; to amuse or inspire; to coordinate movements and activities; or to assert the inherent dignity of all labor, even the most grueling—were seen as no longer adequate, or perhaps even proper, roles for music" by the mid-nineteenth century, he wrote. "Under the old scheme of things, singing workers seemed to acquiesce in their own oppression. . . . The protest song—conceived as a critique of work rather than an accompaniment to it—would now emerge as the quintessential music of organized labor." The former style did not disappear completely, but the older songs were often subsumed within the broader protest approach. That is, there were songs that had been composed to accompany work, and those that referred to working experiences and conditions, perhaps from a critical/political perspective.[5]

Norm Cohen has divided preindustrial occupational songs into six categories: a) domestic work songs; b) agricultural and pastoral work songs; c) sea chanties; d) Afro-American (work gang) work songs; e) songs and chants of direction, where "a primary function of the singer is to direct or organize the actions of other workers"; f) street cries. While some of these types would gradually disappear with industrialization, by the twentieth century they would be replaced by a myriad of labor songs. In Cohen's *Long Steel Rail: The Railroad in American Folksong*, for example, he includes nine songs in the chapter "Working on the Railroad," with most from the later nineteenth century, such as the popular "I've Been Working on the Railroad" and "Jerry, Go Ile That Car."[6]

Labor songs and song-poems continued to be published during the waning years of the nineteenth century, although we do not know how many were sung or how often. But whether popular or not among the working classes, from grassroots or commercial origins, they expressed critical sentiments towards labor and political circumstances that would soon spread among workers, as well as music publishers, collectors, and scholars.

COWBOY SONGS

"Work without music is too modern, too grinding; it was not the life for the Pennsylvania mountaineer whose soul overflowed with melody, 'the joy of living,'" Henry Shoemaker wrote in 1919 in the introduction to his *North Pennsylvania Minstrelsy*. Shoemaker felt that the old songs were dying out, for various reasons. "The coal mines of Kentucky and Tennessee will last longer than the lumber industry of Pennsylvania, which is about ended, though in reality lumbering fostered to a certain extent romantic spirits," he believed, although his interests transcended occupational songs. "Old-time ballad or song singers of the Pennsylvania mountains are now few and far between." He included such work songs as "Canal Boat Song," "Down in a Coal Mine," "The Jam at Gerry's Rock," "The Logger's Boast," and "Lumbermen's Drinking Song." Shoemaker's bent was nostalgia, not class warfare. And, despite his longing for an increasingly lost musical world, he would be joined and followed by numerous collectors, who never seemed to exhaust the number of musicians and songsters who had a wealth of songs, old and new.[7]

A few years before Shoemaker, the budding folklorist John Lomax had scoured the West for cowboy songs. "Out in the wild, far-away place of the big and still unpeopled west,—in the cañons along the Rocky Mountains, among the mining camps of Nevada and Montana, and on the remote cattle ranches of Texas, New Mexico, and Arizona,—yet survives the Anglo-Saxon ballad spirit that was active in secluded districts of England and Scotland even after the coming of Tennyson and Browning," John Lomax wrote in *Cowboy Songs and Other Frontier Ballads* in 1910. He had grown up in Texas, but in 1906, when almost forty, he arrived at Harvard College for some advanced work. Studying with ballad scholars Lyman Kittredge and Barrett Wendell, he had absorbed their belief in the literary substance of antique English and Scottish ballads. But they accepted Lomax's argument that cowboy songs contained "the Anglo-Saxon ballad spirit," if not their substance. For Wendell, in the book's introduction, "To compare the songs collected by Professor Lomax with the immortalities of olden time is doubtless like comparing the literature of America with that of all Europe together. . . . None the less, they seem to me, and to many who have had a glimpse of them, sufficiently powerful, and near enough beauty, to give us some such wholesome and enduring pleasure as comes from work of this kind proved and acknowledged to be masterly."[8]

Lomax published a revised and enlarged edition of *Cowboy Songs and Other Frontier Ballads* with his son Alan in 1938, plus *Songs of the Cattle Trail and Cow Camp*, composed mostly of published song-poems, in 1920. John Lomax's hit and miss approach to collecting songs resulted in a mixed bag of both "traditional" and published examples, drawn from numerous sources. Most he gleaned from letters and scrapbooks, and few from his personal fieldwork, in contrast to his later work in the South. He has also been accused of publishing composite versions. "The ultimate value of Cowboy Songs is measured not in scholarly abstractions," Lomax biographer Nolan Porterfield has argued, "but in what it gave us all, in those lovely, sad, and funny bits of tune and line now embedded in our lives: 'Whoopee Ti Yi Yo, Git Along, Little Dogies,' 'The Old Chisholm Trail,' 'Jesse James,' 'Sweet Betsy from Pike,' and of course, 'Home on the Range,' among dozens of other American favorites which Lomax saved from doom or otherwise helped preserve and popularize."[9]

John Lomax, however, did not pioneer collecting and publishing cowboy songs. Stanley Clark published a few in his 1897 pamphlet *Life and Adventures of the American Cow-Boy.* Brief articles began appearing in the *Journal of American Folklore* in 1901, such as G. F. Will's "Songs of the Western Cowboy" in 1909, and short pieces came out in popular magazines, such as "Cowboy Songs and Dance" in a 1903 issue of *Pearson's Magazine*, and "Songs of the Old Cattle Trails" in *Out West* in 1908. Of more significance was N. Howard "Jack" Thorp's self-published *Songs of the Cowboys* in 1908. A working cowboy, who both wrote his own songs and collected from others, Thorp included "Old Paint," "The Cowboy's Lament (Streets of Laredo)," "The Old Chisholm Trail," and others that would become western standards. "The hundred songs that make up this book are typical and genuine cowboy songs; the river and hobo and outlaw songs that are also a part of the cowboy's repertory having been omitted," Alice Corbin Henderson explains in the book's introduction. "The fact that most of these songs are of known authorship, or that some of them appeared originally in print, in no way lessens their genuine folk-quality." As for the songs' contents, Henderson remarks that they are "naïve records of the hard and free life on the range." Were they, however, directly connected to the cowboy' work experiences? Basically yes, according to historian Douglas B. Green:

> Popular mythology has cowboys crooning soft lullabies and yodels to the cattle on the open range to pacify jittery longhorns, singing old familiar songs and hymns from back home, or creating new songs or new verses to existing songs in the long dark hours of the night. Although this image has long been highly romanticized, the association of music and the cowboy is not purely fictional. Anywhere working men have been isolated for periods of time in particular circumstances, a tradition of song by or about those men and their work develops. Sailors, loggers, railroad workers, boatmen, miners, and others all have musical traditions.[10]

Cowboy songs dealt somewhat with work conditions, but mostly were more general, even romantic. Still, they often captured various aspects of this occupation, which reached its high point in the later decades of the nineteenth century. The singing cowboy would become a staple of movies and recordings, but this creative image was a far cry from the realities of the harsh life of working cowboys. After Thorp and Lomax, Charles Siringo published *The Song Companion of a Lone Star Cowboy* in 1919, followed by Charles Finger's *Sailor Chanteys and Cowboy Songs* in 1923 (republished in 1927 as *Frontier Ballads*, leaving out the chanteys). A merchant seaman, Finger picked up songs around the world, of various kinds. For example, he heard "Stackerlee" on one of his trips, as well as "Jessie James." But he also learned songs in West Texas, among them "Cole Younger," "The Old Scout's Lament," "Roy Bean," and "The Dying Cowboy," a song he heard in Texas but which had also traveled to Australia, New Zealand, and elsewhere. Robert Winslow Gordon wrote about "Cowboy Songs" for the *New York Times Magazine* in January 1928: "The old time cowboy had a code of his own, a diction of his own, a common body of tradition and a common attitude toward life that made him distinctive."[11]

Although Finger does not make an explicit connection between his chanteys and cowboy songs and left-wing politics, there was an implicit link because his book was published as Little Blue Book No. 301 by Haldeman-Julius, a socialist publisher in Girard, Kansas. Indeed, some of the songs had an economic slant, such as "The State of Arkansaw [sic]" and "Root Hog or Die." Finger's predecessors, including John Lomax, were focused on the songs' lyrical language and seemingly romantic verses, harkening back to the lost days of the cowboy's culture, and not their possible political content/intent.

By the 1920s cowboy songs had become ubiquitous in published collections. Louise Pound, Professor of English at the University of Nebraska, featured "Western Ballads and Songs" in *American Ballads and Songs*, published in 1922, with "The Old Chisholm Trail" and "The Dying Cowboy." Five years later Carl Sandburg's influential *The American Songbag* necessarily included a section on "The Great Open Spaces," with such titles as "The Lone Star Trail," "The Tenderfoot," and "Poor Lonesome Cowboy."[12]

Margaret Larkin, despite her left-wing politics, was unable to find any mention of class conflict in the songs. Born in Las Vegas, New Mexico, in 1899, and familiar with cowboy and Hispanic music, she attended the University of Kansas. She became a journalist and covered the striking textile workers in Gastonia, North Carolina in 1929, where she met Ella Mae Wiggins. Wiggins was murdered three weeks later. Larkin moved back to New York and published articles about Wiggins's life and songs, such as "Mill Mother's Lament," and performed her songs for left-wing audiences. She was also performing cowboy songs at the time, leading her to publish *Singing Cowboy: A Book of Western Songs* in 1931. While these songs were somewhat connected with work, they "fall short of being true working songs—they are not geared to the rhythm of the task as a chantey is, or a Negro steel driving song. Perhaps the cowboy's work is not mechanical enough for such intimate connection," she admitted. Moreover, she noted that the songs appeared to be apolitical: "There is a noticeable absence of the rich man—poor man theme so common to folk song, in the cowboy's balladry. . . . The songs record only occasional complaints about the food, and the credit system by which the cowboy drew money in advance against his wages." Still, some of the songs, such as "The Dreary Life," described the cowboy's work as "always hard, uncomfortable, and dangerous." Larkin's collection included both familiar and more obscure numbers.[13]

While cowboy songs were often about work, they have rarely appeared in collections or discussions of work songs. One exception would be Elie Siegmeister's *Work and Sing: A Collection of the Songs That Built America*, published in 1944, whose cover illustration features a farmer, cowboy, miner, fisherman, construction worker, and rural housewife. "The Lone Prairie" section includes "Good-By, Old Paint," "Night-Herding Song," and "The Trail to Mexico." Folklorist Archie Green has also encompassed cowboy songs within his lexicon of workers' culture. In his introduction to Glenn Ohrlin's *The Hell-Bound Train: A Cowboy Songbook*, Green cites a passage from Edward and Eleanor Aveling's *The Working-Class Movement in America* (1888), who quote from "Bronco John" about the hard life of cowboys: "The Avelings were conscious that to literate readers in the 1880s cowboys were not known as proletarians so much as flamboyant personalities. While Glenn in no way uses the word proletarian, he is careful to point out that cowboys continue to labor on ranches and at rodeos." And for Green, "Work, a centripetal force, bonds individuals into folk-like societies, and work songs, broadly defined, encode the behavior of members of such societies. In his remarks on the one hundred songs and poems gathered in this anthology Ohrlin tells much of his life story in terms of work."[14]

Jim Bob Tinsley, a working cowboy, western singer in the 1940s, and author, began his collection *He Was Singin' This Song* with a section on "Work Songs," followed by "On the Trail," "Tragedy," and ending with "The Serious Side." Again, these were not protest songs, but more about life on the range and in the cow towns. Austin and Alta Fife's comprehensive collection *Cowboy and Western Songs* also has a section on "Westerners at Work," which includes "The Strawberry Roan" and "Git Along Little Dogies." They summarize their rather romantic approach: "The best of the cowboy songs came into being after 1870 and before 1930. Their real substance consists of the candid and dramatic way in which they reveal the human condition in those decades of frontier life when men lived, labored, loved, and died, where laws, conventions, and tradition were lacking or ineffectual." But long before the Fifes published their thoughts in 1969, cowboy/western songs had entered popular culture through recordings and movies, particularly those starring Gene Autry and Roy Rogers.[15]

The performer John I. White, along with George Shackley, had published the first commercial song folio, *The Lonesome Cowboy: Songs of the Plains and Hills*, in 1929, and other folios soon followed. Some decades later, White expanded on his thoughts and collections in the fascinating *Git Along, Little Dogies: Songs and Songmakers of the American West*. Here he focused on the composers and collectors, for example D. J. K. "Kid" O'Malley, who wrote "After the Roundup." "His life was probably little different from that of thousands of other rugged men who grew up on the frontier and lived through Montana's memorable open range era of the 1880s and 1890s," White explains. "And, like a few other genuine working cow-punchers such as Andy Adams and E. C. 'Teddy Blue' Abbott, he left behind some choice word-pictures of a time long gone."[16]

While a large percentage of cowboys were of Mexican or African ancestry following the Civil War, there are few published indications of their musical influences. The Lomaxes published *14 Traditional Spanish Songs From Texas* in 1942. The folio included "La Corrida De Kansas," about a cowboy killed by a bull, although the remainder of the songs did not deal with cowboy life. Black cowboys were certainly active, but their output or influence is scarcely known. The African American Charley Willis had learned "Goodbye, Old Paint" on a cattle drive in 1871; a few years later he taught it to the young Jess Morris, whose rendition was later recorded by John Lomax.[17]

The cowboys' prolific musical output, dating from the late 1800s, would enter popular culture, where it would remain for decades. But this was not instantaneous. Bill Malone has pointed out that "this romantic American hero did not come into his own in American music until the 1930s. During that Depression decade, when Americans sought escapist relief from economic anxieties and reassurance that heroes still survived, songs about cowboys began to appear in virtually every realm of American music." Most of these cowboy songs were new compositions, by Jimmie Rodgers and so many others. There was no longer an explicit occupational connection.[18]

SAILOR SONGS

Charles Finger connected "Sailor Chanties" with "Cowboy Songs" in his small 1923 booklet. The title mentioned "Sailor Chanties" in order to differentiate them from logging camp "shanties," where the "shanty" referred to the primitive housing conditions, and a "shantyboy" was another name for a lumberjack. Sea shanties (or chanteys) were shipboard working songs, most dating from the mid-nineteenth century, roughly 1820-1860. There were various types, including long-haul shanties, capstan shanties, and pumping shanties, which accompanied various working conditions, and forecastle (fo'c's'le) songs, those sung for pleasure during the sailors' leisure time. "A sailor chantie [sic], you must know, is not merely sung with an idea of passing the time pleasantly. It is a help, exactly as the brass band is a help to marching soldiers. A few men aloft find that united effort is more easily possible when time is marked by one of their number singing," Finger explained. He also believed the shanties lacked a bitter tone: "The reference to officers is always taken in kind of Pickwickian sense, offense being neither intended nor taken. A crew at odds with its officers would simply refuse to sing and work would suffer in consequence." Finger included "Blow the Man Down," "Reuben Ranzo," "We're Homeward Bound," and even "Stackerlee" as a forecastle song. John Greenway's *American Folk Songs of Protest* included a tiny section entitled "Seamen." Greenway agrees that the "hauling and capstan shanties that comprise the greater part of the sailormen's songs had some complaint against labor administration and social conditions in them, but not impressively much."[19]

Joanna Colcord, the daughter of a sea captain, published her influential *Roll and Go: Songs of American Sailormen*, the first extensive volume of native shanties (as distinct from British publications, such as F. T. Bullen and W.F. Arnold, *Song of Sea Labor (Chanties)*, 1914), in 1924. According to Colcord's introduction, "The greater number of these shanties and forecastle songs have been verified, especially as to music, from the editor's personal recollection. She remembers the tunes as she used to hear them on shipboard, as they were actually sung by sailors in the American merchant marine of her day." Colcord also conducted her own research. She divided the book into four sections—"Short-Drag Shanties," "Halyard Shanties," "Windlass or Capstan Shanties," and "Forecastle Songs"—depending on the songs' functional use. She even included some from black seamen, who were rather common, such as the "negro shantyman [who] contributed" "Mobile Bay." She also inserted "Paddy Works on the Railway," a shanty dating "from the time of the great Irish emigration to America, and in the form in which it was most popular at sea, was undoubtedly taken over bodily from the music-halls," as well as the post-Civil War capstan shanty "Shenandoah" and the "outward-bound" shanty "Rio Grande."[20]

Colcord might have been the most influential early collector, but she was not alone. Frank Shay's *Iron Men and Wooden Ships* also appeared in 1924 and was republished in 1948 as *American Sea Songs and Shanties*, but it did not have Colcord's reach. Shay did, however, include a few water-related songs, along with cowboy tunes and much else, in his salty *My Pious Friends and Drunken Companions* (1927). Frederick Pease Harlow, with a checkered career as a seaman, tried to publish his memoirs, "The Making of a Sailor; Chanteying on the Akbar," in the 1920s, but his editor decided to issue only *The Making of a Sailor* in 1928. Harlow hoped the part on shanties would soon be issued, but this did not occur until the *American Neptune* magazine published the first installment in April 1948, with the entire volume finally appearing in 1962 as *Chanteying Aboard American Ships*. Harlow accompanies each song with his personal comments. "Moreover, his eyewitness accounts of the African-Caribbean roots of sea music are singular," the editor for the 2004 reissue explains. Among the latter songs are "Dixie's Isle," "Gwine to Git a Home Bime By," and "The Darky Sunday School."[21]

There were enough published sources by 1927 for Carl Sandburg to include a section entitled "Sailorman" in his influential *The American Songbag*, although all would not be considered work songs. He ignored the standard academic fascination with Anglo-Saxon ballads and focused instead on a variety of native folk songs from various sources, mostly published. Sandburg published "Whiskey Johnny," "Heave Away," and "The Hog-Eye Man," for a total of nine songs. John and Alan Lomax's *American Ballads and Folk Songs*, published seven years later, also featured a section on "Sailors and Sea Fights." Sea songs were by now considered part of the folksong pantheon. Similar to cowboy songs, they had historic origins, with little connection to 20th century occupations and work experiences. They had attained a romantic tinge, infused with nostalgia, and figured in popular music much more than in working-class culture. This perhaps accounts for the general disinterest of labor folklorists in this material.

Sea songs appeared in a variety of sources throughout the remainder of the 20th century. Fannie Hardy Eckstorm and Mary Winslow Smyth's *Minstrelsy of Maine: Folk-Songs and Ballads of the Woods and the Coast* (1927) included in the section "Songs of the Sea and Shore" such assorted categories as "Deep-Sea Songs," "Chanteys," "Pirate Songs," and "Coastwise Songs." The two independent, zealous collectors were interested in more than just shipboard songs. A bit later, in her 1939 publication, *Folk Songs of Old New England,* Eloise Hubbard Linscott also had a section on "Sea Chanteys and Fo-castle Songs." "The sailors' work was tedious, swabbing down decks, mending tackle, looking over gear, manning the pumps, heaving the lead, and always adjusting canvas to catch a favoring winds," she remarks. "Hard, long hours at monotonous tasks were interspersed with standing watch and brief leisure." With so much difficulty, "the labor of working the ship developed the song that lightened the seaman's task. The sea chantey was sung aboard a sailing vessel to bring speed and efficiency to the performance of work." But with the ships gone, "disappeared the work that made the chantey and the chanteyman necessary."[22]

Interest in sailor songs picked up following World War II. William Doerflinger issued *Shantymen and Shantyboys: Songs of the Sailor and Lumberman* in 1951. Doerflinger, an editor, folklorist, and one-time seaman, explains that he combined songs of the sea and woods because of his interest in the northeastern United States and eastern Canada: "Just as traditional cowboy songs express the spirit of the Western range, or as Negro and mountain ballads illuminate the regional life of the South, even so the folk songs most intimately associated with the Northeast and its adventurous yesterdays are those of the sailor and a woodsman, the shantyman and shantyboy." He was not the first to make such a connection, but he continued the practice. Stan Hugill issued two influential collections, *Shanties from the Seven Seas*, first published in 1961, and *Shanties and Sailors' Songs* from 1969, with the latter having more informational text and songs. Another former British seaman, his collections are most thorough, collected from both oral and written sources. He stressed the trans-Atlantic, indeed trans-world, musical connections. G. Malcolm Laws included a section on "Ballads of Sailors and the Sea" in *Native American Balladry*; he was not particularly interested in shanties, but rather songs about ships and sailing. Through these and other sources, shanties became part of the emerging folk revival by the 1950s.[23]

In contrast with the fascination folklorists and song collectors have had with sea shanties, there have been only a few studies of songs by river boatmen or lake sailors, although they were common. Carl Sandburg's *The American Songbag* included the section "Great Lakes and Erie Canal," with five songs: "The Erie Canal," "Bigerlow," "Red Iron Ore," "Raging Canawl," and "The E-R-I-E." John and Alan Lomax devoted part of *American Ballads and Folk Songs* to the "Erie Canal," with eight songs, but only a single selection for "The Great Lakes," the song "Red Iron Ore." "Canal-boat drivers (the towpath boys) sang for precisely the same reason that cowboys yodeled and sang when riding around the sleeping herds at night," the Lomaxes explained. "The canal boats also moved on at night. The singers made music in order to keep awake and secure entertainment out of their monotonous duties." William Hullfish's *The Canaller's Songbook*, with thirty-seven songs, appeared in 1984, which included the Tin Pan Alley tune "Low Bridge, Everybody Down," the well known "The Er-i-e," as well as selections from the rich Pearl Nye collection at the Library of Congress; Nye had been a captain on the Ohio-Erie Canal. Ivan Walton, Virginia Goodin, and Lee Murdock have also published books of Great Lakes songs.[24]

Blacks and whites sang songs on the docks and southern waterways. "Michael, Row the Boat Ashore" was a pre-Civil War black workers' rowing song. Norm Cohen has connected river songs with sea shanties:

> "Mobile Bay" probably moved from the cotton fields to the shantyman's domain via the intermediary, the riverboat. In the nineteenth century, the major American rivers (including the Mississippi, the Missouri, and the Ohio) were important transportation arteries, and their dock cities bustled with workers loading and unloading rafts and steamboats. "I'm Goin' Up the Rivuh" was a favorite song that the singer could use to extemporize on the hardships of the life of the deck hand. It was sung along the Mississippi by the African American workers.

As for the folklorist Ted Gioia, "The diverse workforce [in the seaport towns] of blacks, European immigrants, and visiting sailors created a rich musical environment. . . . Yet no port or waterway could match the great Mississippi in its abundance of music during the nineteenth century."[25]

Only Mary Wheeler, in *Steamboatin' Days: Folk Songs of the River Packet Era*, seems to have collected many of these songs, which had pretty much vanished by the twentieth century. "The words and melodies of the songs were taken down from the singing of old Negroes who in their youth worked on the boats," she mentions in the preface. She begins with "Work Songs," and includes "Songs of Boats," "Soundings," "Love Songs," and "Dance Songs." "Exhausting labor was required of the roustabout, and it is not surprising that there is a predominance of work songs in his music," she explains. "The hard-driving mate, interested only in getting the freight moved quickly, liked for his men to sing. He would select as a leader a Negro who could 'raise a song,' and then he saw to it that the tune was kept at a fairly rapid pace." Wheeler includes "Ida Red," "Stavin' Chain," and "Carryin' Sacks" among the work songs.[26]

HOBO SONGS AND THE IWW

Hobo songs also related to workers and their experiences, and they have occupied an intriguing niche in the history of labor and protest songs. Although there might appear to be similarities, there are distinct and important differences between a hobo, tramp, bum, and boomer (a laid-off railroad worker). A hobo is, simply, a migratory worker, while a bum is a vagrant or idler, and a tramp is somewhere between the two. That is, a hobo is normally looking for work, while a tramp does not seek out regular work, and might revert to begging; Howard Johnson's "Who Said I Was a Bum," recorded in the 1920s, explains "I may be a hobo, but who said I was a bum?" A hobo, therefore, could easily be classified as a worker, and there is a rather large body of hobo songs. The term seems to date from 1891. Unlike sea shanties and cowboy songs, hobo songs were current and mostly had a political message. They were often complaints about work conditions, bosses, or the economic system. They were not songs to help pace the work, but were about life on the road, and generally without nostalgia.

George Milburn nicely summarized their plight in *The Hobo's Hornbook*, published in 1930, at the onset of the Depression: "Hoboes are migratory workers, while tramps have sources of livelihood other than toil. The tramp ballad is seldom familiar to any but initiates. . . . . The hobo song, on the contrary, is often composed in the hope that it will have wide dissemination, especially when it is designed as a protest against the existing social order." Milburn divided the songs into eight sections, including "Parody and Burlesque," "Hobo Classics," "The Road," and "Wobbly Songs." There are a couple of other sources, such as *The Hobo In Song and Poetry*, and *Hobo: Songs, Poems, Ballads, Recitations, Etc.*, both published in Cincinnati, probably sometime in the 1920s, by small presses. The former contained "Frankie and Johnny Were Lovers," "The Hoboes' Convention," "Wabash Cannonball," and "The Big Rock Candy Mountain."[27]

Milburn described the songs' general substance: "The songs, for the most part, narrate the feats and adventures common to the vagrant life. Hoboes do not have much truck with beauty, but in spite of that sad fact there are occasional fine strains of imagery running through their songs." He begins with "A Convention Song," which lists various hobo meeting places and individual's nicknames, or "monikas," such as Boogie Sam, Wino Bill, and Wingey Red. The songs deal with life on the road, various personalities, job experiences, and other dimensions of their social networks and relationships. Among the titles are "The Boss Tramp," "The Great American Bum," "The Negro Bum," 'The Railroad Bum," "The Dying Hobo," and "The Bindle Stiff." One section is labeled "Wobbly Songs," which includes eleven examples drawn from a rich body of materials from the early decades of the century. Milburn received a complimentary review in the first issue of the *Bulletin of the Folk-Song Society of the Northeast:* "Hoboes and tramps, we may conclude, have the same folk-ways as mountaineers, negroes and cowboys. The veil of silence which the editor casts over the ribald songs in his collection may hide some secrets of hobo authorship, but we have proof of hobo processes of re-creation." Although hobo songs were of recent vintage, the "hobo or tramp is inclusive in his tastes, like all ballad singers."[28]

Fifty years after Milburn's compilation, Norm Cohen's encyclopedic *Long Steel Rail* included ten examples in the section "In a Boxcar around the World." "It is hard to say which of these songs better represented the sentiment of the homeless wanderers," Cohen explained. " 'The Poor Tramp' and 'Because He Was Only a Tramp' offer serious social commentary; 'Wild and Reckless Hobo' and 'Dying Hobo' romanticize somewhat the life of the hobo. The much more recent 'Railroad Boomer' [1929] is a more self-conscious piece with a moral." He includes "The Wabash Cannonball," published in 1904, which also appeared in Milburn. Initially a hobo song, it later lost this meaning when it became popular with Roy Acuff's hit version in 1938.[29]

Work and Sing

The Industrial Workers of the World (IWW), nicknamed the Wobblies, was organized in Chicago in 1905 by a diverse group of activists, including socialists such as Eugene V. Debs and Daniel De Leon, delegates from the Western Federation of Miners, labor organizer Mother Jones, and various other union members and supporters. They dreamed of the "one big union," dedicated to organizing workers, including hoboes, with the goal of transforming the country in the name of workers' rights, as well as racial and gender equality. The IWW promoted strikes and other forms of labor action, including free speech campaigns in communities where they were arrested for street-corner organizing, through their various publications and educational clubs. Songs, in particular, became a powerful organizational tool. The IWW reached its peak of influence by World War I, then began a decline that lasted through the century.

IWW members quickly began to compose poems and songs, the latter set to vaudeville tunes or gospel-hymn standards, with the focus on the words. They originally depended on Charles H. Kerr's *Socialist Songs with Music* (1901), but in 1909 the Spokane branch collected two dozen original songs into the first edition of the *Songs of the Industrial Workers of the World*. Expanded editions soon followed, with titles such as *Songs of the Workers: On the Road, in the Jungles, and in the Shops* and *Songs to Fan the Flames of Discontent*. It was soon nicknamed the "Little Red Songbook," because it had a red cover and was small enough to fit into a shirt pocket. There were a total of 37 editions through the twentieth century. Although there were many anonymous songs, a few prolific songwriters soon emerged, such as T-Bone Slim, Ralph Chaplin, author of "Solidarity Forever," and particularly Joe Hill. Born Joel Hagglund in 1879 in Sweden, he migrated to the U.S. in 1902, changed his name to Joseph Hillstrom, and finally to Joe Hill, while picking up odd jobs around the country. He apparently joined the IWW in 1910 and published one of his most famous songs, "The Preacher and the Slave," the next year. Others quickly followed, such as "Casey Jones, the Union Scab" in 1912. The songbook's fifth edition, in 1913, included nine more, including "Mr. Block" and "There Is Power in a Union." In 1914 he was arrested in Salt Lake City and charged with murder. With much controversy swirling around the evidence and trial, he was executed in 1915. The next year his song "Rebel Girl," perhaps about the labor organizer Elizabeth Gurley Flynn, appeared in the same edition as Ralph Chaplin's tribute song "Joe Hill"; this edition also included Chaplin's "Solidarity Forever," soon to become the anthem of the labor movement.[30]

While most IWW songs related to work experiences and dreams, a few concerned hobo culture, and were meant more for a popular audience. Harry "Haywire Mac" McClintock was born in Tennessee in 1882 and roamed the world for some years as a worker and musician. Along the way he composed "The Big Rock Candy Mountain," already a hit by 1905. His "Hallelujah," soon known as "Hallelujah! I'm a Bum," was probably written not long before it appeared in the first IWW songbook, although Milburn attributed an earlier version to "One-Finger Ellis." It was a hit at the IWW's fourth convention in 1908. Haywire Mac performed it on his San Francisco radio show in 1925, and recorded it three years later for the Victor Talking Machine Company. It had already appeared in Sandburg's *American Songbag.* T-Bone Slim also composed hobo songs, including "The Mysteries of a Hobo's Life," from the tune to "The Girl I Left Behind Me," published in the seventeenth edition of the songbook in the early 1920s. Goebel Reeves was another popular hobo bard. Following World War I he hit the road and soon became a professional musician, initially recording for the OKeh and Gennett record companies, while he frequently appeared on the radio. He specialized in hobo songs, such as "The Drifter," "The Tramp's Mother," "Cold and Hungry, "The Wanderer," and particularly "Hobo's Lullaby." The latter, first recorded by Reeves in 1934, became one of Woody Guthrie's favorites. Jimmie Rodgers, the first country music star, also recorded popular hobo songs, including "Hobo Bill's Last Ride" in 1929 and "Hobo's Meditation" in 1932.[31]

The IWW's belief in syndicalism—the workers' control of the factories rather than trust in the state, shop-floor organizing and emphasis on union organizing while avoiding electoral politics, that is, direct action and worker's autonomy—was at odds with the views of the socialist parties, and later the Communist Party, which emerged following World War I. Nonetheless, those affiliated with the latter championed Joe Hill's songs and memory by the later 1930s. The Manhattan Chorus, a Communist Party-affiliated aggregation in New York, recorded Hill's "Casey Jones" as well as Ralph Chaplin's "Solidarity Forever" for the Timely Recording Company in 1937. The previous year Earl Robinson had written the music for Alfred Hayes's poem "Joe Hill," praising the martyred songwriter, while both were affiliated with the left-wing Camp Unity. It was quickly published by Bob Miller and would later become a folk standard. Barrie Stavis and Frank Harmon (aka Fred Hellerman) edited *The Songs of Joe Hill* in 1955, published by the left-wing People's Artists. A year or two earlier, Labor Arts had issued the first album of IWW songs, *Songs of the Wobblies*, by Bill Friedland and Joe Glazer, who were labor organizers not affiliated with the Communist Party. A decade later Glazer recorded *Songs of Joe Hill* on Folkways Records.[32]

Woody Guthrie (1912-1967), well traveled in boxcars and on foot, would soon specialize in hobo songs. In 1935, Guthrie left Pampa, Texas for California, leaving a wife and children behind. His peripatetic life took him from coast to coast, but the Great Depression and hard traveling led him to compose some of America's finest musical homilies to poverty and life on the road. Such songs as "Dust Bowl Refugee," "Hard Travelin'," "I Ain't Got No Home," and "Dusty Old Dust" (renamed "So Long It's Been Good to Know Yuh") captured the plight of the dispossessed. And "East Texas Red" described the brutality of the railroad bulls who policed the boxcars.[33]

There are some distinctions between black and white contributions to hobo songs. Milburn included "The Negro Bum" in The *Hobo's Hornbook*, noting that "Among the hoboes, the Negro finds something approaching social equality." But few appeared in print until Paul Garon and Gene Tomko published *What's the Use of Walking If There's a Freight Train Going Your Way?: Black Hoboes & their Songs in 2006*. The authors focus on the recorded legacy of mostly blues musicians, with little in the written record. They explain that "African American hoboes specialized in blues: blues about unemployment, blues about the jungles, blues about the police, blues about the highway and the rails, and blues about a woman gone wrong, or just plain gone." They began with "Two Hoboes," collected by Lawrence Gellert in the South in the 1930s. They have one chapter specifically on "Hobo Blues," and another on "Railroad Blues and Hobo Jungles," with the others relating to various work experiences. One example of a hobo song was Alfoncy Harris's "No Good Guy Part II," recorded for Vocalion in 1934, and another, Tony Hollins's "Traveling Man Blues," released by OKeh in 1941. This is a fascinating collection, and captures a vivid slice of African American work experiences and life riding the rails. Hoboing had mostly faded away before the Depression, then accelerated through the hard times, only to recede again with the onset of World War II, except for black migratory workers, who continued to write songs about their experiences.[34]

SOCIALIST AND ANARCHIST SONGS

Socialism and socialist parties had existed in the United States since before the Civil War, and grew by the end of the century. The Socialist Labor Party, founded in 1877, was well established when the Socialist Party, under the leadership of Eugene Victor Debs, emerged in 1901. Both parties overlapped to some degree with the IWW, but with somewhat different political and economic agendas, and they each used songs to spread their messages, particularly in promoting labor unions. Socialist and related labor songs were not new when Charles H. Kerr published the pamphlet *Socialist Songs* in 1899, reissued two years later as *Socialist Songs With Music*. Brisk sales resulted in a second edition within another year. "The first edition of this book was criticized in some quarters as being rather too heavy and sober," Kerr now explained, "and an effort has been made to remedy this defect by the addition of a few lighter songs. The compiler has tried, however, to exclude trashy music and songs without literary merit—his own excepted." Rather than borrowing Knights of Labor songs, Kerr depended heavily on a British publication, Edward Carpenter's *Chants of Labor,* with other songs from a variety of sources. Labor-related songs included Kerr's "Your Work, My Work," William Morris's "The March of the Workers" (to the tune of "John Brown's Body"), and Rose Alice Cleveland's "Hymn of the Toilers."[35]

Harvey Moyer, a socialist author, issued *Songs Of Socialism* in 1905, which had reached its sixth edition by 1910. Moyer was the author of many of the songs, and, using tunes from a variety of sources, he divided the songs into eleven categories, including "National Airs," "Popular Airs," "Humorous Songs," "Marching Songs," and "Christian Socialist Songs." Of course, many had little, if any, relationship to manual labor. Moyer also issued a sampler, *Socialist Song Leaflet From Songs Of Socialism,* with about a dozen selections. These were also not songs for the picket line, or even specifically labor-related, but, as one person noted, were "needed to enliven Socialist meetings and Socialist homes." About the same time, the Young People's Socialist League, which had been formed in Chicago in 1907 and established as the Socialist Party's official youth wing in 1913, issued the pocket-sized *Socialist Songs For Young and Old*. It included mostly political songs, but also "The Jubilee of Labor" (to the tune of "Marching Through Georgia"), with stirring words. The Socialist Party of Rochester, New York issued its own songbook, *Some Songs of Socialism,* in 1912. While borrowing songs from Moyer's collection, there were others from a variety of sources. "As to our own songs they are, for the most part, written to well-known melodies which are easily obtainable," the foreword explained. "Let us all sing and keep singing. Songs have helped to win many battles." It is doubtful if any of these songs entered the workers' musical culture.[36]

Socialist gatherings would continue to sing appropriately ideological songs into the 1930s, when new songbooks appeared, but the members were not much musically active. While their songs might have rallied spirits at organizational meetings, they were hardly known, if at all, within labor circles or sung at union meetings. But labor activists needed their socialist (and later communist) allies. In 1938, more than a decade after Eugene Victor Debs's death, the Socialist Party of Wisconsin published "Spirit of Gene Debs," written by Frank Zeidler, the last Socialist mayor of Milwaukee (Debs had been the Socialist Party's longtime candidate for President).

Various ethnic groups also weighed in with their own labor songs. "Music was of particular importance for German anarchists in New York," Tom Goyens explains. "German working-class culture was steeped in the creation and enjoyment of music, and music played an important role in the early labor movement in Germany. In America too, socialists and anarchists of many ethnicities organized musical groups that enlivened gatherings and festivals while strengthening group identity and cohesion." Anarchist singing societies proliferated, performing a variety of songs and music styles, particularly in the last decades of the nineteenth century. "The most popular songs came from the large arsenal of proletarian ballads, revolutionary songs, hymns to workers' pride and struggle, drinking songs, and traditional German folk songs. Titles such as 'Die rote Fahne' (The red flag), 'Das Lied von der Kommune' (The song of the commune), 'Hoch die Anarchie!' (Long live anarchy!), or Johann Most's 'Arbeitermanner' (Workingmen) were repeatedly performed at all radical gatherings," Goyens continues. "The Marseillaise" and "The Internationale," written by Eugene Pottier in 1874, with music by Pierre DeGeyter in 1888, were also most common.[37]

The historian Bruce Nelson argues that music "was important to Chicago's socialists and anarchists" in the late nineteenth century. Quartets, brass bands, and orchestras entertained at numerous functions. "Socialist festivals featured the performance of singing societies (Gesangvereine in German)," he continues, "whose members came from within the movement." Socialist festivals featured such songs as "The Song of the Flag," "The March of Liberty," "The Seventh of May Song," and "The Internationale." German songs predominated, but there were compositions by Danish, Norwegian, and songwriters from various Eastern European countries. "The cacophony of lyrics, sung in as many as six languages, must have been bizarre," Nelson concludes. "Yet it was the politics of the lyrics that distinguished those socialist singers from their bourgeois counterparts."[38]

Music was also common among the immigrant workers in northern Minnesota. A meeting in Duluth to support local miners on strike in 1907 featured a Finnish band playing "The Marseillaise." In 1922, the Communist-affiliated Workers' Party included its band and male choir during a summer outing. And in 1936, at a rally in Duluth sponsored by the (Communist) Finnish Workers Club, the United Front band performed. Perhaps not all of the music was directly worker related, but it certainly was a common feature at labor functions.[39]

Recently immigrated Jews from Eastern Europe, concentrated on the Lower East Side in New York, also used music to voice their feelings. The Yiddish song "Dem arbiters trer" (The Workers' Tears), for example, expressed their hardships. In 1923, Yankele Brisker's "Der Striker" was published by the J. Leiserowitz Publishing Company. Six years later, Meyer Posner's "Workmen's Circle Hymn," also in Yiddish, appeared; the Workmen's Circle was a Jewish labor fraternal order organized in 1900. International Song Publishers, based in Chicago, issued the song sheet "An Ancient Jewish Lullaby" in 1902. The publisher explained that: "All the great and memorable music of the world came from the common people, the workers singing at their tasks as they tilled the soil or gathered around the hearth when their labor was done. . . . The International Song Publishers are sending out to the world this new music of the awakened workers. . . . There are songs of triumph, songs of hope and encouragement, songs of sadness and sympathy," such as "The Advancing Proletaire," printed about the same time. In 1938, the Education Department of the Workmen's Circle issued Michael Gelbart's songbook *Let's Sing*, with the words in Yiddish.[40]

LUMBERJACKS AND SHANTYBOYS

Similar to cowboys, seamen, and even hoboes, men who worked in the north woods had their own musical vocabulary and culture, which continued into the twentieth century. "The loggers, researchers discovered, were tremendous songsters, as in their ability to remember and share the older music they had heard," Gioia explains. Scholars have been fascinated with this body of music, with numerous books in print, perhaps because, as Gioia points out, the "general tone of gaiety puts the lumber camp songs almost in a class by themselves of work-related music."[41]

Shantyboy, woodsman, or lumberman (later lumberjack) songs have fascinated many collectors. A shanty was a log structure where the loggers generally lived, fifty or more together by the end of the nineteenth century. It was the source of the term shantyboy (there was no connection to sailors' shanties). Logging began in the Eastern woodlands and moved west following the Civil War, particularly into Michigan, Wisconsin, and Minnesota. There was also logging in the South, but collectors have mostly focused on the northern woodsmen and their songs. This was difficult, dangerous, and challenging work, which created close, isolated, all-male communities with accompanying unique cultures.

Henry Shoemaker published one of the earliest collections in 1919, *North Pennsylvania Minstrelsy: As Sung in the Backwoods*

Settlements, Hunting Cabins and Lumber Camps in Northern Pennsylvania, 1840-1910. "Work without music is too modern, too grinding; it was not the life for the Pennsylvania mountaineer whose soul overflowed with melody, 'the joy of living,'" Shoemaker explained, in his romantic image. Among a hodge-podge of poems and songs, he included "The Logger's Boast" (originally from Maine), the ubiquitous "The Jam at Gerry's Rock," and "Lumbermen's Drinking Song."[42]

Roland Palmer Gray published *Songs and Ballads of the Maine Lumberjacks* in 1924, based on his collecting while teaching at the state university. "Their resemblance to the mediaeval English and Scottish popular ballads aroused my interest," he began, with the usual caveat for an academic collector at the time. Gray could date some of the shantyboy ballads to the 19th century, while others were of more recent vintage, and many could not be pinned down. Most of the book included a variety of non-lumberjack ballads, including "The Dying Hobo." "There are, without doubt, many more ballads still sung in the lumber camps or lingering in the memories of the aged woodsmen and seamen," he concluded. "Soon it will be too late to gather them." He included the common "The Jam at Gerry's Rock," as well as "The Logger's Boast," "The Jolly Lumbermen," and "Peter Ambelay."[43]

Logging songs and ballads were often from anonymous composers, but one prolific lumberjack and millhand, Lawrence "Larry" Gorman (1846-1917), became well known. Working in Maine, New Brunswick, and Prince Edward Island, he wrote mostly satires. He "often considered a song as a weapon, a brickbat," his biographer Edward Ives writes. "If he felt that a person had insulted him or 'made little of him,' he was only too likely to make a song." Ives concludes that "among the woodsmen, river-drivers, and sawmill hands of Maine and the Maritimes he was famous." Joe Scott, another Maine woodsman, was also quite productive; and he published his own songs.[44]

Three years after Gray, local collectors Fannie Hardy Eckstorm and Mary Winslow Smyth issued *Minstrelsy of Maine: Folk-Songs and Ballads of the Woods and Coast*, which included several of Gorman's songs. About half of their collection featured "Songs of the Woods," while the rest covered "Songs of the Sea and the Shore" (drawn from their own collecting as well as published sources). "'Making up songs' is a sport among those who work at hard manual labor," they believed. They organized the woods songs into rough chronological periods, including "The Shanty Boys" and "Driving Logs on Schoodic" from the mid-nineteenth century, and "The Jam on Gerry's Rock" and "The Cook and the Teamster" from late in the century. After 1900 many of the old songs had languished. "However musical they might be, Finns and Polackers could not sing in English," Eckstorm and Smyth explained, "and the victrola in camp supplied in part the place of the lusty chorus and the 'good song' by some individual. . . . The woods song is adapting itself to the printed page; and whatever their good points, few of these late productions will be passed down entirely by memory for any length of time." They included among the latter "The Hoboes of Maine" and "Drivers' Lunch."[45]

Franz Rickaby's collection of *Ballads and Songs of the Shanty-Boy* (1926) focused on the Upper Midwest, where he found a rich trove of original material. "The shanty-boy made no appreciable use of his songs while actually at work," Rickaby, an English professor, explained. "He apparently preferred quip and jest, or wordy-by-play of various sorts. . . . But back in the shanty, particularly on Saturday evenings, secure from the outer cold,—his supper stowed safely within him, the old iron stove throwing out its genial heat, and the mellow ministrations of tobacco well begun,—the shanty-boy became story-teller and singer." He noted authors for most of the selections, such as C. L. Clark's "Jack Haggerty's Flat River Girl," Fred Bainter's "Shanty-boy and the Pine," and George Will's "Shanty Teamster's Marseillaise." Unlike Gray, as well as Eckstorm and Smyth, Rickaby added music for most of his selections.[46]

Although Roland Palmer Gray feared that collectors would soon find it increasingly difficult to collect shantyboy songs, this did not turn out to be a problem in Michigan in the late 1930s. Alan Lomax, the Assistant in Charge of the Archive of American Folk-Song at the Library of Congress (1937-1942), heard a group of Michigan lumberjacks at the National Folk Festival in Washington in early 1938 (they had first appeared at the 1934 festival in St. Louis). After recording them for the Library of Congress, he organized a collecting trip later that year to Michigan. While visiting Beaver Island in Lake Michigan, Lomax reported to his boss, Harold Spivacke, on September 1 that he had been "able to obtain a great many ballads that originated on the Lakes and at least three quarters of them are about sailors and ships [and] were much sung by the sailors. But not one chantey!" And he continued, "Upper Michigan is full of old lumberjacks, much to my surprise, and I expect to get this next couple of weeks enough lumberjack songs so that we won't have to go begging to any of the local folk-lorists for material."[47]

Lomax was not disappointed. He wrote again to Spivacke on September 19: "I want a chance now that I have explored lumberjacks & lake sailors a bit to take a whack at the miners." In his official report on the trip, Lomax mentioned that the "Upper Peninsula of Michigan proved to be the most fertile source of material. After six weeks of recording a mass of lumberjack, Finnish and French folk-songs, I felt that there was material enough in the region for years of work." Lomax's productive trip later resulted in a Library of Congress recording, *Songs of the Michigan Lumberjacks* (AAFS L56), as well as a couple of Michigan songs in the "Lumberjack and Teamsters" section of the forthcoming collection with his father, *Our Singing Country: A Second Volume of American Ballads and Folk Songs* (1941).[48]

Lomax had received valuable assistance from Earl Beck, a professor at the Central Michigan College of Education in Mount Pleasant. After a decade of covering the state, Beck published *Songs of the Michigan Lumberjacks* in 1942. "From the time the shanty boys finished their talkless evening meal until nine o'clock, the hour for bed, they had to entertain themselves. Like the salt-water sailors of the old sailing vessels and the cowboys of the Western plains, they learned how to do just that and to do it well. In such an environment and under such circumstances the Paul Bunyan stories and the lumberjack songs were born. Fiddling and dancing as well as storytelling and singing served to amuse them," he explained. Guitars, mandolins, even dulcimers were popular. Beck divided the songs into various categories, beginning with "A-Lumbering Go," then "Shantyman's Life," "The Day's Work," "Men at Play," as well as "Death and the Shanty Boy," with the common "The Jam on Gerry's Rocks." Two years before Beck's inclusive collection, Emelyn Gardner and Geraldine Chickering issued *Ballads and Songs of Southern Michigan*. Among the book's nine sections, such as "Unhappy Love," "Happy Love," and "War," they included twenty-two songs dealing with "Occupations." While not all related to shantyboys, some did, such as "The Lumberman's Alphabet," "The Shantyman's Life," and "The Shanty Boys." Others, for example "David Ward," referred to accidental deaths and terrible working conditions: "Now there was the foreman, a very nice man / He was always at work contriving some plan / Our pockets he'd pick, and our clothes he would sell / And get drunk on the money at the Greenland Hotel."[49]

In 1951, William Doerflinger issued *Shantymen and Shantyboys*, which became an influential collection. "By way of explaining why both salt-water songs and ballads of the lumber woods are presented in the same volume," he began, "be it said at once that this double subject matter is but the natural consequence of the fact that the collection was made in a region long famous throughout the world both for its merchant shipping and for its no less outstanding logging operations." Moreover, he continued, "Preserved in these robust old songs is all the romance of the adventurous callings in which the old-time shellbacks and loggers—unique species now approaching extinction—won their rugged fame." The first half covered sea songs, followed by "The Shantyboys' Life" and other non-sea categories. Doerflinger had a national scope, with music and informative notes for each selection.[50]

In summing up the meaning and value of shantyboy songs, Robert Gordon, avid song collector and the first head of the Archive of American Folk-Song at the Library of Congress, remarked that, aside from bawdy tunes, the lumberjack's "other songs, those that told of his life in the woods, of his courage and of the troubles and accidents with which he met, are more characteristic, more specifically his own property. He did not, as did the cowboy, adopt as his the poems of well-known literary writers." Because of this, they "are lacking in any great literary value, but they are filled with humble, significant, human details." Although they were not technically folk songs, since most had known authors, nonetheless they "deserve inclusion and study in any complete survey of American folk-song." And so they have been since Gordon wrote this in 1927. In his 1960 opus *The Folk Songs of North America*, Alan Lomax included numerous lumberjack songs, along with helpful notes, in the section "Timber Tigers," such as "The Farmer and the Shanty Boy," "The Pinery Boy," "Bold Jack Donahue," and "The Frozen Logger"; the latter was written by James Stevens in 1928. They also became part of popular country music. Elmore Vincent, "The Northwest Shanty Boy," published a folio of *Lumber Jack Songs* in 1932. He included "The Jam on Gerry's Rock," as well as "Song of the Lumberjack," "Yodeling Lumberjack," and "Lonesome Lumberjack."[51]

Songs by and about workers, many sung on the job, others having become part of the country's popular culture, were well established by the eve of the Great Depression. While there was a vibrant legacy from mostly white workers, there was also a deep well of songs by and about black laborers.

(Endnotes)

1 Philip S. Foner, *American Labor Songs of the Nineteenth Century* (Urbana: University of Illinois Press, 1975), 4, 5.

2 Robert E, Weir, "Music and Labor," Robert E. Weir and James P. Hanlan, eds., *Historical Encyclopedia of American Labor* (Westport, Conn: Greenwood Press, 2004), 327; "Mechanics Song," ca. 1820s, broadside in author's possession; Foner, *American Labor Songs of the Nineteenth Century*, 79, and chaps. 2-4 for details of the pre-Civil War period.

3 Eileen Southern, *The Music of Black Americans: A History* (N.Y.: W. W. Norton and Co., 1971), 147-148, 179; Dena J. Epstein, *Sinful Tunes and Spirituals: Black Folk Music to the Civil War* (Urbana: University of Illinois Press, 1977), 161.

4 Henry Edward Krehbiel, *Afro-American Folksongs: A Study In Racial and National Music* (N.Y.: G. Shirmer, Inc., 1914), 46; Roger Abrahams, *Singing the Master:The Emergence of African-Ameican Culture in the Plantation Sout*h (N.Y.: Penguin Books, 1993), 85; William Francis Allen, Charles Pickard Ware, Lucy McKim Garrison, *Slave Songs of the United States* (N.Y.: Peter Smith, 1951 [originally published 1867]), vii.

5 Herbert Halpert, "American Folk Songs," *The American Music Lover*, March 1938, 415; Ted Gioia, *Work Songs* (Durham: Duke University Press, 2006), 229-230; Gioia covers England, Germany and other industrializing countries as well as the U.S. For the remainder of the century, see Foner, *American Labor Songs of the Nineteenth Century*, chaps. 5-13; Clark D. Halker, *For Democracy, Workers, and God: Labor Song-Poems and Labor Protest*, 1865-95 (Urbana: University of Illinois Press, 1991); Bucky Halker, "Solidarity Forever," *Chicago History*, vol. 35, o. 3 (Spring 2008), 30-45.

6 Norm Cohen, "Worksongs: A Demonstration Collection of Examples," Archie Green, ed., *Songs About Work: Essays in Occupational Culture for Richard A. Reuss* (Bloomington: Indiana University, Special Publications of the Folklore Institute No. 3, 1993), 335; Norm Cohen, *Long Steel Rail: The Railroad in American Folksong* (Urbana: University of Illinois Press, 1981), chap. 11.

7 Henry W. Shoemaker, *North Pennsylvania Minstrelsy: As Sung in the Backwood Settlements, Hunting Cabins and Lumber Camps in Northern Pennsylvania, 1840-1910* (Altoona: Altoona Tribune Co., 1919), 18, 20, 26.

8 John A. Lomax, *Cowboy Songs and Other Frontier Ballads* (New York: Sturgis & Walton Co., 1917), unnumbered but first page of "Collector's Note" and last page of "Introduction." See also, John A. Lomax and Alan Lomax, *Cowboy Songs and Other Frontier Ballads*_(N.Y.: Macmillan Co., 1938), for the revised and expanded edition. And for background information on Lomax, Nolan Porterfield, *Last Cavalier: The Life and Times of John A. Lomax*, 1867-1948 (Urbana: University of Illinois Press, 1996), chaps. 8-10.

9 Porterfield, *Last Cavalier*, 153. It has remained in print since 1910. Similar to most collectors at the time, Lomax published only bowdlerized texts.

10 N. Howard Thorp, S*ongs of the Cowboys* (Boston: Houghton Mifflin Co., 1921), xvii, xxiii; Douglas B. Green, *Singing in the Saddle: The History of the Singing Cowboy* (Nashville: The Country Music Foundation Press and Vanderbilt University Press, 2002), 13. On Thorp's life, see Guy Logsdon, *"The Whorehouse Bells Were Ringing" and Other Songs Cowboys Sing* (Urbana: University of Illinois Press, 1989), 296-299. See also the chapter "The Cowboy," Gioia, *Work Songs*, 169-181.

11 Charles Siringo, *The Song Campanion of a Lone Star Cowboy: Old Favorite Cow-Camp Songs* (Sante Fe, N.M.: Siringo, 1919); Charles J. Finger, *Sailor Chanties and Cowboy Songs* (Girard, Kansas: Haldeman-Julius Company, 1923); Robert Gordon, "Cowboy Songs," *The New York Times Magazine*, January 22, 1928, reprinted in Robert Winslow Gordon, *Folk-Songs of America* (Washington, D.C.: National Service Bureau, Publication No. 73-S, December 1938), 101; *Cowboy Songs, Ballads, and Cattle Calls*, Rounder Records Roun 1512, 1999.

12 Louise Pound, *American Ballads and Songs* (N.Y.: Charles Scribner's Sons, 1922); Carl Sandburg, *The American Songbag* (N.Y. : Harcourt, Brace, & Co., 1927).

13 Margaret Larkin, *Singing Cowboy: A Book of Western Songs* (N.Y.: Alfred A. Knopf, 1931), xi, 39. Larkin later married the left-wing Hollywood screenwriter Albert Maltz, and after his blacklisting they settled in Mexico. She died in 1967. There might be subtle complaints buried in some of the lyrics, but rather too restrained for most collectors.

14 Glenn Ohrlin, *The Hell-Bound Train: A Cowboy Songbook* (Urbana: University of Illinois Press, 1973), xiii-xiv. Eleanor Aveling was the daughter of Karl Marx. While Green includes cowboys among workers, there is no essay on cowboy songs in Green, ed., *Songs about Work.*

15 Jim Bob Tinsley, *He Was Singin' This Song: A Collection of Forty-eight Traditional Songs of the American Cowboy* (Orlando: University Presses of Florida, 1981); Austin E. and Alta S. Fife, eds., *Cowboy and Western Songs: A Comprehensive Anthology* (N.Y.: Bramhall House, 1982 [orig. ed. 1969]), xi; and, for the general story, Green, Singing in the Saddle.

16 John White and George Shakley, *The Lonesome Cowboy: Songs of the Plains and Hills* (N.Y.: George T. Worth, 1929); John I. White, *Git Along, Little Dogies: Songs and Songmakers of the American West* (Urbana: University of Illinois Press, 1975), 73.

17 *14 Traditional Spanish Songs From Texas*, Transcribed by Gustavo Duran: From recordings made in Texas, 1934-29 by John A., Ruby T. and Alan Lomax for the Archive of American Folk Song, in the Music Division of the Library of Congress (Washington, D.C.: Music Division, Pan American Union, 1942), 6. Willis's grandson, Artie Morris, would attempt to have a career as a black country singer in Nashville in 1955, but with no luck, although he finally issued a CD in 2001, *Good-bye Old Paint and Other Trail Favorites* (WAM Records).

18 Bill C. Malone, *Don't Get above Your Raisin': Country Music and the Southern Working Class* (Urbana: University of Illinois Press, 2002), 131.

19 http://en.wikipedia.org/w/index.php?title=Sea_shanty; Finger, *Sailor Chanties and Cowboy Songs,* 7, 9; John Greenway, *American Folk Songs of Protest* (Philadelphia: University of Pennsylvania Press, 1953), 233. See also the chapter "Sea and Shore," Gioia, Work Songs, 115-136.

20 Joanna C. Colcord, comp., *Roll and Go: Songs of American Sailormen* (Indianapolis: Bobbs-Merrill Co., 1924), 3-4 of Introduction, 57, 50. Some of the songs were later recorded by Bill Bonyun, *Roll and Go: The Shantyman's Day Aboard a Yankee Clipper*, Heirloom HL-504, 1962.

21 Frederick Pease Harlow, *Chanteying Aboard American Ships* (Mystic, CT: Mystic Seaport Museum, 2004 [original ed. 1962]), xvi.

22 Eloise Hubbard Linscott, *Folk Songs of Old New England* (N.Y.: The Macmillan Co., 1939), 123, 125; *American Sea Shanties and Songs*, Rounder Records Roun 1519, 2004.

23 William Main Doerflinger, *Shantymen and Shantyboys: Songs of the Sailor and Lumberman* (N.Y.: The Macmillan Co., 1951), vii. See also, Gale Huntington, *Songs the Whalemen Sang* (Barre, MA: Barre Publishing Company, 1964); William Cole, *The Sea Ships & Sailors: Poems, Songs and Shanties* (N.Y.: Viking, 1967).

24 John A. Lomax and Alan Lomax, *American Ballads and Folk Songs* (N.Y.: The Macmillan Co., 1934), 453; William Hullfish, *The Canalaler's Songbook* (York, PA: The American Canal and Transportation Center, 1984); Hullfish, *Grand Canal Ballads*, Folkways Records FTS 32318; Ivan Walton, *Windjammers: Songs of the Great Lakes Sailors* (Detroit: Wayne State University Press, 2002); Virginia Goodin, *Sounds of the Lake and the Forest: Michigan Folk Songs* (Ann Arbor: Ann Arbor Press, 1960); Lee Murdock, *Lake Rhymes: Folk Songs of the Great Lakes Region* (np: Depot Recording Publishers, 2004).

25 Norm Cohen, *Folk Music: A Regional Exploration* (Westport, CT: Greenwood Press, 2005), 101-102; Gioia, Work Songs, 129.

26 Mary Wheeler, *Steamboatin' Days: Folk Songs of the River Packet Era* (Baton Rouge: Louisiana State University Press, 1944), ix, 10. Wheeler published a smaller selection in *Roustabout Songs: A Collection of Ohio River Valley Songs* (N.Y.: Remick Music Corporation, 1939).

27 George Milburn, *The Hobo's Hornbook* (N.Y.: Ives Washburn, 1930), xi-xii; *The Hobo In Song and Poetry* (Cincinnati, OH: V. C. Anderson, nd).

28 Milburn, *The Hobo's Hornbook*, xv; "Reviews," *Bulletin of the Folk-Song Society of the Northeast,* Number 1 (1930), 11.

29 Cohen, *Long Steel Rail*, 346. He includes detailed notes and discography for each song.

30 See Franklin Rosemont, *Joe Hill: The IWW and the Making of a Revolutionary Workingclass Counterculture* (Chicago: Charles H. Kerr, 2003); Archie Green et al., *The Big Red Songbook* (Chicago: Charles H. Kerr Publishing Co., 2007), for all of the details; Joyce L. Kornbluh, *Rebel Voices: An I.W.W. Anthology* (Ann Arbor: University of Michigan Press, 1964). IWW songbooks have been published into the 21st century.

31 McClintock's recording of "Hallelujah! I'm a Bum," as well as two versions of "The Bum Song," can be heard on the album *Hallelujah! I'm A Bum* (Rounder Records 1009). Reeves's "Hobo's Lullaby" can be heard on Goebel Reeves, *Hobo's Lullaby,* Bear Family BCD 15680 AH. "Hallelujah! I'm a Bum" was also included on the soundtrack for Charlie Chaplin's *Modern Times* film in 1936.

32 The Manhattan Chorus's recordings can be found in *Songs For Political Action: Folkmusic, Topical Songs, And The American Left*, 1926-1953, Bear Family Records, BCD 15720 JL, 1996, disc one; Bill Friedland, "Labor Arts and the First Recorded IWW Album," in Green et al., *The Big Red Songbook*, 457-462, which has an excellent discography; Joe Glazer, *Songs of Joe Hill*, Folkways Records FA 2039, 1954.

33 For Woody's biography, Ed Cray, *Ramblin' Man: The Life and Times of Woody Guthrie* (N.Y.: W. W. Norton & Co., 2004). Woody's "Union Maid" was his first song to appear in an I.W. W. songbook, the 34th edition in 1973.

34 Milburn, *Hobo's Hornbook*, 249; Paul Garon and Gene Tomko, *What's the Use of Walking If There's a Freight Train Going Your Way?: Black Hoboes & their Songs*, Chicago: Charles H. Kerr Pub. Co., 2006, 8; Mat Haymes, *Railroadin' Some: Railoads in the Early Blues*, York, Euplaud: Music Mentor Books, 2006, Chap. 10.

35 Charles H. Kerr, *Socialist Songs With Music* (Chicago: Charles H. Kerr & Co., 1902), "Note to Second Edition," unpaged. Kerr had published a small edition, *Socialist Songs*, without music, in his Pocket Library of Socialism, No. 11, in 1899. Kerr had founded his publishing company in 1886, and specialized in socialist publishing. Socialism can simply be defined as the belief in the public ownership of the means of production, such as factories, and in extensive public services. Socialist parties are generally anti-business and pro-labor unions, that usually are involved more in political campaigns than labor strikes or agitation. See Allen Ruff, *"We Called Each Other Comrade": Charles H. Kerr & Company, Radical Publishers* (Urbana: University of Illinois Press, 1997).

36 Harvey P. Moyer, *Songs Of Socialism* (Chicago: The Co-Operative Printing Co., 1911); Moyer, *Socialist Song Leaflet From Songs Of Socialism* (Chicago: The Brotherhood Publishing Co., nd), back cover; *Socialist Songs For Young and Old* (N.Y.: Young People's Socialist League, nd), 11; *Some Songs of Socialism* (Rochester: Local Rochester, Socialist Party, 1912),"Foreward" [sic].

37 Tom Goyens, *Beer and Revolution: The German Anarchist Movement in New York City*, 1880-1914 (Urbana: University of Illinois Press, 2007), 168, 171.

38 Bruce C. Nelson, *Beyond the Martyrs: A Social History of Chicago's Anarchists, 1870-1900* (New Brunswick: Rutgers University Press, 1988), 129, 131; Bucky Halker, "Solidarity Forever," *Chicago History,* vol. 35, no. 3 (Spring 2008), 31-45.

39 Richard Hudelson and Carl Ross, *By the Ore Docks: A Working People's History of Duluth* (Minneapolis: University of Minnesota Press, 2006), 53, 93, 235.

40 *"An Ancient Jewish Lullaby"* and *"Child Laborers Spring Song"* (Chicago: International Song Publishers, 1920).

41 Gioia, *Work Songs,* 140, 141.

42 Henry W. Shoemaker, *North Pennsylvania Minstrelsy*, 18.

43 Roland Palmer Gray, *Songs and Ballads of the Maine Lumberjacks with Other Songs from Maine* (Cambridge: Harvard University Press, 1924), xii, xx.

44 Edward D. Ives, *Larry Gorman: the man who made the songs* (Bloomington, IN: Indiana University Press, 1964), 184, 185; Edward D. Ives., *Joe Scott: The Woodsman-Songmaker* (Urbana: University of Illinois Press, 1978). See also, Gioia, *Work Songs*, 145-149.

45 Fannie Hardy Eckstorm and Mary Winslow Smyth, *Minstrelsy of Maine: Folk-Songs and Ballads of the Woods and Coast* (Boston: Houghton Mifflin Co., 1927), 8.

46 Franz Rickaby, *Ballads and Songs of the Shanty-Boy* (Cambridge: Harvard University Press, 1926), xxii.

47 Alan Lomax to Harold Spivacke, September 1, 1938, The Alan Lomax Collection, Archive of Folk Culture, American Folklife Center, The Library of Congress.

48 Alan Lomax to Harold Spivacke, September 19, 1938, The Alan Lomax Collection, Archive of Folk Culture; Alan Lomax, "Archive of American Folk Song: A History, 1928-1939," (Library of Congress Project, Work Projects Administration, 1940), 66.

49 Earl Beck, *Songs of the Michigan Lumberjacks* (Ann Arbor: University of Michigan Press, 1941), 3; Emelyn Elizabeth Gardner and Geraldine Jencks Chickering, *Ballads and Songs of Southern Michigan* (Ann Arbor: University of Michigan Press, 1939), 284. Beck also published Lore of the Lumber *Camps* (Ann Arbor: University of Michigan Press, 1948); James P. Leary, "Woods Men, Shanty Boys , and Bawdy Songs in the American Upper Midwest," unpublished paper in author's possession.

50 Doerflinger, *Shantymen and Shantyboys*, vii.

51 Robert W. Gordon, "American Folk Songs: Shanty-Boy Lays," *The New York Times Magazine*, August 28, 1927, reprinted in Gordon, *Folk-Songs of America*, 56; Alan Lomax, *The Folk Songs of North America* (N.Y.: Doubleday & Company, 1960); *Elmore Vincent's Lumber Jack Songs* (Chicago: M. M. Cole Publishing Co., 1932).

Lawrence Gellert, *Negro Songs of Protest*
(N.Y.: American Music League, 1936)

chapter two

African American Songs

JOHN HENRY AND BLACK WORKERS

"The coming of the railroad into the mountains of Kentucky added a new incentive for the ballad maker," Jean Thomas, a collector and storyteller, explained in *Ballad Makin' in the Mountains of Kentucky*, published in 1939.

> Who has not heard of "John Henry," that legendary figure, the steel-drivin' man, who matched his skill with the sledge against the unbelievable power of the electric drill? Down in the foothills John Henry had been a burly Negro who could swing two sledges at a time, with such speed and ferocity that other workers stood aghast. But when the railroad pressed on and on until it reached Tug Fork, or the Big Sandy, John Henry changed his color. He became a giant mountain man, so powerful he "didn't know his own stren'th." . . . From such "work songs," though mountain singers do not call them by that name, they take a pattern. As soon as they hear of a wreck—and they are frequent as a result of "slides" and "washouts," defective rails, and so on, the disaster is fashioned into song.

In Thomas's view, the John Henry legend had morphed into a discussion of train wreck songs, although they also dealt with work.[1]

Few songs have conveyed the themes of race, work, and the coming of the machine age in as indelible a way as "John Henry." Throughout the twentieth century such issues have highly influenced the scope and meaning of labor songs. There had been much speculation and confusion over the "real" story behind "John Henry," however, arguably the country's most famous labor song. "In southern work camps, John Henry is the strong man, or the ridiculous man, or anyhow the man worth talking about, having a myth character somewhat like that of Paul Bunyan in work gangs of the Big Woods of the North," Carl Sandburg explained, while introducing the song in *The American Songbag*. Having circulated in oral tradition since the 1870s, it was finally published early in the new century, and would eventually number more than fifty variations.[2]

The John Henry story exists as both fact and legend. Who John Henry was, where he worked, what exactly he did, and how and where he died—these are all questions that have remained mostly unanswered. The song has lived a full life for well over a century, although it has often been confused with the ballad of another steel-driving man, "John Hardy." "The ballad 'John Hardy,' although known and sung far beyond the boundaries of West Virginia, without doubt had its origin and development in this state," John Harrington Cox announced in *Folk-Songs of the South* in 1925. "Its hero was a negro whose prowess and tragic end are well remembered and reported by men, both white and black, who saw him and knew him when he was alive." Hardy, while he did work on building a railroad, did not die battling the steam drill, but was executed for murder in 1894. A fragment of "John Henry" appeared in the *Journal of American Folklore* in 1909, about the same time that "John Hardy" was published.[3]

The folklorist Newman White attempted to sort out the controversy over confusing John Henry with John Hardy in his 1928

American Negro Folk-Songs: " . . . the John Henry and John Hardy songs both arose in West Virginia; that they have somewhat coalesced in that state, but are distinctly different songs, and that John Henry is probably the older of the two." While both Henry and Hardy were black, there seems to have developed a racial distinction within their audiences. "Among the Negroes John Hardy does not seem to be known," White continued, "but John Henry seems to have given rise to two types of song, closely related, but fairly distinct. Both are work songs, but the first is purely narrative, while the second is a hammer song, the most widely distributed of all the John Henry or John Hardy songs, and possibly the original of the John Henry story." In 1929, Guy Johnson published *John Henry: Tracking Down a Negro Legend*, followed in 1933 by Louis Chappell's *John Henry: A Folk-Lore Study*. Over seventy years later Scott Nelson issued the much publicized *Steel-Drivin' Man: John Henry, the Untold Story of an American Legend*.[4]

John and Alan Lomax gave prominence to "John Henry" by presenting it as the initial entry in *American Ballads and Folk Songs* in 1934. The song's use as both a historical drama and possible work song has led to its perpetuation in folklore. "There are almost two hundred recorded versions of the ballad of John Henry," Nelson writes. "It was among the first of the songs that came to be called 'the blues' and was one of the first recorded 'country' songs. Folklorists at the Library of Congress call it the most researched folk song in the United States, and perhaps the world." Robert Gordon focused on a variant of "John Henry" as a work song in his 1927 piece "Negro Work Songs From Georgia." "The true work song forms a highly specialized type little known outside of the particular group of workers who sing it," he began. "The following songs were obtained from negroes on the southern part of the Georgia coast during the present collecting trip. All are typical of the coast negro, and fit the particular tasks that he is called upon to do." While he did not name the songs he discussed, one included a "sudden expulsion of breath by the men just as they come down with their hammers [that] makes itself a sort of refrain. Though there is no regular order of verses, the different stanzas are so well known that the whole group joins in after the first line."[5]

"John Henry" can also be labeled a protest song, although this has not been its received identity or legacy. The "real" or imagined steel driving man has mostly been perceived by collectors and scholars as a hero, having proved his strength and stamina against the evil machine. He was not particularly a victim of the terrible working conditions for those, black or white, building the southern railroads. Indeed, collectors of African American songs, secular or religious, have shied away from anything that hinted of unrest or protest. "The Negro, by nature rhythmical, works better if he sings at his labor," Dorothy Scarborough explained in *On the Trail of Negro Folk-Songs*. There was singing in the tobacco factories, in the convict labor camps, among woodchoppers, and while working on the railroad. There was suffering, to be sure, but no real protest, as in "Ain't It Hard to be a Nigger?" In "Railroad Blues," the singer could not afford a ticket to leave town. The historian Marybeth Hamilton has painted a complex picture of Scarborough, a collector who was caught between nostalgia for the "old" South and the realities of modern life: "What Scarborough was hearing all around her, was the sound of her own obsolescence, assertions that reminiscences of black song penned by Southern whites were, at best, inconsequential, revealing little more than sentimental platitudes about African American music's 'heart and spirit'." Still, Scarborough somewhat captured some of the anguish that often seemed to lay just out of the collector's reach.[6]

For some on the political left, however, "John Henry" did have resonance. "It was not difficult to find a proletarian epic in the John Henry story," Scott Nelson has commented. "It was largely a matter of focus." Philip Schatz quoted from "John Henry" in an article on "Songs of the Negro Worker" in the left-wing *New Masses*, but it did not appear in the numerous songbooks connected with the Communist or Socialist parties in the 1930s, or even in *Hard-*

Hitting Songs for Hard-Hit People, compiled by Alan Lomax and Woody Guthrie as the Depression waned but not published until 1967. It took on more of a protest image in the 1960s, however, appearing in Edith Fowke and Joe Glazer's *Songs of Work and Freedom*, as well as Pete Seeger and Bob Reiser's *Carry It On! A History in Song and Picture of the Working Men and Women of America*. In 1939, Paul Robeson appeared as John Henry in the play of the same name by Roark Bradford, along with the bluesman Josh White, but it had a brief run in Boston and an even shorter one in New York. The radical Robeson, a champion of black music, does not seem to have included "John Henry" in his concerts.[7]

SCHOLARLY STUDIES EMERGE

Separating the romantic ideal from the terrible realities of the segregated South plagued many white folklorists. As a graduate student at the University of Mississippi in 1907, Howard Odum packed up his cylinder record player and traveled through northern Mississippi and Georgia collecting African American songs. They were published in 1925 with the assistance of Guy Johnson, his colleague at the University of North Carolina, as *The Negro and His Songs: A Study of Typical Negro Songs in the South*. The bulk of the book was devoted to religious and social songs, but there was also the usual section of work songs. "If the Negro singer in his religious zeal is appealing, the Negro laborer, singing while he works, working while he sings, physically forgetful of routine, is scarcely less characteristic of something indefinable in the Negro's spiritual make-up," they write. Some songs dealt directly with the rhythms and hardships of work, while others were needed to pass the time. "The railroad and section gangs, the contractors, 'hands,' the mining groups and convict labor camps all echo with the sound of shovel and pick and song. The more efficient the song leader, the better work will the company do; hence the singer is valued as a good workman," Odum and Johnson continued. They included a smattering of complaint songs.[8]

Odum and Johnson had some sympathy for their black informants, but, along with most white collectors, they placed them into a mostly ahistorical, romanticized framework. In 1926 they followed up with *Negro Workaday Songs*. Using recently collected songs from North Carolina, South Carolina, Tennessee, and Georgia, they divided the book into fifteen chapters. "It is a day of great promise in the United States when both races, North and South, enter upon a new era of the rediscovery of the Negro and face the future with an enthusiasm for facts, concerning both the newer creative urge and the earlier background sources," they began. "Following the trail of the workaday Negro," they continued, "therefore, one may get rare glimpses of common backgrounds of Negro life and experience in Southern communities. Here were the first real plantings of the modern blues, here songs of the lonesome road, here bad man ballads, here distinctive contributions in songs of jail and chain gang, here songs of white man and captain, here Negro Dr. Jekyls [sic] and Mr. Hydes." Indeed, Odum and Johnson's reach was broad, for they linked the older forms with the "new race blues! Plaintive blues, jolly blues, reckless blues, dirty dozen blues, mama blues, papa blues." They realized that African Americans were not cut off from commercial culture, but were influenced by the "multitude of blues, jazz songs, and others being distributed throughout the land in millions of phonograph records."[9]

They began with a chapter on the blues, but quickly explained that "the lonesome songs of the Kentucky mountaineer, of the cowboy, of the sailor, of any other group, are representative of the blues type." Still, the blues was connected with African Americans because the "Negro wasted no time in roundabout or stilted modes of speech. His tale is brief, his metaphor striking, his imagery perfect, his humor plaintive." This was certainly praise with a touch of paternalism, yet not the condescension found in their previous work. The remaining chapters covered "Songs of the Lonesome Road," "Songs of Construction Camps and Gangs," "Man's Song of Woman," "Woman's Song of Man," "John Henry: Epic of the Negro Workingman," and much else. *Negro Workaday Songs* is a fascinating collection, based on what the authors considered scientific principles.[10]

"While he [Odum] held out some hope that folk blues and formal blues could continue to exist side by side," Marybeth Hamilton argues, "this could only happen so long as black labourers remained uncorrupted, permeated by an essential simplicity." In an essay published in 1935, Guy Johnson noted that the "negro has long been accustomed to sing at work, especially in gang work, and whoever has not seen a group of Negroes swinging picks in perfect rhythm and heard them singing with utter abandon has missed one of the best scenes in the folk field." This struck him as interesting, but certainly not a sign of oppression or anger. "Their tunes may range from an old spiritual to the latest blues hit and their subjects may deal with anything under the sun." Johnson realized, however, that black workers were not always tranquil. "There is one more point which might be worth mentioning, however," he ended his discussion of "Negro Folk Songs." "It is that the Negro in his songs sometimes takes off his mask and gives us that mean look which he would like to give us oftener if he dared."[11]

Newman I. White, a contemporary of Scarborough, Odum, and Johnson, published *American Negro Folk-Songs* in 1928. A professor of English at Duke University, White had students do most of the collecting in 1915-1916 while he taught at Alabama Polytechnic Institute, although he included some songs from other sources. He devoted chapters to "Work Songs—Gang Laborers," "Rural Labor," and "General and Miscellaneous Labor." While boat songs, having originated in Africa, had pretty well died out (because of modern transportation), White believed that the "work song, however, has persisted, and will persist as long as the Negro retains his dominant racial traits." While some were timed to the rhythms of the work, the majority "are merely sung in a way that keeps them from interfering with the work. Their primary function is mental rather than physical." Concerning farm labor, White concluded that "the songs of the rural worker seem to be more decent and more conservative than those of the gang laborer." Mostly concerned with words and phrases, he argued that, "With the laborer at miscellaneous occupations, the thought of woman is connected with food (at least in utterance) more often than with the sex desire which predominates in the woman song of laborers whose utterance is less restricted by circumstance." He hardly touched on complaint songs.[12]

White realized that black workers were race-conscious, with feelings of racial pride and identity, but believed that this did not make them angry or bitter. "Of course, the Negro laborer is sometimes surly; of course, he sometimes growls and is dissatisfied with his lot," he argued. "But the real significance of his songs expressing race-consciousness is the fact that they show little of this mood. Fundamentally they are striking evidence of the deep conservatism, humor, patience, and sense of present realities with which the Negro has contributed probably more than his full share to the concord of the two races n the South." Or so he hoped. But as a product of his times, he was unable to fathom the depths of black repression and potential rebellion, soon to boil to the surface.[13]

LAWRENCE GELLERT AND THE LOMAXES

Although most white collectors avoided any emphasis on black workers' racial discontent, Lawrence Gellert tapped into a rich mine of protest songs. He first published a series on "Negro Songs of Protest" in the left-wing magazine *New Masses* in 1930, and six years later he issued the songbook *Negro Songs of Protest*: "Through Georgia, the Carolinas, way over in Mississippi and Louisiana even, in city slums, on isolated farms out in the sticks, on chain gangs, lumber and turpentine work camps, I gathered more than 300 songs of the black folk—songs that reveal for the first time the full heroic stature of the Negro dwarfing for all time the traditional mean estimate of him." For Gellert, "These songs, reflecting as they do the contemporary environment—the daily round of life in the Black Belt—aside from their musical and literary worth, are human documents. They embody the living voice of the otherwise inarticulate resentment against injustice—a part of the unrest that is stirring the South." Three years later he issued a sequel, "*Me and My Captain": Chain Gang Negro Songs of Protest*. The first volume included such spirited songs as "Out In De Rain." The son of Jewish immigrants from Hungary, Gellert had grown up in New York's left wing culture, and for health reasons moved to North Carolina in 1924. He was certainly not the first to collect songs with a bitter edge, but his work captured the attention of New York's radical left in the midst of the Depression, and influenced such singers as Josh White. Gellert's brother Hugo, an influential artist and active Communist Party member, designed the striking cover for *Negro Songs of Protest*.[14]

While Gellert collected a wide range of African American songs in the South, most of which had no political overtones, John Lomax would be working on his own agenda. He began his interest in African American music and culture when he was young, and it continued while he was publishing *Cowboy Songs* in 1910. Two years later Lomax circulated a notice that he was looking for "songs of the negro—his 'reels,' his spirituals, and his play songs." He was soon giving a lecture on "Negro Plantation Songs," and even planning a book, perhaps with the title of "Ballads of the Cotton Fields and Back Alleys," but it never appeared. He did, however, publish a fragment of his research as "Self-Pity in Negro Folk-Songs" in the *Nation* (1917). After a lengthy delay, while he attempted a career in business and then working with the University of Texas, John and his eighteen-year-old son Alan, in May 1933, began a collecting trip through the South that would leave its indelible mark on both men, as well as on music history. That September he was named "Honorary Curator of the Archive of American Folk Song" at the Library of Congress, but with no compensation except for expenses.[15]

When traveling through Texas and the deep South, the Lomaxes visited black inmates at the Imperial prison farm near Sugarland, Texas, Parchman Farm in Mississippi, and the Angola State Prison Farm in Louisiana. They returned to Washington at summer's end with the first recordings of African American work songs by prisoners and others, including Iron Head and Clear Rock at Imperial; Henry Truvillion, who led a railroad track crew in East Texas; and Huddie Ledbetter, know as Lead Belly, at Angola. "Recordings of these and other Negro songs . . . seem worthy of special comment," they wrote in the introduction to *American Ballads and Folk Songs*, published in 1934. "All the singing was done by Negroes, principally by men. Our purpose was to find the Negro who had had the least contact with jazz, the radio, and with the white man." The idea of isolated prisoners, the nostalgia for a lost musical world, was essentially John's doing, although such isolation was not possible; certainly Lead Belly was steeped in contemporary music. They began with "John Henry," and included numerous songs from their recent collecting trip, including "Ain' No Mo' Cane on de Brazos," "Great God-A'Mighty," and "Goin' Home." Two years later they published *Negro Folk Songs as Sung by Lead Belly*, giving credit and publicity to their most famous "discovery." Thirty years later, Bruce Jackson again recorded black prisoners in Texas, finding an equal number of fascinating songs. By the 1960s, Jackson noted, work songs had all but disappeared, except in "the southern prison, and that is because the southern prison maintained a social institution long dead outside its fences: the culture of the nineteenth-century plantation."[16]

"As he made his work songs, the Negro cleared the land of the South, worked its plantations, built its railroads, loaded its steamboats, raised its levees, and cut its roads," John Lomax explained in his autobiography, which covered the 1933 collecting trip as well as subsequent ones. "When he picked cotton or did some other form of work in which it was not possible to adhere to a regular rhythm, his songs rose and fell with the free and easy movement of his breathing." The Lomaxes did not limit their collecting or understanding of African American work songs to prison labor, although they found this environment to be musically rich and creative. John and Alan were also struck by the music of levee camp workers. "In the thirties, when my father, John A. Lomax, and I were recording across the South, levee camps existed not only along the Mississippi but also on the White River in Arkansas, the Red River in Louisiana, the Brazos and Trinity rivers in Texas, and a score of lesser streams in the vast alluvial plains of the lower South," Alan later wrote in *The Land Where the Blues Began*. Indeed, black work songs were ubiquitous. He now believed that such songs "gave voice to the mood of alienation and anomie that prevailed in the construction camps of the South," and surely elsewhere in that segregated land.[17]

Alan Lomax's southern collecting continued into the 1940s (as did his father's), and picked up again following World War II. He remained fascinated by black (and white) work songs, amid much else. But he was no purist, particularly after he was appointed the Assistant in Charge of the Archive of American Folk Song at the Library of Congress in 1937. He eagerly collected not only field recordings, from throughout the country and the Caribbean, but also recent commercial recordings of blues and other "folk" songs. With Lomax's initial urging, the Archive released a number of recordings from the field, such as *Anglo-American Shanties, Lyric Songs, Dance Tunes and Spirituals* (1942). John Lomax produced a series of radio shows in 1941, "The Ballad Hunter," also released on records, with excerpts of railroad songs, sea shanties, and cowboy songs. Alan Lomax's reach was wide, although some of his work, particularly with the Afro-American music scholar John Work, has come in for some critical attention in recent years.[18]

John Work III, the son and grandson of music scholars and teachers connected with Fisk University in Nashville, joined the college's faculty in 1927. He had a particular interest in the origins of African American music and began his field collecting in

1938. In 1940 he published *American Negro Songs and Spirituals*, which covered spirituals, blues, work and social songs, although he stressed those of a religious nature. He had little to say about work songs, while focusing on "John Henry." "Most of the work songs about John Henry are hammer songs," he explained, "though the narrative song which tells most about this famous character is a social song." This section included "Screw This Cotton" and "Railroad Bill," as well as "John Henry."[19]

On April 29, 1941, Alan Lomax attended a concert at Fisk University, part of the college's seventy-fifth anniversary, where he met Work and Charles S. Johnson, who directed the college's Department of Social Sciences. Lomax and Work discussed two collecting projects, one focused on Nashville led by Work, while Lomax and Johnson would conduct the other in the Mississippi Delta; Johnson had recently published a detailed study of this cotton producing area, *Growing Up in the Black Belt*. Work had earlier thought of a collecting trip to Natchez, Mississippi, which had not transpired, but he did some recording in Nashville.

On August 24, Lomax arrived in Nashville with his wife Elizabeth; they were joined by Lewis Jones of the Fisk Department of Social Sciences, John Ross from the drama department, and Work. During less than a week they recorded a mix of religious and secular songs, some from McKinley Morganfield (later known as Muddy Waters), David "Honeyboy" Edwards, and Son House. Lomax returned to Washington, while Work transcribed the recordings and compiled his unpublished account of the trip. As was his wont, Work devoted little space to work songs, which he easily described:

> Negro work songs may be divided from the standpoint of their functions, and their form, into three types. Some of them are highly rhythmic in character and are sung to coordinate the group efforts of the workmen when precision is necessary. The second type of work song is one in which the individual workman expresses to his fellow workmen, to his "captain"

> and to the world-at-large his immediate sentiments about his woman, his work, or the place where he is living or wants to be. This type of song is given the name "holler" by the folk. The third type of work song is that sung by the group of men for the pure pleasure of singing together.

He included transcriptions of "Lining Railroad Track" and Son House's "Levee Blues." As for Lomax, he clearly realized that, while the Delta appeared rather culturally remote, "Coahoma [a county in Mississippi] blues musicians like Muddy Waters were exposed to the pop music of the day and composed with such models in mind."[20]

BLUES COLLECTORS

By the 1950s music collectors and scholars would increasingly focus on the blues, with less interest in the antiquated spirituals. There was also less interest in work songs. With the decline in sharecropping, as well as less work in the cotton and corn fields, in the mines, on the levees, for the railroads, or on the docks, the focus shifted to industrial work, North and South. Moreover, scholars increasingly studied the plethora of commercial "race" recordings of the 1920s and after, which emphasized newly written songs, often of a topical nature. During the Depression, for example, as Guido van Rijn documented in *Roosevelt's Blues*, there were numerous blues about joblessness, and government jobs through the Civil Works Administration (CPA) and Works Progress Administration (WPA). For example, William "Casey Bill" Weldon recorded "W.P.A. Blues" in 1936. The next year Peetie Wheatstraw (originally William Bunch) released "Working on the Project."[21]

Samuel Charters pioneered the modern study of the blues with *The Country Blues* in 1959. He drew from recordings and focused on individual musicians and their recording companies, rather than on themes or chronology. He discussed the recording of "Workingman's Blues" in the chapter on Brownie McGhee, and "Levee Camp Blues" in the Bluebird Records section. The British scholar Paul Oliver captured how blues lyrics mirrored changing economic conditions for black workers, as he joined others in expanding the blues scholarship after the late 1950s in *Blues Fell This Morning*. He quoted "Rolling Mill Blues" from "Peg Leg" Howell, the Atlanta street singer. "Six-Cylinder" Smith sang about "Working In the Steel-Mills Baby." But by the 1960s blues lyrics were shifting to a focus on personal relationships rather than communal labor.[22]

Harold Courlander drew upon his own research in *Negro Folk Music U.S.A.*, published in 1963. A journalist and zealous field worker, Courlander collected songs and stories in the South and throughout the world. He produced a six-record set, *Negro Folk Music of Alabama*, for Folkways Records, as well as numerous other albums for this eclectic label. In *Negro Folk Music U.S.A.* there is a chapter on "Sounds of Work." "The Negro worksong, particularly the kind sung by railroad gangs, roustabouts (stevedores), woodcutters, fisherman, and prison road gangs, is in an old and deeply rooted tradition," he began. He focused on the older style of songs performed while working, not those about work, its difficulties and dangers. He did not mention any songs about industrial work, and ended with a reference to "Negro shoe shiners, particularly those who plied their trade in the streets, [who] had their own special songs or patter to go along with the percussive shining operation." He separated this chapter from the next on the "Blues," which dealt with more personal matters. The literary and folklore scholar Harry Oster published *Living Country Blues* in 1969. He combined his collecting in Louisiana with a broad selection from recorded blues. Oster found most dealt with love and personal relationships, although he did include some songs about agricultural work.[23]

It is telling that there are few references to work songs in *Nothing But the Blues*, the 1993 collection of original essays and archival photographs. In Sam Charters's introductory essay, he explains: "The work song, with its steady rhythms and its short rhymed phrases, was the other major source [in addition to the 'hollers' or short verses] of the blues." But Charters was more concerned with the influence of the rhythms than the words. In a later essay on the urban blues, Mark Humphrey traced that the music travelled "from the African-American work song to become a new dance and party music of the countryside, replacing slavery-era banjo and fiddle music." John Cowley's informative essay on the field collectors touched on a few work-related songs, but did not focus on them. African American work-related songs had largely vanished from view after midcentury. The blues scholar Elijah Wald has deftly underscored this view: "In fact, when I try to think of examples of rural Southern musicians who reshaped such work songs into professional performance pieces, I come up with as many white banjo players as black blues singers." Among the former he lists Clarence "Tom" Ashley's "Walking Boss" and Uncle Dave Macon's "Buddy, Won't You Roll Down the Line."[24]

If blues performers increasingly shied away from work songs, this did not mean that black labor-related songs had vanished. Indeed, black steel workers, textile mill workers, and others used songs on the picket lines, while performers such as the agricultural organizer John Handcox, Paul Robeson, Josh White, Brownie McGhee, and Big Bill Broonzy continued to sing about oppressive working conditions and political activism for African Americans.

(Endnotes)

1 Jean Thomas, *Ballad Makin' in the Mountains of Kentucky* (N.Y.: Oak Publications, 1964 [orig. pub. N.Y.: Henry Holt Co., 1939]), 120.

2 Carl Sandburg, *The American Songbag* (N.Y. : Harcourt, Brace, & Co., 1927), 24; Scott Reynolds Nelson, *Steel Drivin' Man: John Henry, The Untold Story of an American Legend* (N.Y.: Oxford University Press, 2006).

3 John Harrington Cox, *Folk-Songs of the South: Collected Under the Auspices of the West Virginia Folk-Lore Society* (Cambridge: Harvard University Press, 1925), 175. See Nelson, *Steel Drivin' Man*, for one interpretation of the story, and John Garst for another, http://www.ibiblio.org/john_henry/garst2.html.

4 Newman I. White, *American Negro Folk-Songs* (Cambridge: Harvard University Press, 1928), 190; Nelson, *Steel-Drivin' Man*, however, has not escaped controversy, consult http://www.ibiblio.org/john_henry.

5 Nelson, *Steel Drivin' Man*, 2; Robert Gordon, "The Folk-Songs of America: Work Chanteys," *New York Times*, January 16, 1927, reprinted in Robert Winslow Gordon, *Folk-Songs of America* (Washington, D.C.: National Service Bureau, Publication No. 73-S, December 1938), 16. See also Norm Cohen, *Long Steel Rail: The Railroad in American Folksong* (Urbana: University of Illinois Press, 1981), 61-89.

6 Dorothy Scarborough, *On the Trail of Negro Folk-Songs* (Cambridge: Harvard University Press, 1925), 206, 227, 243; Marybeth Hamilton, *In Search of the Blues: Black Voices, White Visions* (London: Jonathan Cape, 2007), 64, and chap. 3 for an insightful discussion of Scarborough's life.

7 Nelson, *Steel Drivin' Man*, 156; Edith Fowke and Joe Glazer, *Songs of Work and Freedom* (Chicago: Roosevelt University, Labor Education Division, 1960), 82-83; Pete Seeger and Bob Reiser, *Carry It On!: A History in Song and Picture of the Working Men and Women of America* (N.Y.: Simon and Schuster, 1985), 32-34.

8 Howard W. Odum and Guy B. Johnson, *The Negro and His Songs: A Study of Typical Negro Songs in the South* (Chapel Hill: University of North Carolina Press, 1925), 246-247, 255. On Odum see, Lynn Moss Sanders, *Howard W. Odum's Folklore Odyssey: Transformation to Tolerance through African American Folk Studies* (Athens: University of Georgia Press, 2003).

9 Howard W. Odum and Guy B. Johnson, *Negro Workaday Songs* (Chapel Hill: University of North Carolina Press, 1926), 1, 5, 7, 16.

10 Odum and Johnson, *Negro Workaday Songs*, 21, 22.

11 Hamilton, *In Search of the Blues*, 38; Guy B. Johnson, "Negro Folk Song," W. T. Cough, ed., *Culture in the South* (Chapel Hill: University of North Carolina Press, 1935), 564, 569.

12 Newman I. White, *American Negro Folk-Songs* (Cambridge: Harvard University Press, 1928), 250. 251, 281, 292.

13 White, *American Negro Folk-Songs*, 378, 386.

14 Lawrence Gellert, *Negro Songs of Protest* (N.Y.: American Music League, 1936), 6, 14-15, 7; Lawrence Gellert, *"Me And My Captain": Chain Gang Negro Songs Of Protest*, (N.Y.: Hours Press, 1939). Some of Gellert's field recordings were later released as *Collection of Lawrence Gellert: Negro Songs of Protest*, Timely TI-112, 1972, *Negro Songs of Protest: Collected by Lawrence Gellert*, Rounder 4004, 1973, and *Cap'n You're So Mean: Negro Songs of Protest*, Volume 2, Rounder 4013, 1982. See also Steven Patrick Garabedian, "Reds, Whites, and the Blues: Blues Music, White Scholarship, and American Cultural Politics," unpub., PhD diss., University of Minnesota, 2004.

15 Nolan Porterfield, *Last Cavalier: The Life and Times of John A. Lomax* (Urbana: University of Illinois Press, 1996), quote on 169, and see chap. 18 in general.

16 John A. and Alan Lomax, *American Ballads and Folk Songs* (N.Y.: The Macmillan Co., 1934), xxx; John A. and Alan Lomax, *Negro Folk Songs As Sung by Lead Belly* (N.Y.: The Macmillan Co., 1936); Bruce Jackson, *Wake Up Dead Man: Hard Labor and Southern Blues* (Athens: University of Georgia Press, 1999 [originally published in 1972]), 29. See also, Charles Wolfe and Kip Lornell, *The Life and Legend of Leadbelly* (N.Y.: HarperCollins Publishers, 1992), and for the different attitudes between father and son, Patrick B. Mullen, *The Man Who Adores the Negro: Race and American Folklore* (Urbana: University of Illinois Press, 2008), chaps. 3 and 4.

17 John A. Lomax, *Adventures of a Ballad Hunter* (N.Y.: The Macmillan Co., 1947), 113; Alan Lomax, *The Land Where the Blues Began* (N.Y.: Pantheon Books, 1993), 230, 232, 233.

18 *Anglo-American Shanties, Lyric Songs, Dance Tunes and Spirituals*, Library of Congress, Music Division, Recording Laboratory, AFS L2; *The Ballad Hunter: John Lomax (1867-1948), Lectures on American Folk Music*, Library of Congress, Music Division, Recording Laboratory, AAFS L49; and also consult, *Songs of Labor & Livelihood*, Library of Congress, Music Division, Recording Laboratory, LBC 8; *Negro Work Songs and Calls*, Rounder Records Roun 1517, 1999.

19 John Work, *American Negro Songs and Spirituals* (N.Y.: Bonanza Books, 1940), 40.

20 See Robert Gordon and Bruce Nemerov, eds., *Lost Delta Found: Rediscovering the Fisk University—Library of Congress Coahoma County Study, 1941-1942* (Nashville: Vanderbilt University Press, 2005), 8-26, which includes Work's unpublished manuscript, 53-222, with the quote on 97; *John Work, III: Recording Black Culture*, Spring Fed Records SFR-104, 2007, which includes only one work song, "My Captain's Angry, " recorded in South Carolina; Lomax, *The Land Where the Blues Began*, 414, and *passim* for various discussions of this trip. On popular music and the blues in the Delta, see Elijah Wald, *Escaping the Delta: Robert Johnson and the Invention of the Blues* (N.Y.: HarperCollins Publishers, 2004), 57-59, 86-102; Ted Gioia, *Delta Blues: The Life and Times of the Mississippi Masters Who Revolutionized American Music* (N.Y.: Norton, 2008). Following his pioneering study *Work Songs* (Dunham: Duke University Press), 2006, Gioia does touch on work songs in *Delta Blues*, especially see 20-22 for the early collector Charles Peabody and his work in Coahoma County in 1901-1902.

21 Guido van Rijn, *Roosevelt's Blues: African-American Blues and Gospel Songs on FDR* (Jackson: University Press of Mississippi, 1997), 83. See also, John Cowley, "Shack Bullies and Levee Contractors: Bluesmen as Ethnographers," in Archie Green, ed., *Songs*

about Work: Essays in Occupational Culture for Richard A. Reuss (Bloomington, IN: Special Publications of the Folklore Institute No. 3, Indiana University, 1993), 134-162.

22 Samuel B. Charters, *The Counry Blues* (N.Y.: Da Capo Press, 1975 [orig. ed. 1959]). Paul Oliver, *Blues Fell This Morning: Meaning in the Blues* (Cambridge: Cambridge University Press, 2nd ed., 1990), 32, 28.

23 Harold Courlander, *Negro Folk Music, U.S.A.* (N.Y.: Columbia University Press, 1963), 89, 122; Harry Oster, *Living Country Blues* (Detroit: Folklore Associates, 1969). See also, Nina Jaffe, *The Voice For the People: The Life and Work of Harold Courlander* (N.Y.: Henry Holt and Company, 1997); Frederic Ramsey, Jr., *Been Here and Gone* (New Brunswick: Rutgers University Press, 1960).

24 Lawrence Cohn, ed., *Nothing But the Blues: The Music and the Musicians* (N.Y.: Abbeville Press, 1993), 21, 152; Wald, *Escaping the Delta*, 74, and chap. 4 in general. There is no index listing for work songs in two recently published books, Robert Springer, ed., *Nobody Knows Where the Blues Come From: Lyrics and History* (Jackson: University Press of Mississippi, 2006); David Evans, ed., *Ramblin' On My Mind: New Perspectives on the Blues* (Urbana: University of Illinois Press, 2008).

Rebel Song Book (N.Y.: Rand School Press, 1935)

chapter three

Labor/Union Songs

PART 1

EARLY TWENTIETH CENTURY LABOR SONGS

"Organized labor has, in the matter of appropriating well-known songs to its own use, shown a very satisfactory inconsistency and catholicity, and has often strayed far from its ranks and its ideals, selecting and adopting fine poetry and music, however uncongenial and irrelevant its origin, and discarding the mere verse and tune which chanced to bear, so to speak, the union label," social reformer Elizabeth Balch wrote in 1914. "Where, then, has labor found its songs? One element only of the labor movement, the class struggle, and that by no means generally accepted, finds direct natural expression in the war songs of the past." After quoting from a variety of labor songs, focusing on their lyrics, she called for a serious attempt to write poetic, stirring songs. As she concluded, "in part our lack of a great song is because class consciousness in the modern sense, which is leading the workers to self-expression, is a recent development; in part it is because inevitably that movement too often is crude, hard and narrow."[1]

If labor songs lacked much of a poetic flourish, they nonetheless continued into the 1920s. Labor unions, labor colleges, and various radical organizations increasingly published songbooks and encouraged workers to sing while they organized. The tunes were hardly considered important, with most based on familiar religious and popular songs; folk melodies with black or white origins, except for ethnic songs connected with recent immigrants that had a local audience, would not become popular until the later 1930s. There was a brief attempt by left-wing, modernist composers in mid-decade to elevate the masses with stirring, complex words and arrangements, with short-lived results.

During the 1920s, with labor unions on the defensive, seemingly few published songbooks except for the Industrial Workers of the World (IWW). There were, however, numerous occupational songbooks (see chapter 2), including some dealing with miners. "This is a collection of folklore developed among the miners of the anthracite coal region of Pennsylvania during the last century," George Korson explained in the introduction to his first book, *Songs and Ballads of the Anthracite Miner*, published in 1927: "It represents an attempt to salvage from the past a vein rich in the homespun creations of the common people before it is lost forever with the passing of that generation which produced it." For Korson the old life was dying out, but it had a fascinating, invaluable mystique: "These songs and ballads illumined with legends and historical notes, not only mirror the mine and the life that went on around it, but provide an insight into the souls of the men whose hardihood and near-serfdom brought warmth to the country's fireside and fuel to its industry." Korson was one of many at the time to explore occupational songs, but he pioneered the collection of eastern miners' songs.[2]

Born in the Ukraine in 1899, Korson moved with his family to New York in 1906, then to Wilkes-Barre, Pennsylvania, in 1912. With a Jewish background, he nonetheless found this Irish, Welsh, and Slavic community fascinating, and it would eventually consume his curiosity and research. A professional reporter, he first worked for the *Wilkes-Barre Record* in 1917, then the *Pottsville Republican*. He began collecting miners' songs in 1924, including not only the words but also the social contexts. Two years later, now a newspaperman in New Jersey, he began publishing some of his finds in the *United Mine Workers Journal*, which were published in 1927 as *Songs and Ballads of the Anthracite Miner*. Unlike other vocational song collectors, Korson closely identified with organized labor and was keen on focusing on the workers' union affiliations and terrible hardships. The miner's "lot in life has been made much happier by his union," Korson declared, "the United Mine Workers of America [UMW], whose influence in his behalf has been exerted powerfully ever since the great strike of 1902." But he also lamented the pervasive influence of modern technology and entertainments, which had robbed the miners of their traditional cultures: "Not only has the miner of to-day almost forgotten his own songs and ballads, but a note of apology is discernible in the manner with which he sometimes recalls them for the stranger, as if he were just a little ashamed to have been once so naïve. Prosperity always has had a sterile effect on folklore." Korson drew upon collecting in the field, and ignored commercial recordings. *Songs and Ballads of the Anthracite Miner* included seven sections: "Life in the Mine Patch," "When the Heart Was Light," "On Being a Miner," "The Collier Boys," "Four Mine Accidents," "On Strike," and "The Mollie Maguires" (only two songs).[3] "Simple justice compels us to recognize the fact that many concessions which the mine worker has gained from the industry have been wrested from the operators through the medium of the strike," Korson explained, "and the strike has been most effective when the men put up a solid front." Songs helped serve this purpose, during and after, such as "The Long Strike." While the 1875 strike was lost, another in 1902 resulted in forced arbitration between the workers and the company. "Me Johnny Mitchell Man" lauded the United Mine Workers's president from the Slavic perspective. Mitchell (1870-1919) had become the union's president in 1898, and soon its ranks swelled from 34,000 to 300,000. Sheet music appeared in 1906 for "I'm a Johnnie Mitchell Man," which was a different song but also praised the union's leader.[4]

To make the songs more accessible, since *Songs and Ballads* contained no music, Korson followed in 1936 with ten selections in *The Miner Sings*. Melvin LeMon of Bucknell College provided the transcriptions and musical arrangements. "In keeping with the tradition of folk-singing, the miners sang their songs and ballads unaccompanied, and on those rare occasions when there was an accompaniment it was done with guitar," Korson explained. "The fiddle was played in unison with the singer. . . . This collection is intended to serve as a song book for general, everyday use. The songs and ballads are a heritage to be enjoyed by all Americans." The next year the Pennsylvania Folk Festival published Korson's *Pennsylvania Folk Songs and Ballads for School, Camp and Playground*. Among the eight songs was one dealing with mining, "Down in a Coal Mine," but others, such as "The Conestoga Wagoner's Lament" and "The Jolly Lumbermen," described different occupations. Korson helped launched the festival in 1936 at Bucknell University in Lewisburg. Featuring a variety of occupational folklore, such as "Pennsylvania Canal Lore" and "Sea Chanteys of Old Philadelphia," Korson made sure to include singing and folk crafts from the anthracite miners. The next year's program featured Korson's essay, "Humor of the Anthracite Miner," which helped explain the festival's musical section, "Fun in a Mine Patch." In Korson's foreword to the accompanying 1937 songbook, which included a few occupational songs, he explained: "Pennsylvania's folk songs and ballads fall into two broad classifications. There are, first, those that came over from Europe with the early settlers and in the course of several generations were adapted to the Pennsylvania environment. . . . Second, there are the indigenous songs and ballads that sprang from our pioneer basic occupations and industries—farming, Conestoga wagoning, canalling, lumbering, rafting, logging, oil production and coal mining." He preferred the latter group. The 1938 festival, shortened to one day and the last to be held for many years, also featured ballads from miners, Conestoga wagoners, and lumberjacks.[5]

Wasting no time, Korson published an expanded version of *Songs and Ballads of the Anthracite Miner* as *Minstrels of the Mine Patch* in 1938. Drawing upon Irish and Welsh musical influences, the songs were sung at various communal gatherings, at work and at play. "Balladry attained an amazing vogue among the anthracite mine workers," he explained. "From the end of the Civil War to the first decade of the present century, no patch or town escaped the fever of improvising or composing songs, ballads, ditties, and doggerel on some phase or other of the mining theme. Unlettered mine workers seemed to have gone daft thinking, talking, writing, and singing in measured and rhymed sentences." Even children contributed: "One of the best-known ballads in this collection, 'The Driver Boys of Wadesville Shaft,' was improvised by William Keating when he was only twelve years old." (Keating would become one of Korson's prime informants, and performed at both the Pennsylvania and National folk festivals.) The songs deftly captured the miners' brutal lives. "These texts exude sweat and blood, echo every colliery sound, capture every colliery smell," Korson remarked. "They preserve the miners' changing moods, their thoughts and feelings, their fears, heartaches, hopes and deepest longings, and too, their laughter, wit, and humor. Thus intimately bound up with the anthracite industry, the songs and ballads are true Americana." For a relative newcomer to the district, Korson readily empathized with the miners' hardships and cultural lives. Each of the nine chapters included numerous songs and explanatory notes, but again no music.[6]

Having devoted considerable attention to the anthracite miners, he turned his attention in the later 1930s to the bituminous, or soft coal, industry. These mining operations covered not only Pennsylvania, but also a nine hundred mile mountainous strip running through Ohio, Illinois, Indiana, Virginia, West Virginia, Kentucky, Tennessee, and Alabama. Both anthracite and bituminous miners worked underground and lived in miserable shacks, under the control of the mine owners. He again had the cooperation of the United Mine Workers, which had become one of the most powerful of the Committee for Industrial Organization, soon known as the Congress of Industrial Organizations (CIO), unions. *Coal Dust on the Fiddle: Songs and Stories of the Bituminous Industry* appeared in 1943. Over half of the book consisted of Korson's explanatory text for the 140 original songs; Ruth Crawford Seeger supplied tunes for 13. There was singing in the mines, but not for all: "Auxiliary mine workers, like pumpers, chainers, and mule skinners might sing as they worked, but not the miner at the coal face. There the work was much too arduous and dangerous, and the air too thick with coal dust, for singing." Miners might think of a song while working, such as "Harlan County Blues" and "The Dying Mine Brakeman," then write it down later. Mining songs dealt with all facets of the job, the hard work and dangers, miners' unions, their hopes and dreams. The battles between workers and management in Virden, Illinois (1898), Ludlow, Colorado (1913-14), and other mine sites produced numerous songs. At the UMW convention in Columbus, Ohio, in 1940 Korson recorded Charles Langford and the Marvel Quartet from Alabama singing "Union Boys Are We." He also captured Uncle George Jones from Trafford, Alabama, singing "Dis What the Union Done."[7]

Korson's final exploration, *Black Rock: Mining Folklore of the Pennsylvania Dutch*, appeared in 1960. Taking a broad approach to folklore, only one of the book's chapters dealt with songs and ballads. He explained that traditionally in England and Ireland "work songs in which rhythm is attuned to the movement of work performance are missing from the anthracite tradition. Instead we have songs and ballads <u>about</u> work, which are more often sung above ground than below in the coal mines." This style had migrated to the Pennsylvania coal fields. Korson mentioned a handful of anthracite bards and minstrels, including Con Carbon, Ed Foley, Giant O'Neill, and Joe Gallagher: "They not only created ballads of their hazardous occupation, but sang them from one end of the anthracite region to the other, often making the rounds on foot. From mine patch to mine patch they strolled, singing, dancing, fiddling, and storytelling in barrooms, on village greens, or on the porches of general stores." But what about the Pennsylvania Dutch folksong mining tradition? In 1957, Korson embarked on one last field trip to capture this seemingly lost music. In all he collected forty old and new songs, some in German from William "Pop" Shotley, of which fifteen were included in the book, such as "Three Men Came to Coaldale."[8]

While Korson was exploring coal mining songs, others, such as Duncan Emrich and Wayland Hand, were tackling western quartz (metal) mining lore. Emrich was a Denver University English professor (and later head of the Folklore Section of the Library of Congress, 1945-1956), while Hand, who had written his dissertation at the University of Chicago on German folk songs, taught at the University of California at Los Angeles, where he established the folklore department. Emrich published "Songs of the Western Miners" in 1942, covering the continuing output of hard-rock miners. "Whether old or new, popular or folk, the lyrics of the majority of mining songs have been written to the tunes of already existing music, and are in effect parodies," he explained. 'This is curiously true of mining songs to a degree not found among work songs in other occupations, such as the cattle, railroad, or cotton industries." He gave various examples, some with music, including "Casey Jones, Miner," "Only a Miner Killed in the Breast," and "The Hard-Working Miner." A few years later, in an article on the "Songs of the Butte [Montana] Miners," Hand credited Emrich's essay with marking "the beginning of the systematic study of the songs of the hard-rock miner in America. His work is important not only for the variety of songs that it contains and for its general survey of the genre, but also for the challenge held out to workers in the field to pursue, with unremitting zeal, miners' songs of all kinds, wherever they are still to be found." Most songs dated from the last century, Hand argued, since the "practice of singing in the mines has pretty well died out." Still, some of his examples came from the 20th century, such as "Back Home in Butte Montana" and "When I Was a Miner, a Hard-Rock Miner." Moreover, the "absence of ballads commemorating mine disasters, fires, and other stirring events in Butte mining history is one of the disappointments of our collecting experience in Montana."[9]

A few other collectors stumbled upon miners' songs. In 1933, John and Alan Lomax, while in Harlan County, Kentucky, recorded the blind fiddler James Howard performing "The Hard-Working Miner." It appeared the next year in their *American Ballads and Folk Songs*, along with two western mining songs. They would include another four in their subsequent *Our Singing Country*, including "Pay Day At Coal Creek" and Aunt Molly Jackson's "The Coal Miner's Child."[10]

MINERS' SONGS AND THE LEFT

Korson, Emrich, and Hand had little interest in songs with a radical lineage or contemporary focus, even though Korson had strong union credentials. Archie Green, in his magisterial *Only a Miner: Studies in Recorded Coal Mining Songs*, noted Korson's oversights. "Korson was the first American folklorist to present any laborlore to the public," Green explained; "nevertheless, he too rejected some data, for he did not include in his books the contributions of communists to union tradition." Korson was certainly familiar with the coal wars of the time, and the role of Communist party organizers and supporters, but he chose to ignore their musical output. "He wrote to me that in his collecting he distinguished between 'the folk,' the workers themselves [and] union organizers from the outside,'" Green commented. When Korson "found that [a ballad] had been written by an outsider [he] didn't use it. . . . [He] had to be especially careful because in the 1920's and 1930's the Communists were making a determined effort to capture the United Mine Workers of America.'"[11]

Miners' usual unrest in Harlan County, Kentucky, fueled by the escalating depression, led to the outbreak of a strike in early 1931. The UMW did little to assist the striking miners, however, and as conditions worsened a second strike soon broke out. The National Miners Union, affiliated with the Communist Party, sent organizers, including Jim Garland, who had previously worked for the Peabody Coal Company. A group of writers, led by Theodore Dreiser and John Dos Passos, arrived in late 1931, holding hearings in various communities about workers' conditions. They were confronted by Aunt Molly Jackson, Garland's half-sister, a local midwife and songwriter, who performed her composition "Ragged Hungry Blues." "The Dreiser people were so impressed by her that they thought she was just about the whole Kentucky strike," Garland recalled. "In fact, she had done very little in the strike aside from going down into Knox County a time or two to solicit vegetables for the community kitchen." Whatever her role in the strike, she quickly fled to New York City, arriving on December 1, 1931. She was quickly singing her songs before large crowds. In 1935, now ensconced in the city's left-wing community, she recorded seventy-five of her songs for Alan Lomax. She would eventually record over 200 songs for the Library of Congress; some of her 1939 recordings, including "Hard Times in Coleman's Mines," "I Love Coal Miners, I Do," and "Fare Thee Well Old Ely Branch," later appeared on a Rounder Records album. She early recorded four sides for Columbia Records in New York—"Poor Miner's Farewell," "I Love Coal Miners," and "Ragged Hungry Blues," parts 1 and 2, but only the latter was released and quickly became scarce.[12]

The miners' lives worsened in Harlan County as the violence escalated. Sheriff J. H. Blair's men ransacked the home of Florence Reece, searching for her husband Sam, a union leader. She soon scribbled on a page from the wall calendar the song "Which Side Are You On?" based on the hymn "Lay the Lily Low," and it quickly became a standard on the picket line. On February 10, 1932, Harry Simms (aka Harry Hirsch), a union organizer, was shot by a deputy and died the following day; his funeral was held in New York. Jim Garland quickly composed a song in memory of his good friend, "The Ballad of Harry Simms." Garland traveled around the North, raising funds for the striking miners. He returned to Kentucky for a few more years, then moved with his family to New York in 1935, joining Aunt Molly. Garland believed that songs played a vital role in the miners' strikes: "In the course of such fights, songs expressed people's feelings in a manner that allowed them to stand together. The IWW used them, the National Miners Union used them, as did the UMW of A[merica]. . . . Rather than walking up to a gun thug and saying, 'You're a bastard,' which might have resulted in a shooting, we could express our anger much more easily in unison with song lyrics."[13]

"In 1932, my youngest sister (Sarah Ogan was her name at that time, now she is Sarah Gunning) was in the midst of the same tough mine strike that Hazel [Mrs. Garland] and I were so dedicated to," Garland recalled. "Sarah's husband was a striking miner and one of their babies had died, we thought because it had not gotten enough milk to drink. . . . [She soon composed] a fine song which Woody Guthrie later recorded. My sister called it 'I'm Going to Organize, Baby Mine.'" Born in 1910 (her mother was Aunt Molly's stepmother), Sarah married Andrew Ogan in 1925, a coal miner and strong union member. She moved with her family to New York in 1936, where she became caught up in the left-wing folk music scene, joining with her brother and sister, as well as meeting folklorists Mary Elizabeth Barnicle and Alan Lomax. The next year Lomax recorded her songs "Come All Your Coal Miners," "Picket Line," "I Am a Girl of Constant Sorrow," "I'm Going to Organize Babe of Mine," and "I Hate the Company Bosses." He deposited the recordings in the Library of Congress, without her permission; Folk-Legacy Records issued twenty of her songs as "*Girl of Constant Sorrow*," with notes by Archie Green, in 1965. Her first husband having died in 1938, she married Joseph Gunning in 1941.[14]

Jean Thomas, the collector, festival organizer, and writer, unearthed a curious bit of musical lore. In her somewhat fanciful portrait of the blind musician Jilson Setters (originally James William Day), published in *Ballad Makin' in the Mountains of Kentucky*, she captured some of his labor and political songs, such as "Coal Creek Troubles" (recorded in 1937 with Alan Lomax), about a mine strike/lockout in Tennessee in 1891: "When 'trouble' came up in the Coal Creek mines, the valiant old minstrel of the Kentucky mountains promptly declared himself 'in sympathy with the miner.'" The song took on a life of its own, as Archie Green has explained: "During 1891 and 1892 a group of miners—insurrectionists in the eyes of the state, but 'true and honest-hearted' in the view of an itinerant blind fiddler—helped rid Tennessee by direct action of a brutal convict-lease system."[15]

While Korson believed that mining songs had outlived their utility by the 1930s and 1940s, Archie Green, through his heavily illustrated study, well documented that they continued into the 1960s. *Only a Miner* is mostly organized around the recording history of particular songs, such as "Coal Creek Troubles," "Roll Down the Line," "Mother Jones," "Nine Pound Hammer," "Mining Camp Blues, "Coal Mountain Blues," and "Coal Miners Blues." His focus was on early 78 rpm recordings, but he ended with a survey of "coal-song singles only to note the continuity in the music industry's use of mining events and themes." For example, in 1960, soon after a mine disaster in Logan County, West Virginia, the songs "Island Creek Mine Fire" and "Holden 22 Mine" appeared for sale. Green not only noted that Korson had passed over songs with a radical connection, he also reflected on Korson's caution regarding any songs with a bawdy theme. Indeed, it "is our loss that many excellent anthologies of cowboy, hobo, lumberjack, sailor, and soldier songs were marred by total oversight of any obscenity, however defined." Green also explored the curiosity of Gene Autry, the budding cowboy singer with no obvious radical orientation, recording "The Death of Mother Jones" in

1931. The song honored Mary Harris "Mother" Jones, a long-time labor organizer and union hero, who had died in late 1930 at the age of one hundred.[16]

Green devoted one chapter to country songwriter and performer Merle Travis. Born in Muhlenburg County, Kentucky, in 1917, he began recording for Capitol Records in 1946 the album *Folk Songs of the Hills*, released the next year. He included some older songs, such as "Nine Pound Hammer" and "John Henry," as well as three of his own fresh compositions, "Sixteen Tons," "Over By Number Nine," and "Dark as a Dungeon." In *Folk Song: U.S.A.*, John and Alan Lomax praised the album: "Work songs of the East Kentucky coal camps, perfectly performed. A new album, one of the ten best." During early 1948 Alan Lomax also featured *Folk Songs of the Hills* on his Mutual Network radio show, "Your Ballad Man." But the album languished until 1955, when Tennessee Ernie Ford made a hit of "Sixteen Tons," and it gained renewed popularity; it was reissued as an LP in 1957.[17]

TEXTILE SONGS

Radical activists were also active in organizing southern textile workers beginning in the 1920s, which produced a spate of catchy songs. Female workers in the pre-Civil War northern textile mills had used music in their organizing drives. "With the single exception of the miners," John Greenway explained in 1953, "no organized labor group has produced more songs of social and economic protest than the textile workers. Their songs are plentiful from the earliest period of American labor history, and at the present time are richer in sincerity, quality, genuine folk content, and protest, than those emanating from any other industry." John and Alan Lomax had no separate listings for textile songs in their songbooks, although they did include "Cotton-Mill Colic" in *Our Singing Country*.[18]

Textile organizing songs picked up in 1929 during a strike at the Marion Manufacturing Company in Marion, North Carolina, such as "The Marion Massacre" and "The Marion Strike." That same year a strike at the Loray mills in nearby Gastonia produced "Come On You Scabs If You Want To Hear" to "Casey Jones," and "Up In Old Loray" to the tune of "On Top of Old Smokey." "The emergence of songs and the richness of music in mill towns during the 1920s and 1930s—songs and music that spoke directly to the lives and experiences of Piedmont mill workers—should come as no surprise given the importance of such tradition in southern Appalachian mountain culture and the subsequent concentration of mountain folk in the new and growing mill town of the southeast," Vincent Roscigno and William Danaher summarized in *The Voices of Southern Labor*.[19]

The bloody Gastonia strike was partially organized by the Communist-led National Textile Workers Union (NTWU), which generated much controversy. Margaret Larkin, a left-wing journalist and collector of cowboy songs from New York, arrived in Mount Holly, just northeast of Gastonia, in August 1929. Here she met Ella May Wiggins, a union member and spinner at American Mill No. 2 in Bessemer City, near Gastonia, who performed her own songs. "Meetings, speeches, picket lines, the crises of terror—these developed Ell May's latent talents. The immense vitality of the mountain woman," Larkin later wrote, "unquenched by 10 years in the mills, overflowed into 'Song Ballets' about the union and the strike." Mary Heaton Vorse, another radical journalist, collected various ballads familiar to the striking miners, such as "Barbara Allen," "Birmingham Jail," and "Waiting for a Train." "Despite a musical exchange, northern middle-class organizers and southern working-class strikers encountered one another in Gastonia across a vast cultural and class divide," Patrick Huber has explained. Of all the local bards, Wiggins generated the most publicity. The writer Vera Buch noted that she "would write little ballads about the strike, set them to some well-known ballad tune, and sing them from the platform in a rich alto voice." She penned over twenty songs, of which six have survived, including " Chief Aderholt" and "Mill Mother's Song" (later retitled by John Greenway "Mill Mother's Lament"). She was gunned down in September during the strike by company thugs, and was survived by her five children; "Mill Mother's Song" was published the next month in the *Labor Defender*. Women wrote most of the strike songs, such as eleven-year-old Odell Corley with "Up in Old Loray," based on "On Top of Old Smokey," and Daisy McDonald, a Loray spinner, who penned "The Speakers Didn't Mind." "Ballad composing accorded women a status and prestige in their communities usually unavailable to them under peaceful conditions," Patrick Huber has explained. "It also offered women the chance to speak out on issues of importance to them, and no issues figured more prominently in their songs than the plight of wage-earning mothers and their children."[20]

While the strike failed, the songs would live on and influence many others. Dave McCarn, for example, a textile worker who had grown up in Gastonia, recorded "Cotton Mill Colic" in 1930. He had lost his job with the onset of the Depression; he was no radical, only a disgruntled worker. "McCarn's solution to the miseries of textile work is for dissatisfied millhands to quite their jobs and return to their former lives in Southern Appalachia—an untenable plan for many workers," Patrick Huber argued. The record sold well locally, and the song would have a lasting influence. In *Our Singing Country*, John and Alan Lomax included "Cotton-Mill Colic," while attributing it to Joe Sharp of Scottsboro, Alabama, who had recorded it for Alan in 1938, with no mention of McCarn. McCarn also recorded "Poor Man, Rich Man (Cotton Mill Colic No. 2)" and "Serves 'Em Fine (Cotton Mill Colic No. 3)," which laments the decline of the southern textile industry. "While it is true that a great outpouring of textile songs came after 1929 in the wake of the dramatic strikes that swept the Piedmont, and that the most famous cotton mill composer, Ella May Wiggins of Gastonia, North Carolina, was apotheosized after her death by northern radicals, the textile song tradition preceded the ideological conflict of the Depression years and was a product of indigenous conditions," country music historian Bill Malone has maintained. As for McCarn, "More than any other textile song, 'Cotton Mill Colic' entered musical tradition and spread rapidly in the Depression-stricken South, chiefly through the powerful modern medium of phonograph records," Patrick Huber has concluded. "Only five months after its release, Tom Tippett, a labor organizer and activist from Brookwood Labor College in Katonah, New York, heard 'Cotton Mill Colic' sung at a January 1931 union rally during a textile strike in Danville, Virginia."[21]

A short-lived strike at the Marion Manufacturing Company in Marion, North Carolina, in July 1929, also produced a few songs. Frank Welling and John McGhee composed both "North Carolina Textile Strike" and "Marion Massacre," which they recorded for Paramount Records the following October. The latter referred to the murder of six strikers by the deputies.[22]

Howard and Dorsey Dixon grew up in textile families, but had scant connection with the labor movement, although they worked in textile mills much of their lives, while living in Rockingham, North Carolina. They did, however, join the strike against the Hannah Pickett Mill No. 2 in 1932. They began their professional career on a Charlotte radio station in 1934, and recorded for RCA-Victor's Bluebird label two years later. Dorsey composed dozens of songs, including the poignant "Weave Room Blues," "Spinning Room Blues," and "Weaver's Life." Jimmie Tarlton, who also worked at Hannah Pickett Mill No. 2 and often performed with Dorsey, recorded "Weaver's Life" in 1932, and the Dixon brothers followed in 1938. They first recorded "Weave Room Blues" for Victor in 1936, and two years later a somewhat different (and more popular) version; Fisher Hendley and His Aristocratic Pigs also issued the song in 1938 on Vocalion. "Though [Dorsey] Dixon shied away from a sustained critique of southern industrialism," Patrick Huber explained, "his textile mill songs represent a powerful voice of class consciousness and offer important insights into the working conditions and struggles of Piedmont millhands during the 1930s." The Dixons's RCA contact lapsed in 1938, and Dorsey did not record again until contacted by Archie Green and Eugene Earle in 1962. Nineteen of his songs soon appeared in the Testament Records album *Babies in the Mill: Carolina Traditional, Industrial, Sacred Songs*. He had written the title song in 1945, based on his sister Nancy's experiences as a child laborer at the Darlington Manufacturing Company beginning in 1901, while he worked at the Duncan Mill in Greenville, South Carolina. His career was now briefly revived, and he appeared at the Newport Folk Festival in 1963. He died five years later.[23]

There were various other textile-related recordings, for example Lester Pete Bivins's "Cotton Mill Blues" for Decca in 1938. "If these recorded songs are set apart from the strike songs by their failure to suggest alternatives to the unequal relations of labor," Doug DeNatale and Glenn Hinson have explained, "they are joined to each other through a common approach to the problems of mill life. Though they may present grievances, these are generally couched in a joking manner." While their lives were difficult, the songs often touched upon humor and innuendo. Except for "Weave Room Blues" and "Cotton Mill Colic," most of the songs had a limited, local audience.[24]

RADICAL ORGANIZATIONS AND LABOR SONGS

When Aunt Molly Jackson and her family arrived in New York City in late 1931 there was the beginning of a thriving left-wing cultural scene. Within a few years it would grow and flourish. Meanwhile, throughout the country a singing labor movement, fueled by radical organizers and songwriters, was patchy, but clearly visible. This was part and parcel of what Michael Denning termed the "laboring of American culture" during the Depression years and for some time after.[25]

As labor strikes proliferated in the North and South, many union organizers believed that songs could generate greater labor solidarity and passion. This was particularly true for some on the political left, although neither the Communist Party nor any other radical organization, except for the Industrial Workers of the World (IWW), officially promoted folk music as an organizing tool. By the mid-thirties labor songs were becoming ubiquitous at left-wing meetings and also on many, although certainly not all, picket lines.

The Depression and ensuing political upheavals, somewhat reflected in the New Deal legislation of the Franklin Roosevelt administrations beginning in 1933, stimulated a wave of musical responses. Even Jean Thomas found reflections in the southern hills. "There was a time when mountain folk, old and young, looked down upon earning their daily bread at public works," she explained. But with growing economic problems came a changed attitude. "And they learned to their surprise and dismay about the 'Union' and the alphabetically labeled organizations like the C.I.O. Out of their experiences came a new crop of ballads." She gave the example of Bunyan Day's "The Picket Line Blues," relating to a 1937 strike at the Friedman Scrap Yard in Boyd County, Kentucky: "He played the guitar and sang for me one evening, worn out though he was, after doing picket duty for many long, wearisome hours. His tune is quite modern. That is to be expected, for Bunyan Day has a brand-new radio to which he listens avidly." Even Jilson Setters penned labor songs about the CIO and the promises of the New Deal.[26]

In 1932, the Workers Music League (W.M.L.), an offshoot of the Communist Party in New York, published the *Red Song Book*. This was the first party publication to include labor songs with a folk accent. According to the introduction, the "W.M.L., as the music section of the Workers Cultural Federation, is the central organization of all music forces connected with the American revolutionary working class movement. Its aim is to coordinate, strengthen, and give both ideological and musical guidance to these forces." The

W.M.L. soon published a monthly magazine, *The Worker Musician*. Some Communist Party members had formed the League in 1931 to promote proletarian music, and there were chapters in the major eastern cities. They affiliated with the Pierre Degeyter Club (named after the composer of "The Internationale"), which had been formed in 1932 as an organization of left-wing performing artists, publishers, and composers. The latter soon created the Composers Collective, with such musical luminaries as Henry Cowell, Charles Seeger, Marc Blitzstein, Herbert Haufrecht, and Aaron Copland. While many of the composers initially favored a modernist, classical style, as well as songs from outside the U.S., rather than American folk music, the *Red Song Book* significantly included "The Preacher and the Slave," "Hold the Fort" (which the IWW had borrowed from the British transport workers, although it had originated in the United States), Aunt Molly Jackson's "Poor Miner's Farewell," Ella May Wiggins's "I.L.D. Song," and even Maurice Sugar's newly penned "Soup Song."[27]

Critics within the Communist Party were initially confused by the use of the folk idiom. A review of *Red Song Book* in *The Worker Musician*, for example, criticized the "arrested development" of the mining songs. In 1934, Ray and Lida Auville published a handful of their folk-style compositions in *Songs of the American Worker*, such as "the Miner's Son" and "I'm Not Blue Any More (Because I'm Red)." Having moved from the southern mountains to Cleveland, they were now affiliated with the Communist Party. "Members of the Composers Collective reviewed *Songs of the American Worker* in cautiously favorable terms," Richard and JoAnne Reuss explained. "The mere appearance of these more singable topical creations was applauded, yet reviewers Charles Seeger and Elie Siegmeister (using their pseudonyms) both found much that was banal and artificial in the texts and melodies." Mike Gold, the party's culture critic, defended the Auvilles and attacked Seeger for his elitist approach to music: "It is the real thing, folk song in the making, workers' music coming right out of the soul."[28]

The Composer's Collective published its own songbooks in 1934 and 1935. The first *Workers Song Book* included thirteen original songs by Charles Seeger, Elie Siegmeister, Lan Adomian, and others. According to the book's foreword, "The music front of the revolutionary movement in America has been advanced so far by two distinct types of songs: first, well known and popular bourgeois tunes to which revolutionary words have been set; second, original tunes by proletarian composers." The Collective much preferred the latter, which were free "from defeatist melancholy, morbidity, hysteria and triviality." They had listened to Aunt Molly at one of their meetings in 1933, but quickly rejected her folk style. The second songbook included additional songs by Seeger, Earl Robinson, and Hans Eisler, with revolutionary phrases and complex musical arrangements, except for two African American songs collected by Lawrence Gellert. "It is important for the future development of workers' music that this song book have the widest circulation and use," the editors stated, "and that discussions in trade unions, workers' clubs and choruses be organized around the question: 'What is workers' music?' and how far the songs in this volume are satisfactory in answering this question." The response was quite swift—the songs were definitely unsuitable.[29]

But the tide was quickly turning, as a folk style was being adopted by many on the left. Indeed, even Lan Adomian had suggested in early 1934 that workers' choruses should include "Negro songs of protest, work songs, railroad songs, cowboy and hill songs." Jim Garland represented the developing interest in labor songs in the North. "By 1936, I was spending much more of my time singing and picking on the guitar," he recalled. "I was scheduled by the International Workers Order and the Cafe Society [this is probably a general reference, since the progressive nightclub by this name did not open until 1938] to sing before numerous groups, one of them being the Workers Alliance, an organization of the unemployed. With that group we went on demonstrations to the relief office, marched in the May Day parades, and attended mass meetings at

Madison Square Garden." A bit later he briefly had his own local radio program, with his sister Sarah and others. Garland was in the thick of the Popular Front cultural movement, when the Communist Party reached out to others on the left and within labor unions to help promote labor organizing, civil rights, economic equality, and world peace. Folk music would play a growing role in this struggle. The International Workers Order (IWO) People's Chorus, directed by Earl Robinson, included folk songs in its concerts. "The choristers, who made their debut at the New Masses concert a few short months ago, concentrate on such native ballads as 'Casey Jones,' 'Wanderin',' and 'The Tarriers Song,'" explained a *Daily Worker* review in May 1938. "They have performed at union, I.W.O. and American League for Peace and Democracy functions." Robinson recalled he "felt happiest and most fulfilled when the National Seamen's Union invited us to sing in their soup kitchen as part of their strike activity."[30]

In addition to the southern mining and textile struggles, folk-style songs also emerged from various other union organizing drives, North and South, both black and white, by mid-decade, particularly with the founding of the CIO in late 1935. The CIO heavily organized industrial workers and advocated strikes and other forms of worker activism. One example was the sit-down strike in Flint, Michigan, promoted by the newly formed United Automobile Workers Union (UAW). "Music and singing played a major role at Flint, largely because of the nature of a sit-down strike," Timothy Lynch has explained. "The very fact that workers were together, occupying a number of plants for over six weeks, made boredom and idleness commonplace. Writing and singing songs were effective ways of maintaining morale and passing the time." Songs quickly appeared, such as "The Fisher Strike," published in the local UAW newspaper, which explained how the strike began in the Fisher Body Factory Number One. "The Battle of Bull's Run" celebrated a workers' victory over the local police. Some of the songs, such as "Oh, Mister Sloan," derided the company's management.[31]

The strikers' meetings usually had entertainment. "But best of all the strikers liked their own hillbilly orchestra which broadcast its nightly programs over the loudspeaker for the benefit of the many outsiders who gathered each evening to listen," Henry Kraus, managing editor of the Flint union newspaper, explained in his history of the strike. "The hopeful spirit of the strike was expressed by the orchestra's sprightly 'theme song,' which had been adapted on the first night of the strike to the music of the well-known southern folksong, 'The Martins and the Coys," The song was entitled "The Fisher Strike." When some of the strikers were arrested, "the men revived their courage incessantly through singing of 'Solidarity [Forever],' whose eight-worded elementary but evocative refrain brought them a steady, heartening echo from the friendly hosts outside. . . . 'We sang it four thousand times a day,' Charley Hammer later reported. 'We sang it at midnight, at three in the morning or at any time it came into our heads.'" When the sit-in ended, "wives and children rushed to husbands and fathers who had not been seen for ten fear-filled days. Strong, heavily-bearded men were unashamed of tears. Then someone began to sing 'Solidarity' . . . and as all joined in, the moment was carried beyond its almost unbearable tenseness and emotion."[32]

Striking autoworkers and their wives composed some of the songs, while others were borrowed from various sources. "Hold the Fort" and "We Shall Not Be Moved" were particularly popular. Kraus noted that ten songs from the *Rebel Song Book*, published by the socialist-oriented Rand School in 1935, were popular, in particular "The Soup Song," "Hold the Fort," and "Solidarity Forever." The Detroit labor lawyer Maurice Sugar first wrote "The Soup Song" in 1931. According to Christopher Johnson, Sugar's biographer, "Very few songs of the Depression enjoyed such wide currency. Its easy rhythms (sung to the tune of 'My Bonnie Lies over the Ocean') and biting ironies encompassed both the despair and the dark humor that marked the workers' outlook in those years." Indeed, when Sugar visited the Fisher Body plant during the sit-in, as he later informed Pete Seeger, "I was taken to the plant kitchen where long lines of workers with soup bowls in their hands, [were] waiting to have them filled from the gigantic soup cistern. . . . and all the time they were singing the 'Soup Song' with gusto." The *United Automobile Worker* published a page of songs, entitled "Strike Songs: Battle, Victory, Joy," in January 22, 1937. The newspaper's editors believed, though "basing their verse on other tunes, the songs, nevertheless, express a collective creative activity that is rare enough in American life."[33]

Sugar became caught up in the auto sit-in. He composed "Bring Me My Robe and Slippers, James," about the workers' living conditions, and especially "Sit Down." A decade later he vividly recalled the setting: "I wrote the song 'Sit-Down' [sic] during the avalanche of sit-down strikes, which occurred in the early months of 1937. . . . 'Sit-Down' was sung by the strikers in their meeting halls, and in the plant while the strike was in progress. In the plants, singing was part of the organized recreation of the workers, and they frequently improvised musical bands, featuring accordions, mandolins, guitars, mouth organs, and now and then saxaphone [sic]. These bands went sled-length for folk songs." As sit-downs spread to other industries, so too did "Sit Down." It was as popular among the strikers as "The Soup Song." The Timely record company, affiliated with the Communist Party, issued an album of labor songs by the New Singers in 1935, which contained "The Soup Song"; its second album, by The Manhattan Chorus, included "Sit Down." While Timely records had limited circulation, Sugar's songs did reach a somewhat larger audience.[34]

STRIKE SONGS IN STEEL

The Homestead strike in Pennsylvania in 1892 was musically different from the southern mine and mill strikes, with more of a British than southern influence, yet with popular overtones. Members of the Amalgamated Association of Iron and Steel Workers

(AA) struck against the Carnegie Steel Corporation's Homestead Steel Works, just upstream from Pittsburgh. There were earlier mill-related songs, such as the 1875 "March of the Rolling-Mill Men." Archie Green has found twelve connected with the Homestead strike, and has examined two in detail, William Delaney's "Father Was Killed by the Pinkerton Men" and John Kelly's more influential "A Fight for Home and Honor at Homestead, Pa." He also has brief notes for "The Homestead Strike," "Stand by the Workmen at Homestead," "The Strike at Homestead," and others.[35]

The Steel Workers Organizing Committee (SWOC), forerunner of the United Steelworkers of America, emerged in mid-1936 as part of the CIO; six years later SWOC merged with the moribund AA to form the United Steel Workers of America (USW). The steelworkers were not much of a singing union, at least judging from the seeming dearth of songbooks. One from the mid-1950s (with the drawing of a barbershop quartet on the cover) included an assortment of folk and popular songs, with the likes of "America the Beautiful," "Casey Jones," "Joe Hill," "Oh Susanna," "The Blue Tail Fly," and "You Are My Sunshine." Only a few related to the union, such as "Strong Men of Steel," "It's a Good Thing to Join a Union," "Mammy's Little Baby Loves a Union Shop," and "A Song for Steelworkers." But none were particularly catchy, such as "The Soup Song" or "Roll the Union On," which were also included.

But other steel-connected songs surfaced during the labor upheavals of the 1930s. Joe Gelders, working for the National Committee for the Defense of Political Prisoners in Birmingham, Alabama, penned "The Ballad of John Catchings" in 1936. Catchings worked for Republic Steel's Thomas Furnace and was charged with assault during a strike in 1934. Gelders and his wife Esther recorded the song for Alan Lomax in New York in November 1937. Singing among black union members increased by mid-decade. "During the late 1930s, SWOC even had its own labor vocal group known as the Bessemer Big Four Quartet," according to the historian Robin D.G. Kelley. "Made up of black gospel singers who had sung with the West Highland Jubilee Singers during the 1920s, the Bessemer Big Four Quartet performed at union meetings and was heard occasionally on local radio broadcasts. Singing eventually became the Alabama CIO's cultural cornerstone." The collector Robert Sonkin recorded the Bessemer Big Four singing "Good Evening Everybody" in 1941. "The importance of the unions to black industrial workers in Birmingham District was expressed through the medium of gospel music," Brenda McCallum has explained, "which, like some earlier British and American labor song traditions, had a strong ideological commitment to unionism that was grounded in Christian theology and proclaimed unionism as a holy cause." By this time labor songs, derived from a variety of sources and influences, had become part of popular culture.[36]

(Endnotes)

1 Elizabeth Balch, "Songs for Labor," *The Survey*, January 3, 1914, 408, 428.

2 George G. Korson, ed., *Songs and Ballads of the Anthracite Miner: A Seam of Folklore Which Once Ran Through Life in the Hard Coal Fields of Pennsylvania* (N.Y.: Frederick H. Hitchcock/Grafton Press, 1927), ix-x.

3 Korson, ed., *Songs and Ballads of the Anthracite Miner*, xix; Angus K. Gillespie, *Folklorist of the Coal Fields: George Korson's Life and Work* (University Park: Pennsylvania State University Press, 1980), chap. 1.

4 Korson, ed., *Songs and Ballads of the Anthracite Miner*, 157, 161, 181; *I'm A Johnnie Mitchell Man* (Williamsport, PA: Vandersloot Music Pub. Co., 1906).

5 Melvin LeMon and George Korson, *The Miner Sings: A Collection of Folk-Songs and Ballads of the Anthracite Miner* (N.Y.: J. Fischer & Bro., 1936), 3; *Pennsylvania Folk Songs and Ballads for School Camp and Playground* (Lewisburg: Pennsylvania Folk Festival, 1937), 1. The National Folk Festival, beginning in St. Louis in 1934, also included occupational performers, such as retired seamen from Sailor's Snug Harbor on Staten Island, two cowboy singers, and retired lumberjacks from Michigan.

6 George Korson, *Minstrels of the Mine Patch: Songs and Stories of the Anthracite Industry* (Philadelphia: University of Pennsylvania Press, 1938), 4-5, 7; George Korson, "Coal Miners," in Korson, ed., *Pennsylvania Songs and Legends* (Baltimore: The Johns Hopkins Press, 1949), 354-400. Some of these recordings were issued by the Library of Congress in 1947, *Songs and Ballads of the Anthracite Miners*, Library of Congress, Music Division, Recording Laboratory, LC 16; *Songs and Ballads of the Anthracite Miners*, Rounder Records, Roun 1502, 1996.

7 George Korson, *Coal Dust on the Fiddle: Songs and Stories of the Bituminous Industry* (Philadelphia: University of Pennsylvania Press, 1943), 119; Ray Funk, "Birmingham Quartets Celebrate the Union Movement," *Spirit of Steel: Music of the Mines, Railroads and Mills of the Birmingham District* (Birmingham: Sloss Furnace Association, 1999), 11-18 (the accompanying CD includes both recordings). See also, *Songs and Ballads of the Bituminous Miners*, Library of Congress, Music Division, Recording Laboratory, LC 60, which appeared in 1965; Nimrod Workman, *I Want to Go Where Things Are Beautiful*, Twos & Fews/Drag City, DC379, 2008.

8 George Korson, *Black Rock: Mining Folklore of the Pennsylvania Dutch* (Baltimore: Johns Hopkins Press, 1960), 350, 355.

9 Duncan Emrich, "Songs of the Western Miners," *California Folklore Quarterly*, vol. 1, no. 3 (July 1942), 214; Wayland Hand, Charles Cutts, Robert C. Wylder, Betty Wylder, "Songs of the Butte Miners," *Western Folklore*, vol. 9, no. 1 (January 1950), 1-2, 3, 49.

10 John A. Lomax and Alan Lomax, *American Ballads and Folk Songs* (N.Y.: Macmillan Company, 1934), 437; Lomax and Lomax, *Our Singing Country: A Second Volume of American Ballads and Folk Songs* (N.Y.: Macmillan Company, 1941), 271-278. And see, in general, Ted Gioia, *Work Songs* (Durham: Duke University Press, 2006), chap. 10.

11 Archie Green, *Only a Miner: Studies in Recorded Coal-Mining Songs* (Urbana: University of Illinois Press, 1972), 17, 18.

12 *Welcome the Traveler Home: Jim Garland's Story of the Kentucky Mountains*, ed. Julia S. Ardery (Lexington: University Press of Kentucky, 1983), 149-150; Shelly Romalis, *Pistol Packin' Mama: Aunt Molly Jackson and the Politics of Folksong* (Urbana: University of Illinois Press, 1999), chaps. 1-3; *Aunt Molly Jackson*, Rounder Records 1002, 1972. "Ragged Hungry Blues" appeared in *Songs For Political Action: Folk Music, Topical Songs, and the American Left*, Bear Family Records BCD 15720, 1996. See, in general, John W. Hevener, *Which Side Are You On? The Harlan County Coal Miners, 1931-39* (Urbana: University of Illinois Press, 1978).

13 Romalis, *Pistol Packin' Mama*, 38; *Welcome the Traveler Home*, 161; Timothy P. Lynch, *Strike Songs of the Depression* (Jackson: University Press, of Mississippi, 2001), chap. 2.

14 *Welcome the Traveler Home*, 159; Romalis, *Pistol Packin' Mama*, chap. 5; Sarah Ogan Gunning, *"Girl of Constant Sorrow,"* Folk-Legacy Records FSA-26, 1965.

15 Jean Thomas, *Ballad Makin' in the Mountains of Kentucky* (N.Y.: Henry Holt Company, 1939), 195; Green, *Only a Miner*, 188, and chap. 5 in general.

16 Green, *Only a Miner*, 409, 20, and chap. 7 for the Mother Jones story; Elliott Gorn, *Mother Jones: The Most Dangerous Woman in America* (N.Y.: Hill & Wang, 2001).

17 John A. Lomax and Alan Lomax, *Folk Song: U.S.A.* (N.Y.: Duell, Sloan and Pearce, 1947), 401; Bob Richards, Erasie Palmer, Dick Milton, *The Miner's Song* (N.Y.: Quality Music Co., 1947); Green, *Only a Miner*, chap. 8.

18 John Greenway, *Folksongs of Protest* (Philadelphia: University of Pennsylvania Press, 1953), 121.

19 Vincent J. Roscigno and William F. Danaher, *The Voice of Southern Labor: Radio, Music, and Textile Strikes, 1929-1934* (Minneapolis: University of Minnesota Press, 2004), 65.

20 Margaret Larkin, "We'll Never Let Our Union Die," *Daily Worker*, September 14, 1938; Patrick Huber, " 'Battle Songs of the Southern Class Struggle': Songs of the Gastonia Textile Strike of 1929," *Southern Cultures*, vol. 4, no. 2 (Summer 1998), 115, 118; Patrick Huber, *Linthead Stomp: The Creation of Country Music in the Piedmont South* (Chapel Hill: University of North Carolina Press, 2008), 195-196.

21 Huber, *Linthead Stomp*, 206, and chapter 3 in general; Bill Malone, *Don't Get above Your Raisin': Country Music and the Southern Working Class* (Urbana: University of Illinois Press, 2002), 39; Patrick J. Huber, "'Cain't Make a Living at a Cotton Mill': The Life and Hillbilly Songs of Dave McCarn," *North Carolina Historical Review*, vol. 80, no. 3 (July 2001), 328.

22 Greenway, *Folksongs of Protest*, 130-133.

23 Huber, *Linthead Stomp*, 218, and chap. 4 in general on Howard and Dorsey Dixon; Dorsey Dixon, Howard Dixon, and Nancy Dixon, *Babies in the Mill: Carolina Traditional, Industrial, Sacred Songs*, Testament Records T-3301, 1965.

24 Doug DeNatale and Glenn Hinson, "The Southern Textile Song Tradition Reconsidered," Archie Green, ed., *Songs about Work: Essays in Occupational Culture for Richard A. Reuss* (Bloomington, IN: Special Publications of the Folklore Institute No. 3, Indiana University, 1993), 82. On the General Textile Strike of 1934, which seems to have pro-

duced few, if any, songs, see Roscigno and Danaher, *The Voice of Southern Labor*, chap. 7. Roy Harvey, a member of Charlie Poole's North Carolina Ramblers, wrote the song "The Virginian Strike of '23," "which remains one of only a few songs about southern labor struggles to appear on commercial hillbilly records before World War II," according to Huber, *Linthead Stomp*, 132; it was recorded by Harvey and Earl Shirkey for Columbia Records in October 1929 and released the next May. Harvey had been an engineer on the Virginian Railroad and joined the strike by the Brotherhood of Locomotive Engineers, which lasted for six years. For a discography of recordings of early "Occupational and Protest Songs," see Guthrie T. Meade, Jr., Dick Spottswood, Douglas S. Meade, *Country Music Sources: A Biblio-Discography of Commercially Recorded Traditional Music* (Chapel Hill: Southern Folklife Collection, University of North Carolina at Chapel Hill Libraries, 2002), 410-419.

25 Michael Denning, *The Cultural Front: The Laboring of American Culture in the Twentieth Century* (N.Y.: Verso, 1996).

26 Thomas, *Ballad Makin' in the Mountains of Kentucky*, 238.

27 Workers Music League, *Red Song Book* (N.Y.: Workers Library Publishers, 1932), [3]; Ann M. Pescatello, *Charles Seeger: A Life In American Music* (Pittsburgh: University of Pittsburgh Press, 1992); Elizabeth B. Crist, *Music for the Common Man: Aaron Copland During the Depression and War* (N.Y.: Oxford University Press, 2005).

28 Richard A. Reuss and JoAnne C. Reuss, *American folk Music and Left-Wing Politics, 1927-1957* (Lanham, MD: Scarecrow Press, 2000), 52 (first quote), 74, 75 (second quote).

29 *Workers Song Book 1934, No. 1* (N.Y.: Workers Music League, 1934), 2; *Workers Song Book No. 2* (N.Y.: Workers Music League, 1935), inside front cover.

30 Lan Adomian, "What Songs Should Workers' Choruses Sing," *Daily Worker*, February 7, 1934; *Welcome the Traveler Home*, 183; Irene Tennenbaum, "Mass Folk Music Aim of Workers Order Chorus," *Daily Worker*, May 27, 1938; Earl Robinson with Eric A. Gordon, *Ballad of an American: The Autobiography of Earl Robinson* (Lanham, MD: The Scarecrow Press, 1998), 74.

31 Lynch, *Strike Songs of the Depression*, 86.

32 Henry Kraus, *The Many & the Few; A Chronicle of the Dynamic Auto Workers* (Los Angeles: The Plantin Press, 1947), 104, 151, 290.

33 Christopher H. Johnson, *Maurice Sugar: Law, Labor, and the Left in Detroit, 1912-1950* (Detroit: Wayne State University Press, 1988), 117; "So-o-o-o-up," *People's Songs*, vol. 2, nos. 1 and 2 (Feb.-March 1947), 22; quote in Lynch, *Strike Songs of the Depression*, 114.

34 So-o-o-o-up," *People's Songs*, vol. 2, nos. 1 and 2 (Feb.-March 1947), 22. See also, Johnson, *Maurice Sugar*, 212-213 and *passim*. Both Timely albums are included in Ronald Cohen and Dave Samuelson, comps., *Songs for Political Action: Folk Music, Topical Songs and the American Left, 1926-1954*, Bear Family Records BCD 15720, 1996.

35 Archie Green, "Homestead's Strike Songs," in Green, *Wobblies, Pile Butts, and Other Heroes: Laborlore Explorations* (Urbana: University of Illinois Press, 1993), chap. 7; see also, Jacob E. Evanson, "Folk Songs of an Industrial City," in George Korson, ed., *Pennsylvania Songs and Stories* (Baltimore: The Johns Hopkins Press, 1949), 423-466.

36 Joyce Cauthen, "The Ballad of John Catchings," *Spirit of Steel*, 27-36 (the accompanying CD includes the recording); Robin D. G. Kelley, *Hammer and Hoe: Alabama Communists During the Great Depression* (Chapel Hill: University of North Carolina Press, 1990), 149; the Bessemer Big Four's "Good Evening Everybody" is quoted in *Spirit of Steel*, 64-66 (the accompanying CD includes the song); Brenda McCallum, "Songs of Work and Songs of Worship: Sanctifying Black Unionism in the Southern City of Steel," *New York Folklore*, vol. 14, nos. 1-2 (1988), 27. See also, Elizabeth Morgan, *Socialist and Labor Songs of the 1930s* (Chicago: Charles H. Kerr Publishing Company, 1997).

COMMONWEALTH
LABOR SONGS

A COLLECTION OF OLD AND NEW SONGS
FOR THE USE OF LABOR UNIONS

Published Spring Quarter
1938 by Commonwealth
College Mena Arkansas

Price: 5 cents

Commonwealth Labor Songs (Mena: AR: Commonwealth College, 1938) *chapter four*

The Later 1930s and the War Years

LABOR SCHOOLS

By the mid-1930s, there were some elements in place for a singing labor movement, particularly within those industrial unions with left-wing connections. Much of this impetus came from the proliferating labor schools. The creation of Ruskin College at Oxford University in England in 1899 sparked a growing interest in workers' education in the United States. Some schools, such as the International Ladies Garment Workers Union's "Worker's University" in New York, met in a public school building at night. By the 1930s there were summer programs for women affiliated with colleges and universities, such as the Bryn Mawr Summer School for Women Workers, the Barnard Summer School, and the University of Wisconsin Summer School. There were also residential labor colleges, such as Brookwood in Katonah, New York, and Commonwealth College in Mena, Arkansas, and most of them included music as part of their programs.

A group of socialist and pacifist activists founded the Brookwood Labor College in Katonah, New York, in 1921 as the first residential labor school. Although not officially sponsored by the American Federation of Labor (AFL), over a dozen international unions were supportive. Until its demise in 1937, labor songs were integrated parts of its curriculum and it published a handful of songbooks. For example, *Brookwood Chatauqua Songs*, with the subtitle "A Singing Army Is a Winning Army," was published in 1936 or 1937. Beginning with "Solidarity Forever," it included a spirited collection of songs, some with a Communist connection, such as "The Internationale," "Anthem of the I.L.G.W.U.," and "Hold the Fort," as well as "We Shall Not Be Moved," which school organizers had learned from the West Virginia Miners' Union.[1]

Kate Richards O'Hare and William Zeuch organized Commonwealth College in 1923 in western Louisiana, which soon moved to Mena, Arkansas. Another residential school, it combined workers' education with a cooperative lifestyle; it lasted until 1940. Agnes "Sis" Cunningham arrived during the summer of 1931 as a student. She later recalled: "At suppertime we sang 'The Internationale.' Somebody remembered how much I loved the song; it had been eons, so it seemed, since I'd sung it or heard it sung. Now I would see that it was sung every day." Sis was a gifted musician and organizer of musical dramas, and the college published her small songbook, *Six Labor Songs*, including Reginald Kaufman's "March of the Hungry Men," for which she composed the music. In 1938 the school issued two additional songbooks, *Commonwealth Labor Songs* and *Commonwealth Labor Hymnal*. The former was divided into four sections: "Songs For Labor," "Songs For the Picket Line," "Southern Labor Hymns," and "Folk Songs." The latter included both IWW songs, such as "Casey Jones, the Union Scab" and "The Preacher and the Slave," as well as "Song of the Red Air Fleet" and "Red Front." In the summer of 1937, a few years after leaving Commonwealth, Sis taught briefly at the Southern Summer

School for Women Workers near Asheville, North Carolina. Initially founded in 1927 at Sweet Briar College in Virginia, it had moved to Asheville. While there she published a songbook for the students, which included "There Are Strange Things Happening," partially written by her father, Chick Cunningham.[2]

Various other labor schools published songbooks, such as the University of Wisconsin School for Workers, begun in 1924. *The School For Workers Song Book* featured a section with "Union Songs," including "Joe Hill," "Preacher and the Slave," "My Darling CIO," and "Union Maid," as well as chapters for "Good Fellowship Songs," "Spirituals and Folk Songs," and "Patriotic Songs." In 1938, Caroline Wassermann compiled a songbook for the Pacific Coast School For Workers in Berkeley, California. An expanded version in 1939 included a wide variety of tunes, including "Sing Me a Song of Social Significance" from the ILGWU musical *Pins and Needles*, "The Popular Wobbly," and "Solidarity Forever." The following year, the Hudson Shore Labor School in West Park, New York, formerly the Bryn Mawr Summer School, published its own songbook.[3]

The Kentucky Workers Alliance (KWA), a branch of the Workers Alliance of America, promoted labor songs through the work of Don West, born in North Georgia in 1906. After a brief stint at the Hindman Settlement School in Knott County, Kentucky, in 1930, he graduated from the Vanderbilt School of Religion. Along with Myles Horton, West helped launch the Highlander Folk School, in Monteagle, Tennessee, in 1932, but he was gone within the year. The KWA was formed in 1936, with West as its organizational secretary and then state organizer until his departure in late 1937. The KWA published his small songbook, *Songs For Southern Workers*, in 1937. A published poet, West adopted various tunes, such as "Study War No More" which now became "Not Going to Work and Starve No More," while "Jacobs Ladder" turned into "We Are Building a Strong Union." He also included his friend Jim Garland's "Give Me Back My Job Again," "Solidarity Forever," and "The Internationale." West's biographer James Lorence has captured the songbook's essence: "Drawing freely on familiar music as well as many songs that originated in 'bloody Harlan,' West substituted locally relevant words that articulated the sentiments of the downtrodden toward the elite who dominated their lives and inspired them to collective action."[4]

Meanwhile, the Highlander Folk School (HFS) developed an emphasis on workers' education, particularly through the use of labor songs. Zilphia Mae Johnson began as a student in January 1935; she married Myles Horton two months later, and quickly became the school's music director. "Music and folk dancing were forms of entertainment as well as education at HFS," John Glen has written in his history of the school. "They instilled a sense of solidarity among students, fostered a feeling of cultural pride, offered inspiration and hope, and contributed to the development of leadership, if only for group singing." Ralph Tefferteller, the square dance instructor, had also arrived in 1935. Folk music became such a vital part of the school's program that it published a steady stream of songbooks during the 1930s into the 1940s. The list included *Workers Songs* (1935), *Let's Sing* (1937), *Songs of the Southern Summer School* (1938), *Songs for Workers* (1939), and *Songs of Field and Factory* (1940). Zilphia Horton also edited *Labor Songs* for the Textile Workers Union of America in 1939. "Most of the songs in this collection were written by people who work in the mines, mills, factories, and on the farms," she explained in the introduction. "It is hoped that this book will encourage workers to write and sing their own songs," which was her life's work.[5]

Lee Hays, a friend of Zilphia Horton, occasionally visited Highlander before joining the faculty of Commonwealth College in late 1937, when Claude Williams, a radical Presbyterian minister, became its director. Hays organized social-action dramas and led the singing. Both Hays and Horton had come under Williams's influence during his stay in Paris, Arkansas, and he had influenced Horton to move to Highlander. Waldemar Hille, dean of music at Elmhurst College in Chicago, met Hays during a visit to Commonwealth. In 1938, Hille and Hays performed for striking newspapermen in Chicago. When Hays's biographer, Doris Willens, interviewed Hille on the subject he recalled, "Lee participated in meetings and sang union songs, labor songs, radical songs. . . . He had all this wonderful material that he and Claude had created with a few word changes out of gospel songs, making them into inspirational labor-organizing songs. Such as 'Organize, Organize, Let the Will of the Lord Be Done.'" At the time Hille planned an "American Workers Song Book," covering "Songs of the American labor front," "International Workers Songs, "Negro Songs," "Youth Group Songs," "Sailor Songs," "Jail-Convict-chain gang" songs, and much more. While that project was never completed, Hille soon compiled a similar songbook for Commonwealth College that would be more expansive than *Commonwealth Labor Songs*, but it too was stillborn. Hays also proposed to Zilphia Horton that the two of them put together their own labor songbook in late 1938. "We want to get out a good workers' songbook," he explained, "as an anniversary publication. It must have music, and it must be representative. . . . I am wondering how we could cooperate with you folks on this project. It would be an admirable way to get together, it seems to me, on a specific service to the labor movement."[6]

There is no indication that this Hays-Horton songbook appeared, although Hays did compile the ten-page mimeographed *Commonwealth Labor Songs—A Collection of Old and New Songs for the Use of Labor Unions*. He specialized in combining theater and music. "We wrote and produced many plays for sharecroppers and Farmers Union audiences," Hays recalled. "It was in the plays that we first sang 'No More Mourning' and 'Roll the Union On' and 'What is that I see yonder coming?' And always we sang songs like 'Let the will of the Lord be done' and 'When the struggle's over we shall all be free, in the new society.'" Williams left Commonwealth in 1939, and the college closed the following year, just when Hays moved to New York.[7]

In 1939, Hille summed up his fervent interest in worker's songs, by now shared by many: "Because I believe America's problem No. 1 today is the true understanding of the workers: among themselves, in relationship to professionals and intellectuals and other middle class elements, and in relation to the upper '400.' . . . American worker's songs are one of the many channels of human persuasion that must be put into the service of a common cause of humanity—the brotherhood of man." He would devote his life to such music. "Since music as an art has the power to communicate just at the point at which words fail," he concluded, "it is easy to understand the potential value of the study, assimilation and reproduction of American worker's songs in an attempt to identify ones-self [sic] with their cause."[8]

SONGS AND UNION ORGANIZING

Labor schools did their part in connecting music with a labor consciousness, and they were strongly assisted by a variety of newly emerging farmers and industrial unions. For example, the interracial Southern Tenant Farmers Union (STFU) published their undated *Song Book*. Organized in 1934 in Tyronza, Arkansas, the STFU joined briefly with the CIO-affiliated United Cannery, Agricultural, Packing and Allied Workers Union (UCAPAWA). The STFU attracted the thirty-one-year-old black sharecropper John L. Handcox in 1935, then living in St. Francis County in eastern Arkansas. As an organizer for the union until 1937, he composed various poems and songs. During a trip to Washington, D. C. in March 1937, Charles Seeger and Sidney Robertson recorded eight of his songs for the Library of Congress, including "Raggedy, Raggedy Are We," "We're Gonna Roll the Union On," and "Mean Things Happening in This Land." Sis Cunningham attended the STFU 1937 convention in Muskogee, Oklahoma. "Each session opened with singing," she recalled, "usually led by A.B. Brookins or John Handcox or a choir from a local church. We sang one or several of the most loved songs: 'Before I'll Be a Slave, I'll Be Buried In My Grave,' 'Hungry, Hungry Are We,' 'Roll the Union On,' 'Strange Things Happening in This Land,' and, of course, 'We Shall Not Be Moved.'" While Handcox vanished from history until his reemergence in 1980 (he died in 1992), "Roll the Union On" had become a labor standard.[9]

Various CIO unions issued their own songbooks, particularly those with a left-leaning orientation. The United Office and Professional Workers of America (UOPWA), for example, issued two flimsy songbooks in the 1940s. They included a variety of domestic and foreign songs, including "Careless Love," "Freiheit," "On Top of Old Smokey," "Spring Gong" (China), and "Anthem of the Soviet Union." The pocket-sized *Let's Sing!*, published by the International Ladies' Garment Workers' Union (ILGWU), with its socialist orientation, included many selections from the *Rebel Song Book*. "A victorious army is a singing army," the introduction proclaimed. "The I.L.G.W.U., ever marching on to win a better life for the workers, has its own songs, some of which are given here. These, like the others in this collection, have been born on the picket line. They mock our foes, remember our martyrs and hymn faith in our union and international solidarity." In addition to the standards, such as "Soup Song" and "Bread and Roses," there was also "Song of the Dress Striker" and "No More Sweatshops." The Textile Workers Organizing Committee (TWOC) of the CIO produced the small book of *Songs* in the mid-thirties. It included "The C.I.O.'s In Dixie," "Write Me Out My Union Card," "Picket Parade," and "Put On Your New TWOC Bonnet." Out of the TWOC emerged the Textile Workers Union of America (TWUA), which issued *Labor Songs* in 1939. It included songs for various occasions, such as "Workers Lullabye," "Workers' Funeral Hymn," and "Oh, Mister Boss Man, Don't Cry For Me!"[10]

In 1940, the Amalgamated Clothing Workers of America (ACWA) issued *Sing, Amalgamated!*, subtitled *A Book of Songs for Picket Lines, Meetings, Parties, and Other Union Occasions*, which about covered the ground. Beginning with the usually requisite "The Star Spangled Banner," the book contained "Hold the Fort," "Casey Jones," "Hallelujah I'm a Bum," and "We Honor Our Union." The list was not particularly radical, except perhaps for "Joe Hill." A few years later, the UAW-CIO Education Department in Detroit published *UAW-CIO Sings*, with sections for union songs, songs of fellowship, patriotic songs, and folk songs. "Our union is a singing union," the text proclaimed. "We can hear our members sing of their struggles, of their fights in organizational days, of why they think 'it's a good thing to join the union.'" It included "We Shall Not Be Moved" and "The Spirit of the CIO." Folk songs were incorporated because the "UAW-CIO is a union of Negroes and whites, Jews and gentiles, Catholics and Protestants, Alabamans and Michiganders, Jerseyites and Californians, people whose parents were born in Poland, in Canada, in Russia, in Sweden, in Germany, in Finland. You can hear it in the stories they tell, sometimes it is plain from their accents, most of all you hear it in their songs, their folk songs." Most union songbooks were not so inclusive. The small *Songs for Seamen*, issued by the National Maritime Union (NMU) in 1947, opened with "Commonwealth of Toil" and also featured the IWW-connected "The Preacher and the Slave."[11]

Union songbooks covered a wide range of topics, but all had one aim, as the Birmingham [Alabama] Industrial Union Council's *CIO Songs* explained: "Keep in the Rhythmic Swing of the Labor Movement—Enliven Your Meetings and Join the Grand March to Victory by Singing." Some songs had national resonance, such as "We Shall Not Be Moved," but most in *CIO Songs* had more of a local connection, such as "The C.I.O.'s In Dixie," "We're Gaining In Steel," and "The Miner's Strike Song." The ILGWU also produced a volume of *Dixie Union Songs*. Some unions, in particular the ILGWU, issued numerous songbooks over many years, while other, such as the United Oil and Petroleum Workers of America, the Amalgamated Meat Cutters and Butcher Workmen of North America, and the United Rubber Workers of America, published infrequent editions.

Many labor leaders, but certainly not all (far from it), believed that "A singing army is a winning army!" as union organizing escalated through the late 1930s.[12]

LABOR SONGS REACH BROADWAY

In 1934, Aaron Copland, a modernist composer and member of the Workers Music League (WML), favorably reviewed the first volume of their *Workers Song Book* for the left-wing *New Masses* (he had no song in this copy, but his "Into the Streets May First" appeared in the 1935 edition). He agreed that "every participant in revolutionary activity knows from his own experience that a good mass song is a powerful weapon in the class struggle." Copland's optimism did not translate into reality, and the WML's compositions had scant, if any, influence in the wider world of the working class. The numerous labor songs using folk and popular melodies were considerably more popular at union meetings and on the picket line. But there was another form of seemingly rarified musical expression which connected workers' experiences and dreams with a popular audience: the Broadway musical.[13]

Stage plays and musicals had a venerated past, but had usually shied away from overt support for labor's complaints and causes. Beginning with the onset of the Depression, however, left-wing musical expressions took various forms. Perhaps most surprising were the popular musicals that began to appear. "In truth, the most effective agit-prop [agitation and propaganda] verse produced in the northern labor movement during these same years was cast in an essentially popular vein," Richard Reuss has argued. "Such songs as 'Picket on the Picket Line,' 'Oh, Mister Sloan,' and 'There Was a Rich Man Who Lived in Detroitium' emphasized humor, cleverness, and 'cute' lyrics for the most part. They frequently had a jingle-like quality different from the folk-derived union music of the South, which was by comparison unpretentious and straightforward, manifesting a gut militancy absent in the majority of urban labor songs created in the 1930s." Workers' musicals joined the myriad of left-wing plays, novels, murals, poetry, and other forms of radical cultural expression by the mid-1930s.[14]

During the early years of the Depression radical theatrical groups in New York and elsewhere began staging plays with music, such as *Art is a Weapon* (1931), *Sweet Charity* (1932), *Worlds Fair* (1933), *Who's Got the Baloney* (1933), and *Parade* (1935) (for which "Aunt Molly Jackson's Coal Mining Blues" was written, but apparently not performed). They were not memorable and had no catchy tunes. By mid-decade, however, when the League of Workers' Theatres became the New Theatre League and promoted workers' theaters throughout the country, such musicals became more influential. *Sit-Down!* (1937), for example, was drawn directly from the recent Flint strike, and included the performers as workers singing "Solidarity Forever," "Sit Down," "and "Hold the Fort." Marc Blitzstein's *The Cradle Will Rock* (1937), while politically controversial, had considerably more popularity and impact. The play's setting in a steel town focused on the current labor strife, with a strong anti-boss message. The songs propelled the plot forward, and while too complicated to be popular on a picket line, one in particular, "The Cradle Will Rock," long remained a Broadway standard.[15]

Pins and Needles, which opened in late 1937, would serve, along with *The Cradle Will Rock*, as the preeminent labor musicals. "Today a person has but to wander into a trade union meeting and as likely as not he will encounter a phonograph playing the music from labor's 'Pins and Needles,'" Kenneth Hunter explained in the *Daily Worker*. "The gathering then joins and sings the songs with lusty relish." Music of various sorts appeared to be ubiquitous at radical gatherings, such as the chorus of 500 voices at the Tenth National Communist Party convention at Madison Square Garden in May 1938. "In the Communist Party, in the Socialist Party, to some extent in the YCL [Young Communist League], songs written as satire on popular numbers and originals have been produced at small meetings," Hunter added. *Pins and Needles* had been written and performed by members of the International Ladies Garment Workers Union (ILGWU) Players, with the music by the composer Harold Rome, at the Princes Theater, now called Labor Stage. Originally featuring union members, the performers soon became professionals as they staged *Pins and Needles* in New York and throughout the country for almost four years. The songs, topical and satirical for the most part, included "We'd Rather Be Right," "Sunday in the Park," "Men Awake," "One Big Union for Two," "When I Grow Up (The G-Man Song)," although they changed over the years. "Sunday in the Park" made the Hit Parade.[16]

Left musicals declined following *Pins and Needles*, as energies were diverted elsewhere. Langston Hughes wrote *Don't You Want to Be Free?*, which was performed in April 1938. With poetry and music, the play covered the history of oppressed African Americans, ending with a call for racial unity. Traditional spirituals were featured, but with new lyrics. The next year Paul Robeson starred in the short run production of *John Henry*, along with the theatrical newcomer and blues musician Josh White. Despite the cast and story potential, it received poor reviews and closed within a week. After a stellar academic and sports career at Rutgers University, and obtaining a law degree from Columbia University Law School, Robeson had pursued a successful acting and musical career through the 1920s before moving to England in 1931. When he returned to the United States in 1939, while not abandoning a hectic performing schedule, he plunged into supporting various CIO unions. He preferred integrated unions, such as the United Auto Workers, and performed at a monster rally at Cadillac Square in Detroit in May 1941. "From the spring of 1941 on, Robeson made regular appearances before union conventions and union rallies, urging labor leaders to fight racial discrimination at the workplace, and urging Blacks to strive for union leadership," Mark Naison has written. He became an honorary member of the National Maritime Union (NMU) and performed at their July 1941 convention, singing "Water Boy," "Joe Hill," and "Old Man River."[17]

The musical *We Beg to Differ*, a Canadian import, enjoyed limited success when performed in Philadelphia in December 1939. More popular were the Theatre Arts Committee (TAC) Cabarets in New York in the late 1930s. From 1937 to 1939 each midnight production had various songs and performers, such as Will Geer, Francis Farmer, Imogene Coca, Tony Kraber, and Michael Loring, doing "Casey Jones," "Old Paint (The Horse With the Union Label)," and "Capitalistic Boss." The labor-oriented *Sing for Your Supper* in 1939, one of the final Works Project Administration (WPA) productions, included both song and dance. Indeed, the left-wing dancer Edith Segal had been involved with the Red Dancers and the Dance Group of the Needle Trades Workers Industrial Union; she was also the Social Director of Unity House, the ILGWU's resort. There were scattered agit-prop theater groups around the country, such as the Red Dust Players in Oklahoma, which featured Sis Cunningham. A singing (and dancing) labor movement had glimmers of hope, as the quickly expanding CIO and rejuvenated AFL assured workers increasing influence, but with the coming of war and a somewhat reviving economy, its future seemed less than bright.[18]

THE ALMANAC SINGERS

Labor songs and performers had deep roots in New York when a rag-tag group of young singers and writers formed the Almanac Singers on the verge of the United States entry into World War II. "I returned to New York City in the fall of 1940, after having spent five or six months hitchhiking around the South and West, and most recently to New England," Pete Seeger would recall. "I believe it was the month of December, but it might have been early January, when I tackled the problem of the manuscript to the book, 'Hard-hitting Songs,' and wondering whether I should try and find a publisher for it." Seeger had met Woody Guthrie, who had just arrived in New York from California, at the "Grapes of Wrath" benefit concert at the Forrest Theatre the previous March 3.[19]

Seeger and Guthrie were brought together by Alan Lomax after the concert, and it proved to be a fateful meeting. The songbook that would eventually be published as *Hard Hitting Songs for Hard-Hit People* began soon after. Guthrie took the next two months to write the head notes, Seeger transcribed the melodies from songs that Lomax had collected from recordings, field work, and publications; there were also a few written by Guthrie. The 150 selections, the cream of the crop of contemporary labor and protest songs, were grouped under thirteen headings, such as "Hard Luck on the Farm," "Some From the Old Wobblies," "Hell Busts Loose in Kentucky," "Detroit Sets Down," "The Farmers Get Together," and "One Big Union." "Working people sing of their hopes and of their troubles," John Steinbeck wrote in the foreword, "but the rhythms have the beat of work—the long and short bawls of the sea shantys with tempos of capstan or sheets, the lifting rhythms, the swinging rhythms and the slow, rolling songs of the southwest built on the hoof beats of a walking horse. The work is the song and the song is the people." It would take until 1967, however, when Irwin Silber, editor of *Sing Out!*, finally published this monument to work songs and Alan Lomax's collecting skills. Indeed, as Lomax wrote on the eve of the book's publication, "Most of these songs would probably have disappeared if they had not been collected or recorded at the time. . . . In a sense we treasured these songs, because to us they were symbols of the fighting, democratic spirit of a whole sector of the population that is too often viewed as faceless, voiceless, supine and afraid."[20]

Seeger met some of the "faceless, voiceless" workers as he traveled around with Guthrie for a few months starting in May 1940, and then roamed around by himself until November (not December as he later remember it). He had heard that Lee Hays was also working on a book of labor songs, and the two soon met. "I don't know whether I called him up first or he called me," according to Pete, "but I remember coming around to a small dark one-room apartment where Lee and Mill Lampell were staying. . . . And we hit it off right away, Lee and me, and Mill too. . . . So we teamed up together and started singing at some little fundraising parties I guess in January, 1941. And pretty soon Mill was joining us, although Mill made no claim to being a singer or musician." Seeger and Hays began at the Jade Mountain Restaurant in December, a fundraiser for Spanish Loyalist refugees. Millard "Mill" Lampell had grown up in New Jersey, attended the University of West Virginia, then moved to New York in mid-1940 as a budding writer. He soon met Lee and they began sharing an apartment in Hell's Kitchen. "Pete talked ardently about his dream of using singing to help unions organize, but didn't volunteer much about himself," Mill later wrote. "And I didn't ask. . . . In his faded workshirt and thick-soled clodhoppers, Pete looked like a poor kid just off the farm."[21]

They soon began singing together. "The first night Pete appeared at our apartment, the three of us stayed up until dawn," Lampell would recall. "I sat there listening to him and Lee trade ballads, blues, gospel hymns, sea chanteys, field hollers, cowboy laments, breakdowns. After a while, I found myself joining in on the choruses, the songs echoing a wild mix of moods." Woody Guthrie soon appeared at their door with his family, but didn't stay long. By February, Pete (often using the surname Bowers in any publicity in order to protect his father, who was working for the government), Lee, and Mill were living together in a loft on 12th Street near Fourth Avenue, the first Almanac House. They came up with the name Almanac Singers for their fledgling group. They were now temporarily singing anti-war songs, which quickly appeared on the Keynote label's *Songs for John Doe* album, but they focused on labor union songs.[22]

Adding a new member, Peter Hawes, they participated in the May Day parade, and then appeared at the "Sign of the Times" labor review at Finnish Hall in mid-month. "In this little show they do all of their familiar popular numbers but some new ones as well, blasting the enemies of labor and of peace and telling the story of the great strike struggles of this very year," according to the *Daily*

COMMITTEE for MINERS

presents

FOLK MUSIC

for

HAZARD

Benefit for Unemployed Hazard, Kentucky Coal Miners

Polytechnic Auditorium
Baltimore, Maryland

February 28, 1965

Program of Folk Music for Hazard, Kentucky, coal miners, Baltimore, Maryland, February 28, 1965, with Phil Ochs, Tom Paxton, Buffy Sainte-Marie, Patrick Sky, Jim & Jean, Alix Dobkin, and the Greenbriar Boys.

John A. Lomax and Alan Lomax, *Cowboy Songs and Other Frontier Ballads* (N.Y.: Sturgis & Walton, 1917 [orig. ed. 1910]); N. Howard *Thorp, Songs of the Cowboys* (Boston: Houghton Mifflin Company, 1921 [orig. ed. 1908]).

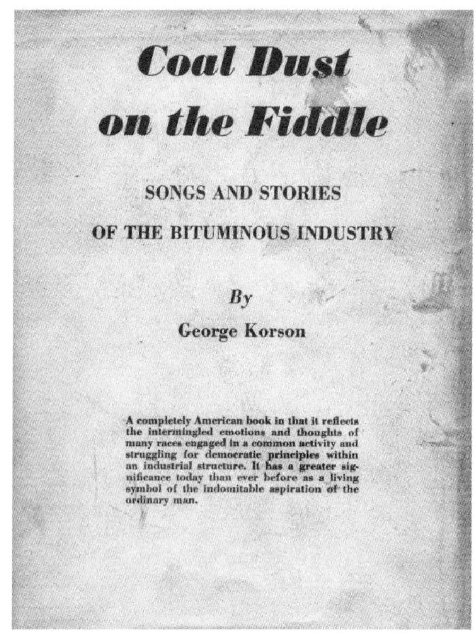

Coal Dust on the Fiddle

SONGS AND STORIES OF THE BITUMINOUS INDUSTRY

By George Korson

A completely American book in that it reflects the intermingled emotions and thoughts of many races engaged in a common activity and struggling for democratic principles within an industrial structure. It has a greater significance today than ever before as a living symbol of the indomitable aspiration of the ordinary man.

George Korson, *Coal Dust on the Fiddle: Songs and Stories of the Bituminous Industry* (Philadelphia: University of Pennsylvania Press, 1943).

Songs: Knowledge Is Power (N.Y.: Educational Department, International Ladies' Garment Workers' Union, nd); Zilphia Horton, comp., *Labor Songs* (N.Y.: Textile Workers Union of America, 1939).

CIO Songs (Birmingham, Ala.: Birmingham Industrial Union Council, nd.); *UAW-CIO Sings* (Detroit: UAW-CIO Education Department, ca. 1941).

Henry W. Shoemaker, comp., *North Pennsylvania Minstrelsy* (Altoona, PA: Altoona Tribune Company, 1919); *The March of the Workers and Other Songs* (Chicago: Young Workers League of America, ca. 1925).

Rebel Song Book (N.Y.: Rand School Press, 1935.)

Red Song Book: Prepared in Collaboration with the Workers Music League (N.Y.: Workers Library Publishers, 1932).

Workers Song Book No. 1 (N.Y.: Workers Music League, 1934).

Almanac Singers, Talking Union: 8 Union Songs of the Almanac Singers. N.Y.: New Theatre League, ca. 1941.

Caroline Wassermann, comp., *Song Book of the Pacific Coast School For Workers.* Berkeley: Pacific Coast School for Workers, 1939.

Yankele Brisker, "Der Striker," sheet music, 1923.

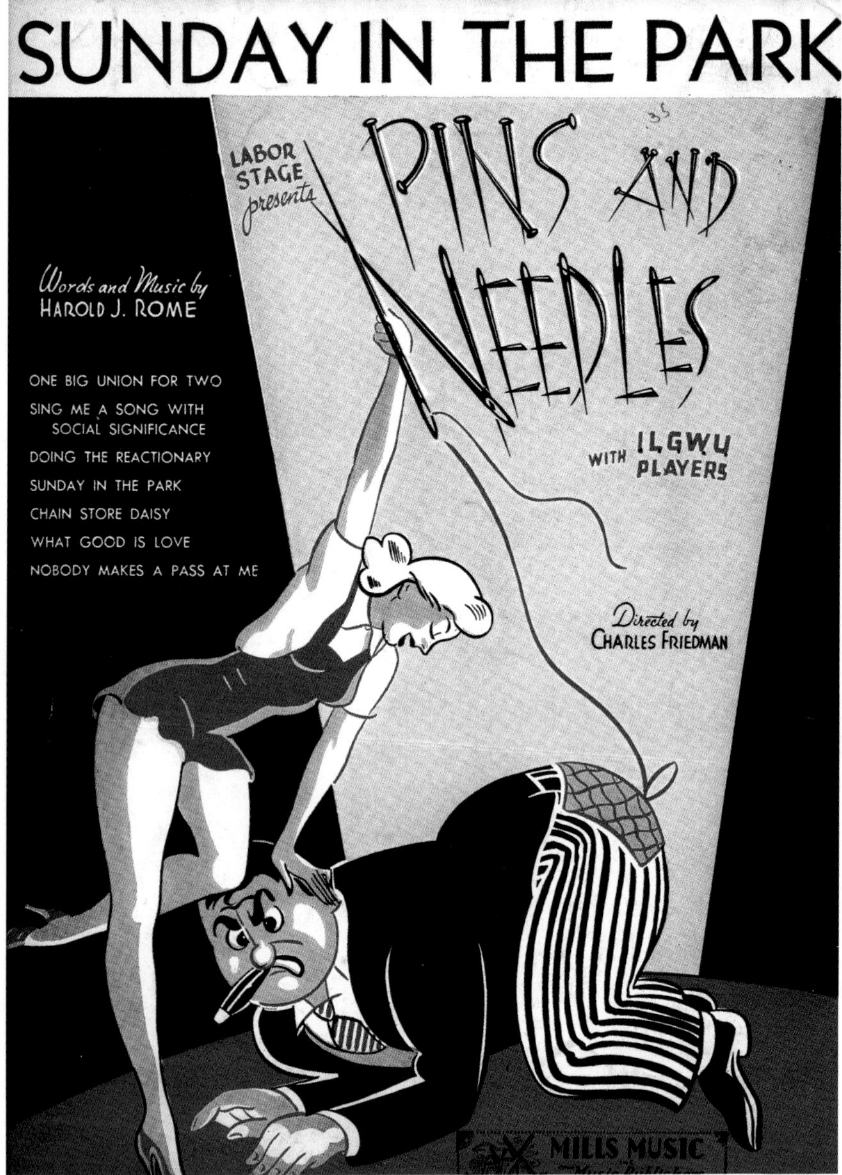

"Sunday in the Park," Pins and Needles, sheet music, 1937.

S. R. Lang, "The Union Parade," sheet music, 1904.

Pierre Degeyter, "The Internationale," sheet music, 1934.

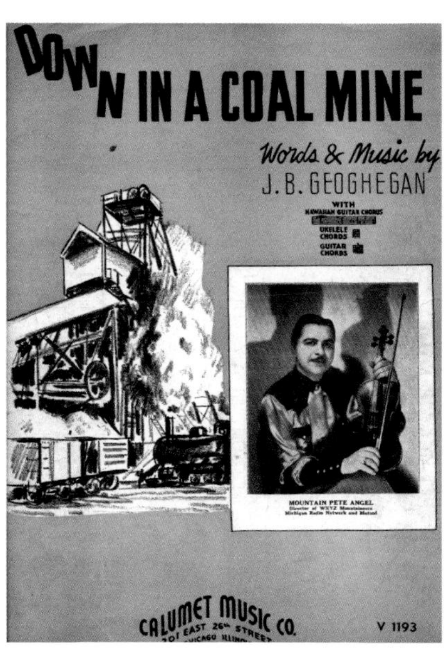

J. B. Geoghegan, "Down In a Coal Mine," sheet music, 1937.

Douglas and Liebich, "The Advancing Proletaire," sheet music, ca. 1920.—

Chas. Fern, "I'm a Johnnie Mitchell Man," sheet music, 1906.

Rudolph Leonhart, "Labor March," sheet music, 1895.

Joe Hill, "Workers of the World Awaken!," sheet music, 1916.

I.W.W. Songs to Fan the Flames of Discontent. Cleveland: I.W.W. Publishing Bureau, December 1914; Charles J. Finger, *Sailor Chanties and Cowboy Songs.* Girard, KS: Haldeman-Julius Company, 1923.

Barrie Stavis and Frank Harmon, *The Songs Of Joe Hill.* N.Y.: People's Artists Inc., 1955.

Kathy Kahn and Danny McMahan, *Coors Brewery Strike Songs,* Dare to Struggle Music 1977.

AMERICAN
FOLK SONGS
OF PROTEST

By John Greenway

John Greenway, *American Folk Songs of Protest.* Philadelphia: University of Pennsylvania Press, 1953.

Edith Fowke and Joe Glazer, *Songs of Work and Freedom.* Chicago: Labor Education Division, Roosevelt University, 1960.

Elie Sigemeister, *Work and Sing: The Songs That Built America.* N.Y.: William R. Scott, 1944.

William Doerflinger, *Shantymen and Shantyboys: Songs of the Sailor and Lumberman.* N.Y.: Macmillan Co., 1951.

Ad for The New Singers, Workers Songs, Timely Records 1935.

Joe Glazer, comp., *Songs for AFSCME.* [Washington, D.C.]: AFSCME, 1978.

AFL-CIO Song Book. Washington, D.C.: AFL-CIO Department of Education, Revised 1974.

May Day Songbook. Workers Party & Labor Action, ca. 1950.

Worker article. Aunt Molly Jackson, Lead Belly, and Josh White began regular visits to Almanac House. "It was all inspiring," *Daily Worker* writer Mike Gold enthused, "Remarkable in New York, this spontaneous gathering of folk-singers. Here above the rolling trucks and grimy factories of Fourth Avenue, an Americana folk legend was being made right under one's nose. Yet hasn't the revolutionary workers' movement thus stimulated folk-art in every land?" Soon after, in late May, they performed for the giant rally of twenty thousand striking Transport Workers Union members at Madison Square Garden. Around this time the group recorded the album *Talking Union* on the Keynote label, which included "Union Train," "Talking Union," "All I Want," "Union Maid," "Which Side?," and "Get Thee Behind Me Satan." Pete, Lee, and Mill were joined by Josh White and his wife Carol, Sam Gary, and Bess Lomax. Originally issued in July 1941 as an album of 78 rpm records, Folkways Records reissued it as a single LP in 1955. This was the first time that recordings of these songs were readily available in libraries, scattered record stores, and people's homes.[23]

June began with a rousing gathering of performers at Town Hall, organized by Earl Robinson and Will Geer, and titled "A Cavalcade of American Song." It was a benefit for the N.Y. Committee to Aid Agricultural Workers. Scattered among the traditional songs, such as "Bennington Riflemen" (Almanac Singers), "Haul Away Joe" (Burl Ives), and "Working on the Railroad" (Tony Kraber), were such labor songs as "John Henry" (Josh White and Lead Belly), "Hard Working Miner" (Aunt Molly Jackson), "Weave Room Blues" (Pete Bowers/Seeger), and "T. B. Blues" (Lead Belly). The Almanacs continued their busy schedule, recording two albums of traditional songs for General Records in early July, soon released as *Deep Sea Shanties and Whaling Ballads* and *Sod Buster Ballads*. They included a variety of older occupational songs, including "Blow Ye Winds, Heigh Ho," "I Ride an Old Paint," and "Haul Away, Joe." Just after the recording session Seeger, Lampell, Hays, Guthrie, and Pete Hawes left for a western road trip, but the latter soon became ill and dropped out. They had already written to Saul Mills of the New York CIO Council, wondering "if you could send us the names of any union people in the cities listed, to whom we could write and try to arrange bookings." Mills obliged by writing to Louis Goldblatt of the California State Industrial Council: "In addition to composing, the Almanac Singers also have been singing these songs at union meetings and rallies in and about New York. They are very popular and in great demand. . . . They wear work clothes and may be described as [a] typical, American homey singing group. They are not New Yorkers and much of their singing is in the Western twang."[24]

Beginning in Philadelphia, the quartet (they were now minus Hawes) performed before labor groups in Cleveland, Detroit, Akron, Chicago, Milwaukee, and Denver, before hitting San Francisco. Their album *Talking Union* was now out, along with a songbook, *Talking Union: 8 Union Songs of the Almanac Singers*, published by the New Theatre League. "Our *Talking Union* album didn't hit the juke boxes, didn't cause Victor or Columbia any sleepless nights, but it was being distributed by a lot of CIO affiliates," according to Lampell. "As a wildfire of strikes raged across the country, two and a half million American were walking picket lines. It excited us to hear that (Union Maid) was being sung by cotton mill workers in North Carolina, by strikers at the International Harvester tractor plant in Minneapolis, by hospital workers in Chicago and aircraft workers in Los Angeles. . . . New York was no longer the heart of union action." Perhaps their songs had spread, but Seeger had a different recollection of the group's prominence: "We had no great fame except in this narrow group of left-wingers; but we sang for a few hundred here and a few hundred there across the country. We stayed in peoples' homes or the cheapest hotels."[25]

They performed before a large NMU convention in Milwaukee. "Standing against the wall, we surveyed the crowd, looked at each other, and grinned. The hall was packed to overflowing with five or six hundred delegates, row after row of craggy, weathered faces, Great Lakes sailors and riverboat men. It was what we had dreamed of since Madison Square Garden, a chance to be part of the crash and surge of a tidal wave of union organizing that was sweeping across the nation," Lampell later rhapsodized. While the men had never heard of the Almanacs, when they began with "Which Side Are You On?" the delegates were soon joining in. "We got a standing ovation and an unbelievable collection of $135 when we passed the hat." In Detroit they sang in Cadillac Square before an autoworkers' rally. In Minneapolis they appeared alongside pickets at an International Harvester plant, then were gassed by the National Guard.[26]

One memorable evening in Chicago they performed for the Chicago Repertory Group, and were welcomed by the budding actor and writer Louis "Studs" Terkel. In 1931, a group of actors had formed the Chicago Workers' Theater, which became the Chicago Repertory Group in 1935 when it staged *Waiting for Lefty*, which included in the cast the recent law school graduate Terkel. Three years later they produced *The Cradle Will Rock*, and were well established when the Almanacs arrived. Terkel and Win Stracke, another regular cast member, readily promoted the music of the Almanacs, and following the war would be key figures in the local People's Songs chapter.

Lampell had met Harry Bridges, head of the International Longshoremen's and Warehousemen's Union on the West Coast, before they left New York, so they had a contact when they reached San Francisco. Just prior to their departure, the Almanacs had recorded two songs for Keynote, "Song For Bridges" and "Babe O' Mine," the former written by Lampell, Hays and Seeger, the latter by Sarah Ogan Gunning, and the single 78 rpm quickly appeared. At their performance at the Longshoremen's Union Hall, "There was Harry Bridges and some other union leaders up front," Seeger recalled, "and some of the Longshoremen in the crowd, maybe 500 or more, turned around and I think I heard one mutter, 'What the heck is a bunch of hillbilly singers coming in for. We've got work to do here today.' But Harry Bridges introduced us, and when we finished singing, 'The Ballad of Harry Bridges,' we got a standing ovation. The applause was deafening. We sang several more songs, and when we walked down the aisle, they slapped Woody on the back so hard, they nearly knocked him over." They also performed for the Miscellaneous Workers Local 110, the Marine Cooks and Stewards, and the International Workers Order (IWO). The *Daily Worker* article pointed out that they "are touring the country now, singing workers' songs to working people—mainly to trade unions—but to the common people everywhere."[27]

Hays soon returned to New York, while Guthrie, Seeger, and Lampell moved on to Los Angeles, "where once again left-wingers and the C.I.O. arranged for one booking after another," according to Seeger. "I remember marching in the Labor Day Parade in early September, and they all loved to join in on, 'Oh, You Can't Scare Me, I'm Sticking to the Union." Lampell had a similar memory: "Our record albums had found their way out there, people had heard about us, and there was as much work as we could handle. Singing in picket lines at the aircraft plants. Singing in union halls. Singing at fund-raising parties. . . . And we got paid at each one." Lampell also soon returned to New York, leaving Guthrie and Seeger to venture to Portland and Seattle, after stopping first in the Central Valley of California to perform for some migratory workers. They arrived back in New York in early October, having joined with mineworkers in Butte, Montana, and lumberjacks in northern Minnesota.[28]

They had discovered somewhat of a singing labor movement, but with difficulty and in scattered spots. Most unions were more interested in bread and butter issues, rather than a few scraggly troubadours, and had little time for songs. This was particularly the case with the older AFL unions, although many of the new CIO locals also had little, if any, interest in folk-style union songs. The Almanacs had hoped for more, although where possible they had encountered a responsive crowd. While in Los Angeles they (probably mostly Guthrie) had written an article for the local left-wing magazine *The Clipper*, entitled "Hard hitting songs by hard hit people": "Anywhere there's worry, trouble, misunderstanding, you'll find plenty of songs. The Union men and women haven't just fallen heir to their Union cards and higher wages. They stopped work, went out on strike, marched on the picket line, and fought wind and weather," and sometimes sang labor songs. But they were disappointed that there was not a broader interest. "The woods are full of good honest musicians and song writers, artists, and actors of all kinds," they continued, "who would like to be on the side of the workers in this battle. Why is it that the work of these progressives hasn't really grabbed a hold in the Unions?" They had hope that popular culture—radio, theater, movies, popular music—would pick up on the workers' plight, since the "history is being sung in songs and ballads in the Union halls, and the Union hall is the salvation of real honest-to-God American culture."[29]

Soon after returning, the Almanacs moved to a townhouse at 110 West Tenth Street, then to 430 Sixth Avenue. The flexible group now included Bess Lomax, younger sister of Alan, and Baldwin "Butch" Hawes, the younger brother of Peter. But now Hays moved out, replaced by Arthur Stern, another bass singer. The floating group appeared before various union and radical gatherings into the winter, as the U.S. plunged into the war in early December following the Japanese attack on Pearl Harbor. They had earlier switched to pro-war songs, and in January 1942 recorded the album *Dear Mr. President* for Keynote, which included "Reuben James," "Round, Round Hitler's Grave," and Sis Cunningham's "Belt Line Girl," about women working in a war plant. Sis Cunningham and her husband Gordon Friesen had fled from the "Red Scare" in Oklahoma the previous fall and moved into Almanac House in early December; they lived there and later in the Sixth Avenue quarters until October 1942. The Almanacs struggled through the winter and into the spring, with shrinking finances and engagements. At an organizational meeting in April, Lampell wondered whether "there really can be 'just trade union singers.' Because unions now are going into other groups—defense setups for instance." After a lengthy discussion, little was settled. Late in the month five Almanacs, including Cunningham and Seeger, performed in Detroit, Chicago, Milwaukee, and Rochester.[30]

They only recorded once more, in early June, "Boomtown Bill" (by Woody) and "Keep That Oil A-Rollin'" (by Woody and Butch Hawes), a record commissioned by the Fort Worth-based Oil Workers International Union (UWIC-CIO), then trying to organize Standard Oil. Keynote Records produced 1,000 copies for the union, which controlled the limited distribution.[31]

By the summer of 1942 the Almanac Singers had begun to splinter; Guthrie had moved on, Seeger was drafted in July, and with Detroit appearing as a promising location, Bess Lomax, Butch Hawes, Arthur Stern, and Charlie Polacheck moved there in June. They had received an invitation from the UAW-CIO for some appearances. As Ford Local 600 Education Director Frank Marquart wrote to local organizers, the "Almanac Singers will be in Detroit during June and arrangements can be made to have them appear at union meetings in the Ford and other locals. These singers have done some excellent work in producing union songs and have made a hit wherever they appeared. I think you could swell the attendance in your June meeting if you arranged to have these singers present and advertised the fact to the members." But things did not go as planned. "We have not succeeded in doing what we came out to do—that is, to get ourselves made an official part of the UAW educational staff," Bess Lomax wrote to her brother Alan from Detroit. "We've failed in this due primarily to the confused and unwieldy politics of the UAW International. So far as we can tell, they seem to be scared of us now, although we have done nothing that hasn't been right up their alley and their educational program. However, we've made several hundred bookings ranging in size from private parties to Cadillac Square rallies, and not one of them has been a flop." They also performed at the United Rubber Workers (URW) convention in Akron, and the United Cannery, Agricultural, Packing and Allied Workers of America (UCAPAWA) Convention in Chicago. As Lomax concluded, "our situation is not so bad. We have lots of opportunities and we seem to be nicking the surface in more than one direction," despite their internal bickerings.[32]

In his commentary near year's end to Seeger and the Almanacs in New York, Arthur Stern also had a mixed view of their experiences. "The Almanac Singers between the dates of June 10 and November 1, 1942, made 107 separate bookings which have gotten us successfully into and out of debt a number of times (we are now in debt)," he reported. Trade unions sponsored almost seventy of their appearances, heavily UAW locals that paid $30 for 30 minutes. "Our program material has consisted of our own songs, one song popularized by the 'Priority Ramblers' of Washington, 'Looking for a Home,' and folk material. In general, at a straight union meeting or political rally we use no folk material." At union gatherings they performed "Solidarity Forever," "Hold the Fort," "UAW-CIO," "The Union Maid," and "Boomtown Bill." As performing prospects continued to dim, the four Almanacs took war industry jobs, then Bess Lomax and Butch Hawes returned to New York to get married. But Cunningham and Friesen had decided they would move to the motor city, and they arrived in early December 1942. Cunningham joined Stern and Polacheck in a rump Almanacs, but they faced rough times and the group had collapsed by the spring. They had issued a small songbook, *Anti-Fascist Songs of the Almanac Singers*. Securing jobs, Cunningham and Friesen remained in Detroit until May 1944, when they also returned to New York.[33]

The Almanacs had made their mark by early 1943, then faded from the scene. They had left a vibrant legacy, however, having produced a few dozen recorded songs, written many clever lyrics, and demonstrated that a group of city-based musicians could engage audiences while adapting contemporary topics to traditional folk tunes. And they would cast a long shadow. But their aim to stimulate a singing union movement had been only dimly realized.

At the time they disbanded, however, they did have one group that followed their lead. The Priority Ramblers in Washington, D.C. were composed of Jackie Gibson, Bernie Asbell (originally Asbel), Tom Glazer, Edna Crumply Nell, Josephine Schwartz, and Helen Schneyer, and they were all members of the United Federal Workers of America (UFWA). "The 'Priority Ramblers' . . . have become famous in the past few weeks for their old and new folk songs," one contemporary article commented. "Performing at many square dances, socials and meetings, they have brought special significance to songs that have been sung and will continue to be sung by the people. Under the direction of Alan Lomax, the group has appeared in Baltimore and Philly as well as in the District. The singers compose their own songs to express the feelings and experiences of government workers."[34]

With their floating membership, similar to the Almanacs, the Priority Ramblers, initially under Lomax's tutelage, kept active. Asbell, a New York native, had attended the folk gatherings at Almanac House before securing a clerical job in Washington in early 1942. Gibson worked for Lomax, who would leave the Library of Congress for the Bureau of Special Operations, at the Office of War Information (OWI), in October 1942. Lomax and Gibson pulled the group together, and they became favorites of Eleanor Roosevelt, who invited them to perform for the White House's military guard in July. They participated in a songbook, *Songs to Fight By*, issued for the UFWA's second constitutional convention. "The songs in this book are union songs," noted the introduction. "Many of them have grown out of the activities of the two United Federal Workers' song groups—the UFWA Chorus and the Priority Ramblers." The selections included a few by the Priority Ramblers, such as "Amsterdam Maid," which they updated as a pro-war song, Asbell's "Talking UFWA," and Glazer's "A Dollar Ain't A Dollar Any More." They also had a Saturday night radio show on local station WOL. On September 6, 1943, the folklorist Benjamin Botkin, who had replaced Lomax as the Assistant in Charge of the Archive of

American Folk Song, assembled the group in the Library's recording studio. With Asbell in the Army, the group now included Gibson, Glazer, Nell, and Schwartz. Among the ten songs they recorded were "I'm Looking For A Home," "Song of the Free," and "Overtime Pay." "We recorded ten songs by the Priority Ramblers this week and they came out very well as you may hear from Tom and Jackie," Botkin wrote to Lomax. "We are also hoping to record Edna Nells' folk songs." They disbanded in early 1944.[35]

While no other organized singing groups emerged, Alan Lomax recorded an all-star pick-up group, labeled the "Union Boys," in New York on March 11, 1944. The racially mixed assembly included Pete Seeger (just before shipping out to the South Pacific), Burl Ives, Tom Glazer, Brownie McGhee, Sonny Terry, Josh White, and Lomax himself. Of the twelve songs recorded, five were quickly issued by Moe Asch on the album *Songs for Victory: Music for Political Action*, which was promoted by the CIO Political Action Committee. Labor songs included "Hold the Fort" and "UAW-CIO." There were very few recordings of labor songs made during the duration of the war, as most of the performers scattered. The newspaperman and labor organizer Vern Partlow recorded six songs in 1943, including "Join the U.A.W.-C.I.O.," "The U.A.W. Train," and "Susan's in the Union," for private distribution and as campaign songs for the UAW. Josh White and Tom Glazer, along with Bess and Butch Hawes, recorded six songs for Asch on June 19, 1944, which appeared in the album *Songs of Citizen C.I.O.* Sponsored by the National CIO War Relief Committee, it included the title song, "GI Joe and the CIO," "Social Workers Talking Blues," and "Freedom Road." "Composed in folk style," one review explained, "the songs are an expression of the basic needs and dreams of the working man, of his desire for work and dignity after the war, of his yearning for peace and a chance to raise his family in security, of his eagerness to be an integral part of the community in which he lives." Woody Guthrie also recorded a few labor related songs for Asch, such as "Farmer Labor Train." Most unions had by now put aside their militant rhetoric and strike activities to focus on the war effort. But this was only temporary, and when the war ended in the summer of 1945 labor activism, and accompanying tunes, would reemerge. Labor songs were far from dead, but the difficult, frustrating struggle to promote a singing labor movement would continue.[36]

In 1942, Lead Belly contributed his share of occupational songs with a southern focus in an album for Asch, *Work Songs of the U.S.A.* Among the six sides were "Take This Hammer," "Haul Away, Joe," "Rock Island Line," and "Ol' Riley." These were part of his repertoire that also included "Cottonfields," "Pick a Bale of Cotton," "Boll Weevil," "John Henry," "Bring Me Lil' Water Silvy," and "The Cotton Picking Song." They would all become part of the folk music lexicon within a few years.

(Endnotes)

1 *Brookwood Chautauqua Songs: A Singing Army Is a Winning Army* (Katonah, NY: Brookwood Labor Publications, *ca.* 1937).

2 Agnes "Sis" Cunningham and Gordon Friesen, *Red Dust and Broadsides: A Joint Autobiography* (Amherst: University of Massachusetts Press, 1999), 114; Agnes Cunningham, *Six Labor Songs* (Mena, AR: Commonwealth College, nd); *Commonwealth Labor Songs* (Mena, AR: Commonwealth College, 1938); *Commonwealth Labor Hymnal* (Mena, AR: Commonwealth College, 1938); *Songs of the Southern School for Workers* (Asheville, NC: Southern School For Workers, 1940), which might be the book Sis edited; William H. Cobb, *Radical Education in the Rural South: Commonwealth College, 1922-1940* (Detroit: Wayne State University Press, 2000). "There are Are Strange Things Happening" should not be confused with Sister Rosetta Tharpe's "Strange Things Happening Every Day," her hit on the "race" charts in 1945.

3 *The School For Workers Song Book* (Madison: The University of Wisconsin School For Workers, nd, probably early 1940s); Caroline Wasserman, comp., *Song Book of the Pacific School For Workers* (Berkeley: Pacific Coast School for Workers, 1939).

4 Don West, *Songs For Southern Workers* (np: Kentucky Workers Alliance, 1937), reissued by the Appalachian Movement Press in 1973; James J. Lorence, *A Hard Journey: The Life of Don West* (Urbana: University of Illinois Press, 2007), 72, and *passim.*

5 John M. Glen, *Highlander: No Ordinary School, 1932-1962* (Lexington: The University Press of Kentucky, 1988), 37; Zilphia Horton, ed., *Labor Songs* (N.Y.: Textile Workers Union of America, 1939), 2.

6 Doris Willens, *Lonesome Traveler: The Life of Lee Hays* (NY: W.W. Norton & Company, 1988), 56; Waldemar Hille, "Prospectus of the American Workers Song Book for publication spring 1939," Waldemar Hille file, Archie Green Papers, Southern Folklife Collection, University of North Carolina, Chapel Hill, North Carolina; Lee [Hays] to Zilphia, November 28, 1938, Zilphia Horton letters, Highlander Folk School Collection, Tennessee State Library and Archives, Nashville, TN.

7 Robert S. Koppelman, *"Sing Out, Warning! Sing Out, Love!": The Writings of Lee Hays* (Amherst: University of Massachusetts Press, 2003), 69-70.

8 Waldemar B. Hille, "Why All the Interest in Americana Folk and Worker's Songs," *Elmhurst Student Paper*, Elmhurst College, 1939 (copy in author's possession).

9 Cunningham and Friesen, *Red Dust and Broadsides*, 158; Rebecca B. Schroeder and Donald M. Lance, "John L. Handcox: 'There Is Still Mean Things Happening,'" Archie Green, ed., *Songs about Work: Essays in Occupational Culture for Richard A. Reuss* (Bloomington, IN: Special Publications of the Folklore Institute No. 3, Indiana University, 1993), 184-207; *John L. Handcox: Songs, Poems and Stories of the Southern Tenant Farmers Union*, West Virginia University Press Sound Archive Volume VI, 2004, which includes all of his early Library of Congress recordings as well as some done in 1985 for the Smithsonian's Center for Folklife and

Cultural Heritage; Ronald D. Cohen, "Agnes 'Sis' Cunningham and Labor Songs in the Depression South," Chris Green, Rachel Rubin, James Smethurst, eds., *Radicalism in the South Since Reconstruction* (NY: Palgrave Macmillan, 2006), 83-96.

10 *Let's Sing!* (NY: Educational Department, International Ladies' Garment Workers' Union, nd), 1.

11 *Sing, Amalgamated!* (NY: Amalgamated Clothing Workers of America, 1940); *UAW-CIO Sings* (Detroit: UAW-CIO Education Department, nd), 1, 50.

12 *CIO Songs* (Birmingham: Birmingham Industrial Union Council, nd), back cover,16-17.

13 Copland review quoted in Elizabeth B. Crist, *Music for the Common Man: Aaron Copland during The Depression and War* (NY: Oxford University Press, 2005), 29.

14 Richard A. Reuss with JoAnne C. Reuss, *American Folk Music and Left-Wing Politics, 1927-1957* (Lanham, MD: The Scarecrow Press, 2000), 107; Marc E. Johnson, "The Masses Are Singing: Insurgency and Song in New York City, 1929-1941," unpub. PhD dissertation, Graduate Faculty, The City University of New York, 2003.

15 Eric W. Trumbull, "Musicals of the American Workers' Theatre Movement—1928-1941: Propaganda and Ritual in Documents of a Social Movement," unpub. PhD dissertation, University of Maryland, 1991; Erik Gordon, *Mark the Music: The Life and Work of Marc Blitzstein* (N.Y.: St. Martin's Press, 1989).

16 Kenneth Hunter, "20,000 Voices in Mass Chorus at C.P. Convention," *Daily Worker*, May 24, 1938.

17 Mark D. Naison, "Paul Robeson and the American Labor Movement," Jeffrey C. Stewart, ed., *Paul Robeson: Artist and Citizen* (New Brunswick: Rutgers University Press, 1998), 181-182.

18 Malcolm Goldstein, *The Political Stage: American Drama and Theater of the Great Depression* (NY: Oxford University Press, 1974), 198-203; Victoria Phillips Geduld, "Performing Communism in the American Dance: Culture, Politics and the New Dance Group," *American Communist History*, vol. 7, no. 1 (June 2008), 39-65.

19 Pete Seeger, "History of the Almanac Singers 1941-42," October 1987, manuscript in author's possession.

20 Alan Lomax, Woody Guthrie, Pete Seeger, *Hard Hitting Songs for Hard-Hit People* (NY: Oak Publications, 1967), 8, 366; David King Dunaway, *How Can I Keep from Singing? The Ballad of Pete Seeger* (NY: Villard Books, 2008).

21 Pete Seeger, "History of the Almanac Singers 1941-42," October 1987, manuscript in author's possession; Millard Lampell, "Home Before Morning," November 1997, manuscript in author's possession.

22 Millard Lampell, "Home Before Morning," November 1997, manuscript in author's possession; Reuss and Reuss, *American Folk Music and Left-Wing Politics*, chap. 7.

23 Ralph Warner, "'Sign of the Times' Spirit Labor Revue," *Daily Worker*, May 17, 1941; Mike Gold, "Change the World," *Daily Worker*, May 27, 1941.

24 The Almanac Singers to Saul [Mills], nd, copy in author's possession; Saul Mills to Brother Goldblatt, June 25, 1941, copy in author's possession.

25 Millard Lampell, "Home Before Morning," November 1997, manuscript in author's possession; Pete Seeger, "History of the Almanac Singers 1941-42," October 1987, manuscript in author's possession.

26 Millard Lampell, "Home Before Morning," November 1997, manuscript in author's possession.

27 Pete Seeger, "History of the Almanac Singers 1941-42," October 1987, manuscript in author's possession; Don Russell, "Meet the Almanac Singers: They Sing Hard-Hitting Songs That Belong to the People," *Daily Worker*, August 14, 1941.

28 Pete Seeger, "History of the Almanac Singers 1941-42," October 1987, manuscript in author's possession; Millard Lampell, "Home Before Morning," November 1997, manuscript in author's possession.

29 The Almanac Singers, "Hard hitting songs by hard hit people," *The Clipper*, vol. 2, no. 7 (September 1941), 5, 6.

30 "The Almanacs Reorganization Meeting, April 12, 1942," copy of minutes in author's possession.

31 Archie Green, "Woody's Oil Songs," Archie Green, ed., *Songs about Work: Essays in Occupational Culture for Richard A. Reuss* (Bloomington, IN: Special Publications of the Folklore Institute No. 3, Indiana University, 1993), 208-220; all of the Almanac Singers's recordings can be found in Ronald Cohen and Dave Samuelson, comps., *Songs for Political Action: Folk Music, Topical Songs and the American Left, 1926-1954*, Bear Family Records BCD 15720, 1996; Reuss and Reuss, *American Folk Music and Left-Wing Politics*, chap. 7.

32 Frank Marquart To All Building Chairmen, May 12, 1942, copy in author's possession; Bess to Alan, *ca.* early July 1942, Alan Lomax Collection, Archive of Folk Culture, American Folklife Center, The Library of Congress.

33 Arthur Stern, "The Almanac Singers in Detroit," ca. November 1942, copy of manuscript in author's possession.

34 "Singing (with photo of Priority Ramblers)," April 30, 1942, unidentified article, copy in author's possession.

35 *Songs to Fight By*, [Washington, D.C.]: United Federal Workers of America, nd, copy in author's possession; Botkin to Lomax, September 9, 1943, Alan Lomax Collection, Archive of Folk Culture, American Folklife Center, The Library of Congress; for five of their songs, see Cohen and Samuelson, comps., *Songs for Political Action*.

36 "Social Work Blues Recorded by CIO," *Community Services Newsletter*, October 1944. Some of the Union Boys recordings and most of the others, are included in Cohen and Samuelson, comps., *Songs for Political Action*. Soon after the war ended Tom Glazer recorded an album of *Favorite American Union Songs* for the CIO Department of Education and Research.

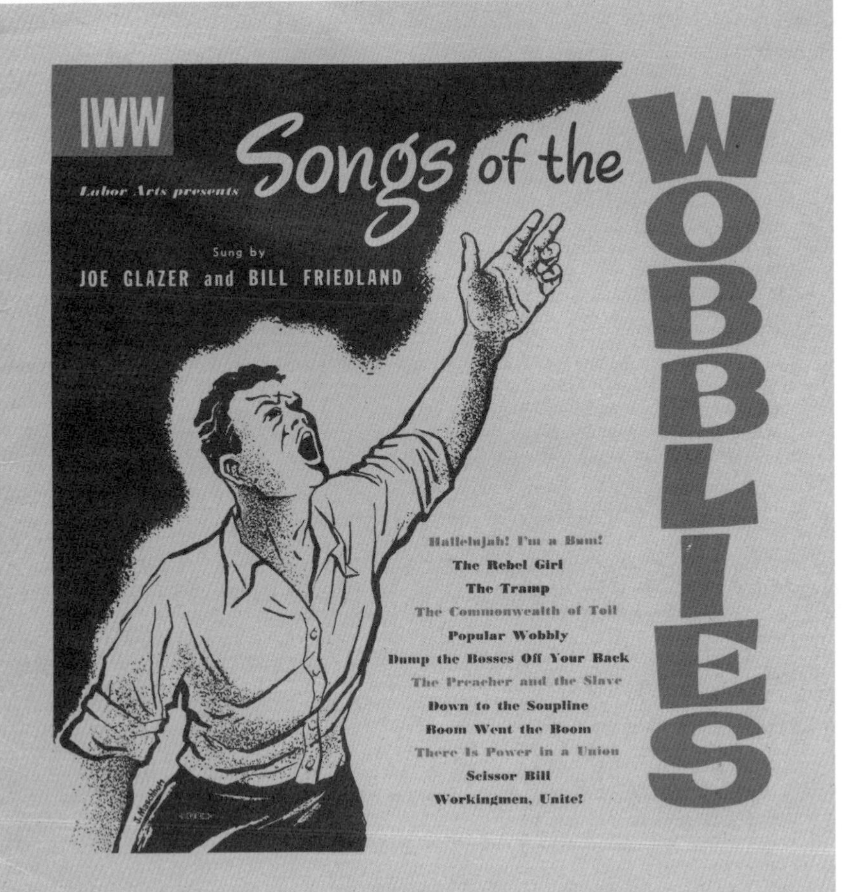

PROGRAM NOTES

AND LYRICS FROM THE LATEST LABOR ARTS ALBUM OF SIGNIFICANT AMERICAN LABOR SONGS

Songs of the Wobblies: Program Notes and Lyrics From the Latest Labor Arts Album of Significant American Labor Songs. (Detroit: Labor Arts, 1953)

chapter five

The Postwar Years to 1960

Work songs, generally without political or radical overtones, had entered popular culture by the end of World War II. This trend could be seen in some of the selections in folk song books for children that had begun to appear, such as Ruth Crawford Seeger's *American Folk Songs for Children*, published in 1948. The wife of Charles Seeger and step-mother of Pete, Ruth Seeger was a prominent modernist composer and folk song expert who had transcribed songs for John and Alan Lomax. Thoroughly familiar with a wide range of songs from the Library of Congress, she had begun circulating rough drafts of her children's book among parent-cooperative nursery schools around Washington, D.C. starting in 1941. As finally published by Doubleday & Company, *American Folk Songs for Children* included a section entitled "Work, Hammers, Trains, Boats," with such selections as "Pick a Bale of Cotton," "This Old Hammer," "John Henry," "Every Monday Morning (More About John Henry)," and "Blow, Boys, Blow." Seeger stressed the songs' rhythmic qualities, suitable for children's play, and not their historical contexts and connections.[1]

Young People's Records (YPR), a maverick mail order children's record company founded in New York by Horace Grenell in 1946, issued folk, classical, and talking records. Scattered among the hundreds of recordings over the coming years were a few that included work songs, such as the record titled *Yankee Tars*, performed by Tom Glazer. "Here are three sea ballads—real sea ballads—that were sung by American seamen many years ago," explained the liner notes for the songs "The Cumberland's Crew," "Yankee Tars," and "Yankee Man of War." Oscar Brand performed "Takes Everybody to Build This Land," "Chisholm Trail," "Erie Canal," and "John Henry" on the recording *Let's All Join In*, released in 1947. The next year *Chisholm Trail* appeared, with Will Geer serving as the narrator and Tom Glazer as the singer; it included "Chisholm Trail," "Poor Lonesome Cowboy," "I Ride an Old Paint," and "Get Along Little Dogies." According to the notes: "Here's a record that will tell you a real story about the life of a cowboy. When you put on your chaps and spurs and high cowboy boots you will really know how a cowboy spent his time and be able to sing the songs that he sang as he drove his cattle the many, many miles from the range to the railroad depot." Pete Seeger recorded a few sea songs for YPR, such as "Boston Come All Ye," "Cruise of the Bigler," and "New Bedford Whalers."[2]

Among the company's many supporters was the children's music educator Beatrice Landeck. In her book *Songs To Grow On* published in 1950, she included a smattering of work songs, such as "I've Been Working on the Railroad," "Whoopi Ti-Yi-Yo," and "Night Herding Song." "The easiest way for a child to understand the very complex civilization in which he lives is for him to pretend, for short periods of time, that he, himself, is one of the objects of that civilization . . . ," she explained. "When he play-acts as the sailor or the cowboy or, on the other hand, gallops like a horse or hops like a rabbit, he is trying to gain further understanding of his environment." Four years later, *More Songs To Grow On* contained "I Ride an Old Paint," "Haul Away, Joe," and "Good-Bye, Old Paint."[3]

In 1947, Tom Scott's *Sing Of America* was full of occupational tunes, such as "Steel-Linin' Chant," "The Erie Canal," "John Henry," and "The Old Chisholm Trail." That same year Margaret Boni published the ubiquitous *Fireside Book of Folk Songs*, with a long section of work songs, including "Lowlands," "Shenandoah," "Blow the Man Down," and "A-Roving." "American and English work songs are ballads, too," Boni explained to her broad audience, something that folklorists had long confirmed, "but they serve a more definite purpose. The principle of 'music while you work' was discovered long ago when men first saw that rhythm and unity of action helped to perform a task with greater swiftness and efficiency. . . . The sailing ships are gone, and the era of laying new rail lines has come to a halt. But during the war, factory workers in many countries found their speed stepped up, their nerves quieted, and their efficiency increased if they worked to music which was rhythmically stimulating." So, work songs might have more than just nostalgia value.[4]

Through the later 1940s there were scattered recordings of occupational songs. For example, the opera baritone Leonard Warren, backed by an orchestra and chorus, recorded an album of *Sea Shanties* for RCA Victor in 1948, while Decca released Carl Sandburg's *Cowboy Songs and Negro Spirituals*. Indeed, there were numerous cowboy recordings by the Rangers, Tex Ritter, Bing Crosby, and so many others. Some were listed in Ben Gray Lumpkin's *Folksongs on Records*, an expansive discography that appeared in a third edition in 1950: By now such songs, lacking any radical overtones or connections, were becoming part of the musical mainstream.

PEOPLE'S SONGS

While children and their parents were exposed to a variety of work songs, an activist group of musicians and their supporters attempted to spark an enhanced interest in labor songs for organizational purposes. The Almanac Singers had splintered then vanished by 1944, with Pete Seeger winding up on the island of Saipan in the western Pacific. There he met Betty Sanders, a singer with the USO, Felix Landau, and Mario "Boots" Casetta, who worked for the base radio station. They began discussing how to initiate a singing labor movement once peace was at hand. By the end of 1945 Seeger had returned to New York, along with Sanders and Landau, while Casetta was back in Los Angeles.

On December 31, 1945, a rather large group of folk music enthusiasts gathered at the home of Seeger's in-laws, the Ohtas, to form People's Songs, Inc. "The unions have cried for the material that we've got, they need our several thousand songs, and they need new ones made up on the jump as we go along," Seeger explained, according to Woody Guthrie. "The bosses and the monopoly folks own their leather lined offices, pay clerks big money, pay experts, pay detectives, pay thugs, pay artists to perform their complacent crap, pay investigators to try to keep our stuff beat down, and the only earthly way that we can buck against all of this pressure is to all get together into one big songwriters and song singers union, and we will call our union by the name of Peoples Songs." The quote might have been more Guthrie than Seeger, but it surely expressed the mood of the few dozen who were gathered. The group's constitution began: "We believe that the songs of any people truly express their lives, their struggles and their highest aspirations." *Daily Worker* columnist Mike Gold reported "that a group of former Almanac singers, plus others concerned with labor music, started to organize something again the day before New Year. Songs, songs, songs of, by and for the people!"[5]

An organization was soon in place and the first issue of the monthly *People's Songs* bulletin appeared in February 1946. "The people are on the march and must have songs to sing. . . There are thousands of unions, people's organizations, singers, and choruses who would gladly use more songs," the bulletin announced, with much optimism. Each issue would include songs and articles. The first song to be printed was Ralph Chaplin's "Solidarity Forever," which connected the activist present with the IWW, labor-organizing past. Indeed, with the war's end there were escalating labor strikes, with two million on the picket lines in January. Hootenannies soon sprang up in New York and elsewhere, featuring Guthrie, Seeger, Sonny Terry, Brownie McGhee, Bernie Asbell, Tom Glazer, Betty Sanders, Lead Belly, and others. While not officially connected to the Communist Party, People's Songs received constant publicity in the *Daily Worker* and many of its members were somehow affiliated and often appeared at party-connected functions.[6]

People's Songsters appeared in a series of concerts and labor rallies into the spring. "With the growth of People's Songs, the hootenannies, too, have come back to New York," Felix Landau explained in *Union Voice*, a local union publication. "On May 9, a 'Union Hootenanny,' a regular jam-session of union songs will be presented. . . . As Pete explained to me: 'We're interested in getting the union people to come and hear our songs. And take them back to their union, and get everybody there to sing them.'" Seeger, Guthrie, and Lee Hays performed before thousands of striking CIO United Electrical, Radio & Machine Workers (UE) members in Pittsburgh in late March. "The Westinghouse strikers were both bitter and full of fun as they jammed the roped-off street in front of City Hall yesterday," as the local press covered the story. "They grinned as a 'hill-billy' trio sang their lusty new labor songs that have an old-fashioned camp meeting appeal. . . . There were about 5000 in the crowd, and they all roared their approval when the 'hill-billy' soloist extemporized with a new song that had more meaning than rhyme." Such a rally captured the essence of People's Songs, but would not last long. "Speakers spoke between our songs," Guthrie explained. "The mayor dished out a nice plate of broad and liberal words into the faces of several thousand sore and anxious strikers. We sang two songs made up this day for the situation here at Westinghouse. The crowd roared like the ocean in a rock cavern. Good to see and feel."[7]

Seeger preferred to perform before striking union members and political activists. He worked hard for People's Songs through the year, serving as their Executive Secretary, but he also had to make a living because of his growing family. By late 1946 he was performing at the Village Vanguard nightclub in Greenwich Village. But Seeger mostly focused on promoting labor, civil rights, and other radical songs. A nagging problem for People's Songs was how to get the music to the union members. Landau got some suggestions from Walter Sassman, the UAW-CIO's Midwest educational representative. "'First of all,' he began, 'you have to have an idea of what meetings in our locals are like. Generally the men discuss shop news; every once in a while there are local issues to talk about—and that's the whole meeting. Most locals do not have even a phonograph to play records on.'" Moreover, he continued, they are mostly "used to popular music. They know a few of the famous old union songs, like 'Solidarity Forever,' but in general I feel that parodies to pop-tunes would be the best medium to get them singing labor songs." Sassman also recommended issuing only single records, since albums were generally too expensive, and he "would like to know how to go about getting labor records put into juke-boxes in bars and cafeterias where workers congregate." Despite such difficulties, Alan Reitman, Public Relations Director for the CIO-PAC, believed that the "CIO Political Action Committee is happy to cooperate with People's Songs and work with it toward attainment of our mutual goals." They would work together to help elect union-friendly representatives to Congress in the fall.[8]

As part of their commitment to a singing labor movement, in 1945 the CIO had organized the racially integrated New York City CIO Council's Chorus. "Director Simon Rady has a long union history," an article in the *CIO News* explained. "He led the famous 'Pins and Needles' chorus, as well as those of the Amalgamated Clothing Workers and the N.Y. Port of Embarkation." An accompanying photo of chorus members Betty and Robert DeCormier noted that the chorus "features [a] wide repertoire of folk, union and classical songs."[9]

Notwithstanding some reservations about issuing albums of labor songs, the CIO-PAC released *Songs For Political Action* in September 1946, just in time for the fall elections. Seeger, Tom Glazer, Hays, and Hally Wood Faulk performed "Voting Union," "A Dollar Ain't A Dollar Any More," "A Dollar For Pac," and ten more, to be used at rallies, broadcasts, and on sound trucks. Their hopes were soon crushed, however, as a right-wing backlash emerged. "The left-wing songsters, who put class struggle jingles to folksong [sic] melodies, will carry CIO-PAC's election message to voters throughout the nation, via mass rallies, radio and phonograph records," the conservative columnist Frederick Woltman warned. He should not have worried, for the Republicans swept the congressional races and took over Congress. Soon after, Moe Asch inaugurated a new label, Union Records. "Basic in the history of the American people from Revolutionary days through World War II and the efforts of labor, has been the struggle to keep and preserve the spirit of democracy," he announced. Among the first three albums were *Roosevelt's Inaugural Address of 1933* and *Picket Line Songs* by the Jefferson Chorus, which included "Hold the Fort," "Write Me Out My Union Card," and "Roll the Union On." By the end of 1946 the album *Roll the Union On*, produced by People's Songs and directed by Alan Lomax and Bess Lomax Hawes, appeared on the Union label, although issued by Asch Records. Seeger, Hays, Dock Reese, Hally Wood Faulk, Butch Hawes, Lou Kleinman, with Bess Hawes performed "Listen, Mr. Bilbo," "Roll the Union On," "This Old World," and three more.[10]

While labor musicals had pretty much faded before the war, in November 1947 *Thursdays Till Nine*, written by Henry Foner and music by Norman Franklin, opened in New York. The "show was presented by the Department Store Employees Union, CIO, and featured a cast of 55 behind-the-counter workers of Macy's, Gimbels, Hearns, Namms, and a host of other New York stores," ran the notice in *People's Songs*. "Set in the R.H. Maybe Department Store ('Don't say no, say maybe') the musical depicts the tribulations of a homeless haberdashery salesman who learns the lessons of unionism the hard way. Fifteen songs, including 'Selling Union' and a 'Ballet of the Shirts' dot the production." The bulletin printed the lyrics to "Selling Union," with the words "So get your orders ready, for I'm selling union now, Just one to ev'ry customer is all we can allow."[11]

People's Songs remained nationally active through 1946 and into 1947. In Detroit, Rolf Cahn and Barbara Spillman Cahn performed at soup kitchens and on picket lines during a Chrysler workers strike. According to Rolf Cahn, "we were sent out by the [UAW] International to various locals. . . . We sang in the line, or from a sound car to the line, or gave a real concert with pop stuff and blues from within the sound car. . . . There was tremendous gratitude among the workers." In Cleveland about thirty organizations were somehow involved in the People's Songs chapter, while in Minneapolis-St. Paul the local group tried to recruit Scandinavian workers in the cities and miners in the Iron Range towns. A continuous stream of concerts in New York kept the performers busy. A packed stage at Irving Plaza, including Josh White, Guthrie, and Lead Belly, featured the benefit show "Songs From the Mine Fields" for the Centralia miners killed in the Illinois mine disaster. But People's Songs attempted to promote more than just labor and political songs. "We have based our program largely in the rich and democratic tradition of American folk music," Alan Lomax wrote to the conductor Leonard Bernstein, wondering if he would lend his name to the national board of directors. "We feel that the whole American folk tradition is a progressive people's tradition. For that reason our concerts, our new songs, our artists are, in great measure, rooted in the fertile soil of American folk music." A key figure in organizing People's Songs events, Lomax was not only expressing the organization's lofty goals, but more broadly his lifelong commitment to promoting a democratic musical culture, grounded in equality and tradition. As one example, in early March 1947, People's Songs "presented to Boston its first Hootenanny Friday night: their spirituals, work songs, and blues; Spanish songs of New Mexico; American soldier songs; and English, Irish, and Scottish ballads."[12]

In addition to distributing the bulletin and song sheets, People's Songs also produced a few filmstrips, with accompanying recorded sound tracks, to show at political and union meetings. For example, in mid-1947 they distributed one for the National Maritime Union-CIO recruiting drive. Seeger, Glazer, Hally Wood Faulk, and Ronnie Gilbert performed "Talking Union," "Solidarity Forever," "The Whole Wide World Around," and "Hold the Fort." Glazer had written "The Whole Wide World Around" for the World Federation of Trade Unions. Josh White and Tom Glazer recorded a few songs for use on sound trucks during strike activities, including among steelworkers in Pittsburgh and Gary, Indiana, and a garment workers strike in Kearney, New Jersey. Glazer also recorded an album for the CIO Department of Education and Research, *Favorite American Union Songs*, including "Solidarity Forever," "Casey Jones," and "Which Side Are You On." While Seeger performed heavily in New York, he also took time to travel around the country, spreading the word. For example, on August 17 he appeared at the Challenge Folk Festival in Denver, Colorado, held at the American Legion Park (Earl Robinson had been featured the previous year). He was joined by "local cultural groups, presenting the culture of the West, the Mexican people, Jewish people, and other nationality groups." People's Songs and its friends throughout the country promoted an international agenda, along with their labor union musical activities.[13]

Aside from New York, People's Songs was most active in California. Boots Casetta anchored the Los Angeles branch. In December 1946, along with the composer Fred Warren, he launched Charter Records. The label first produced an album by the calypso singer Sir Lancelot, followed by five satirical songs by Morry Goodson and Sonny Vale. A string of singles followed, as well as an album by Seeger which featured "Black, Brown, and White Blues," "The Death of Harry Sims," and "Winnsboro Cotton Mill Blues." (In mid-July 1948, Casetta moved to New York to help run the music desk of the Henry Wallace Progressive Party presidential campaign.) Bob and Adrienne Claiborne, based in New York, traveled across the country in mid-1947. "We sang to unions, to PCA [Progressive Citizens of America] groups, to parties and rallies. Everywhere we found plain people beginning to get together, work together, sing together," they reported after returning to New York in October. In San Francisco they were sponsored by the California Labor School, which was "doing a wonderful job in servicing the unions out there."[14]

Organized in 1942, the California Labor School was supported by dozens of CIO and AFL local unions. Four years later the school looked to broaden its music program. "The main emphasis in the proposed program will be on the development of an Interracial Chorus, a Music Workshop to prepare arrangement of American labor and folk music for production, group classes in instrumental music, and several courses to enhance the understanding and enjoyment of good music," music critic Alfred Frankenstein and violinist Isaac Stern noted in their fundraising proposal. In 1944, Leo Christiansen had organized a labor chorus, and by 1947 it was made up of "more than 40 longshoremen, street car conductors, waitresses, office workers, welders and working men and women ad infinitum." In January 1947, Casetta, along with Goodson and Vale, traveled north from Los Angeles to stage two hootenannies, which served as the start of the San Francisco People's Songs chapter. Led locally by Lou Gottlieb, Barbara Cahn, and Jerry Walter, they affiliated with the California Labor School. In July 1948, *People's World*, the West Coast Communist paper, reported that in "the past month Walter has performed on picket lines for the CIO Warehousemen and CIO Office Workers." The school continued to promote folk music and workers' culture until its demise in 1957, a victim of increasing government harassment.[15]

Vern Partlow, a journalist and active member of the Los Angeles Newspaper Guild, performed a number of songs in support of the Food, Agricultural and Allied Workers (FTA), who were striking

Northern California canneries in mid-1946. "We presented a regular show . . . with union and folk stuff, jive with PAC lyrics, Mexican songs, and some popular stuff," Partlow reported in *People's Songs*. "Once a goon squad at a remote plant gate came out and scowled ferociously, and tried to pick a fight, but we kept on singing and nothing happened." He recorded a number of original songs, including "Talking F.T.A.," "Round and Round the Canneries," and "My Name Is Cannery Bill," which were heard at local rallies.[16]

People's Songsters from around the country gathered in Chicago in October 1947 for their first (and last) national convention. Earl Robinson, Seeger, Guthrie, Big Bill Broonzy, Win Stracke, and others performed at the main hootenanny at the plush Orchestra Hall. Jenny Wells traveled from New Mexico to participate. "Folk Music, as the democratic heritage of people's singers today was the theme of the discussion led by Alan Lomax, outstanding folklorist, who advanced the concept that people's songs of today, the union and topical songs, are in keeping with the best tradition of American music," the bulletin explained, in a roundup of convention activities. "Chicago union leaders participated in the discussion on 'MUSIC IN THE TRADE UNIONS,' which was contributed by Pete Seeger and Bernie Asbel[l], who outlined some of their experiences in singing for union groups throughout the country." The convention ended with high expectations.[17]

In addition to printing songs in each issue of the bulletin, and distributing song sheets, People's Songs promoted songbooks. The August 1947 issue posted a notice that the "UAW is the first major union to issue a full-fledged songbook since the end of the war." It is not clear which songbook was mentioned, since many were undated, perhaps *UAW CIO Union Songs*. People's Songs soon issued its own *A People's Songs Wordbook No. 1*, which was pocket-sized, with fifty-seven songs and no music. This was followed in early 1948 by *The People's Song Book*, edited by Waldemar Hille. "Here is a big, clean wind of a book that will blow the mists of doubt and discouragement right out of your heart," Lomax announced in the foreword. And in his preface, the folklorist Ben Botkin explained that there "have been many song books before this—folk song books, labor song books, community song books. But there has never been a book that combines all three, and draws upon the greatest of folk song traditions—the freedom song—as successfully as this one does." It was divided into four parts: "Songs that helped build America," "World freedom songs," "Union songs," and "Topical-political songs." Labor songs were scattered throughout, such as "Paddy works on the railway," "Tarrier's song," "Hold the fort," "Picket line Priscilla," "Roll the union on," "Talking union," and so much more, each with music so they could be sung and shared. While working on the songbook, Seeger wrote to Zilphia Horton at the Highlander Folk School, who was in the midst of pulling together yet another of the school's compilations: "It seems to me that the song book should include as many favorite tunes of everybody as possible. When I say everybody, I mean everybody in the labor and progressive movement, of course—labor, plus the millions of Americans we want to draw into it." The Amalgamated Clothing Workers of America (ACWA) in New York even distributed *The People's Song Book*, and included some of the songs in its own *Amalgamated Song Book*.[18]

People's Songs struggled to remain alive through the spring of 1948, while they were caught up in the Progressive Party's presidential campaign. Labor and political songs filled the pages of the bulletin, such as "We Are Building a Strong Union," written by West Virginia miners in 1934. People's Songsters Seeger, Ernie Lieberman, Fred Hellerman, and Bob DeCormier led the singing during the large May Day parade in New York from the back of a truck, with such songs as "Roll the Union On," "Solidarity Forever," and "Hold the Fort." With the former Vice President Henry Wallace as their candidate, the Progressive Party had high hopes that disgruntled union members and many others would flock to this third party. One tactic was to use folk music as an organizing tool, so People's Songs was hired to run the campaign's music desk. Alan Lomax headed the project, with assistance from Casetta, who had moved to New York, Seeger, and Irwin Silber. People's Songs Cleveland launched the campaign with a small *Wallace for President Song Book*, which was the prelude for the national office's larger *Songs for Wallace*. Among the twenty-five songs, all related to the campaign, there were some with a union focus, such as "The Farmer-Labor Train" and "Union Train (For Wallace)." People's Songs also published the small folio of Woody Guthrie's *Three Songs For Centralia*, in memory of the 111 miners killed in a March 1947 Illinois mine explosion. Following the Progressive Party's dismal showing in the November election, as union members flocked to vote for President Harry Truman's reelection, People's Songs fell on hard times and disbanded early the next year. At their December 1948 board meeting, Seeger believed that their "major shortcomings . . . are the continued lack of activity in the labor movement, [and] the still tremendous limitations of audience and participation imposed by monopoly control of the main channels of communication."[19]

After People's Songs collapsed in early 1949, People's Artists emerged from the ashes to organize musical events; in May 1950 it began publishing *Sing Out!*, a small monthly magazine of songs and news. Labor songs remained important, although other matters, such as world peace, political repression, and civil rights, took on increasing importance. Labor unions now rarely welcomed left-wing folk singers. In September 1951, however, the United Electrical, Radio, and Machine Workers of America (UE), staged a Freedom Festival as part of its national convention in New York. The UE had been purged from the CIO in 1949 because of its radical image (and replaced by the International Union of Electrical, Radio and Machine Workers), but it managed to survive, although with a shrunken membership. The Freedom Festival "was reminiscent of the Thirties, when unions were a beehive of cultural activity: Pins and Needles, TAC [Theater Arts Committee], the drama competitions between the UOPWA [United Office and Professional Workers of America], Furriers, Warehouse Workers, etc.," according to one account. "Here, indeed, was the labor movement supporting and strengthening its economic and political struggles with the power of song, the might of satire, the strength of drama." Among the entertainers were Earl Robinson, calypso singer Duke of Iron, actor Howard DaSilva, a jazz trio, and the People's Artists Quartet—Laura Duncan, Betty Sanders, Osborne Smith, and Ernie Lieberman. "You might say that this was a union meeting, only the business of the meeting was conducted in song and the voting was done by applause," the article continued. "Many of the old union songs: 'Talking Union,' for instance, and some newer ones: [Bernie Asbell's] 'Song of My Hands,' brought voice to 3,000 throats." Members of People's Artists participated in scores of events in New York through the early 1950s, but rarely performed for labor unions.[20]

OTHER LABOR SONGS AND SONGSTERS IN THE LATER 1940s

Those connected with People's Songs did not have a monopoly in spreading labor union songs following the war. In September 1948 *People's Songs* published "We Will Overcome" with this message: "It was learned by Zilphia Horton of the Highlander Folk School, in Tennessee, from members of the CIO Food and Tobacco Workers Union. . . . Zilphia writes: 'It was first sung in Charleston, S[outh] C[arolina].'" Originally composed by the Reverend Charles Tindley early in the century as a hymn, it was picked up in 1946 by striking workers, mostly African American women, at the American Tobacco Company in Charleston. Horton learned it when some of the strikers visited Highlander, and passed it on to Seeger, who published it in the bulletin. A few years later it became "We Shall Overcome" and emerged as a staple of the civil rights movement.[21]

People's Songs organized a number of music caravans in conjunction with the Wallace campaign, which often featured Seeger in the East and South, and Bernie Asbell in the Midwest. But they were not alone in using a traveling group to reach into the hinterlands with labor songs and skits. During World War II the CIO's United Packinghouse Workers of America (UPWA) began organizing workers in the Midwest, particularly in Iowa, which passed an anti-union right-to-work law in 1947. Teaming with the Iowa Farmers Union (IFU) to promote farmer-labor cooperation, the UPWA sponsored a Union Caravan during three months in mid-1949 featuring the performer Marianne "Jolly" Smolens, the actor Hershel "Hesh" Bernardi, his wife Betty Bernardi, Ray Stough, Henrietta Fisher, and Juanita Griffin. They had "a forty-five minute performance of comic skits, folk dances, and topical lyrics set to well-known music. All members of the troupe were on stage for the entire show, but each performed in various combinations or as solos backed up by the group," according to a later account. Their songs included "The Farmer is the Man," "It's My Union," "Oh, Freedom," and "Solidarity Forever." They preferred fairs and work sites where farmers and workers gathered during the summer months in Iowa and eastern Nebraska. The tour ended in Chicago, where they recorded a two-disc 78 rpm album, *It's My Union*. The UPWA soon released a seventeen minute film, *They Met at the Fair*. After a short break, the Caravan traveled east to perform for the International Fur and Leather Workers Union in Pennsylvania and New York. Unfortunately, the audiences were small, since most of the men were off hunting, and the women and children were less radical than the union's leadership.[22]

While Smolens and her colleagues were briefly touring the fairs, Joe Glazer was promoting labor songs for various mainstream unions. Born in New York in 1918, the son of Eastern European immigrants, with a father in the International Ladies Garment Workers Union (ILGWU), Glazer attended Brooklyn College. He developed a love for folk music in the mid-1930s, but he had no affiliation with the Communist Party, and he was careful to avoid any sectarian political attachments. Beginning as a teacher at Truax Air Field and graduate student at the nearby University of

Wisconsin during the war, Glazer was happy to accept a job with the education department of the CIO Textile Workers Union of America (TWUA) in May 1944. During a textile strike in Maine in late 1945, he began using songs for the workers, such as "Roll the Union On" and "Solidarity Forever." "We sang and we sang," he would recollect. "We must have gone on for an hour or more on a picket line that seemed to stretch for miles around the plant. . . . After singing for an hour or more in the snow and the bitter cold, we marched back to the union hall, exhilarated and ready to do battle with mill owners for another week or two—or for another month if we had to." This was the beginning of the half-century career of labor's troubadour, who quickly learned that a singing labor movement was somewhat feasible, if not widespread.[23]

Glazer organized for the TWUA until 1950, mostly in New England, but also in the South: "At the southern textile training institutes we always did a lot of singing. We would open each evening with a half-dozen union songs from the little songbook I had put together. After the formal meeting, which might consist of a speaker or perhaps a movie followed by a discussion, there would be a lot of informal singing, more union songs plus lots of hymns that everybody seemed to know." With guitar in hand, Glazer continued to travel and use music to stimulate labor union members, just as it appeared that music was no longer part of a worker's culture. "During the six years I worked for the Textile Workers Union I led textile workers, North and South, in old labor songs and wrote new songs and parodies for training institutes, rallies, picket lines, and meetings," he boasted in his autobiography. "A hair raising ride in an airplane early in 1950 moved me to cut a record with eight of these songs." *Eight New Songs for Labor* was issued by the CIO Department of Education, including "We Will Overcome," and Glazer's compositions "The Mill Was Made of Marble" and "Too Old to Work." He was accompanied by the Elm City Four and the guitar player Fred Hellerman, whose involvement with the Communist-tinged People's Songs did not seem to faze Glazer (and this was just before Hellerman began recording with the Weavers). This was the first of dozens of Glazer's albums that would appear through the end of the century.[24]

In mid-1950, Glazer became the education director of the United Rubber Workers (URW), another CIO union, where he led their activities until 1961. He continued to write and sing, including "Automation," which he performed at the United Automobile Workers Union (UAW) convention in 1955, along with "The Song of the Guaranteed Wage." Soon after he regaled the last CIO gathering with "Let's Call the Roll of the CIO," just before their merger with the AFL on the following December 8. By now there was barely a singing labor movement. AFL-CIO president George Meany had little interest in such stuff, "although he would react positively when he heard union songs that someone else had put on a program," according to Glazer. Although not as politically conservative as the union's leader, Glazer somewhat expressed his politics in the album *Ballads for Sectarians*, recorded with Bill Friedland, a staff member of the Michigan CIO, in 1952. Full of musical satires on the Community Party, which he loathed, the album was recorded in Detroit and issued on the small Labor Arts label headed by Bill Kemsley, Education Director of the Michigan CIO, and the labor organizer Ethel Polk. Labor Arts followed in 1954 with Glazer and Friedland's *Songs of the Wobblies*, the first recordings of IWW songs, including "Hallelujah, I'm a Bum," "Popular Wobbly," and "Dump the Bosses Off Your Back." That year Folkways Records also issued Glazer's *The Songs of Joe Hill*, with "Casey Jones," "Scissor Bill," and "Mr. Block."[25]

Friedland was part of the non-Communist left, which issued such songbooks as the Workers Party and Young People's Socialist League's *Sing!*, while the Los Angeles section of the Workers Party (WP) issued its own *Sing!: Labor and Socialist Songs* in 1945. About the same time the *May Day Songbook* by the Workers Party (WP) and Labor Action appeared. The WP, formed in 1940, was an offshoot of the Trotskyist Socialist Workers Party, which issued the newspaper *Labor Action*.

Glazer continued through the 1950s and after to turn out one album after another, while giving numerous concerts and editing, along with the Canadian folklorist Edith Fowke, *Songs of Work and Freedom*, which was published in 1960. "The best union songs come out of the bitter times: the great struggles and the hard-fought strikes, out of triumphs won against overwhelming odds," they wrote in the introduction. "Peaceful, prosperous times on the labor front rarely bring forth a song worth singing or saving." And they went on to explain "why such a high proportion of good union songs come from the coal mines and textile mills. . . . The textile workers and the coal miners have worked mostly in lonely mine patches and mill villages, many of them located in the rural south or in isolated mountain communities. Many of these workers come from a great singing tradition—secular or religious, or both. Miners and mill workers have had a long, fierce, and often tragic struggle to build a union. This combination of isolation, singing tradition, and bitter struggle has provided what might be called the perfect climate for the production of protest songs." While the majority of the songs were of an older vintage, a few were by Glazer. He simultaneously issued the album *Songs Of Work And Freedom*, accompanied by jazz guitarist Charlie Byrd, and banjo player Mike Seeger, half-brother of Pete and a member of the New Lost City Ramblers. He included among the fourteen songs "Solidarity Forever," "Talking Union," "Hard Times In The Mill," and his own compositions "The Mill Was Made of Marble" and "Automation." Moreover, "The Mill Was Made of Marble" appeared in the *CIO Song Book*, issued by the CIO Department of Education and Research in 1951, along with such labor standards as "We Shall Not Be Moved," "Union Maid," "Take Me Out To the Ball Game," and "Daisy."[26]

THE 1950s

While Joe Glazer worked hard to stimulate a singing labor movement in the midst of increasing union torpor and conservative resistance, and while the Cold War escalated, Pete Seeger and various others continued the struggle to spread labor songs from a more radical perspective. As part of the Weavers, the popular quartet that had a number of song hits before facing the blacklist by 1953, Pete Seeger and his radical colleagues, Ronnie Gilbert, Lee Hays, and Fred Hellerman, had to mute their political message. With the Weavers's collapse, however, Seeger continued to record and document the history of work songs. In 1955 Folkways Records released the album *The Talking Union with the Almanac Singers & other Union Songs with Pete Seeger and Chorus*. The first side, with a new chorus, the Song Swappers, included fresh recordings of "We Shall Not Be Moved," "Roll the Union On," "Casey Jones," "Miner's Lifeguard," "Solidarity Forever," "Join the Union," and "Hold the Fort," while side B featured all of the songs from the original 1941 Keynote release. "Unlike most hymns and patriotic songs, union songs are usually composed by amateurs to suit a particular occasion, and have a short life," Seeger explained in the accompanying booklet. "More often than not, they are simply new words to an older melody. A few of such songs, however, prove worthwhile enough in melody and lyrics to warrant being passed on by one generation of workers to the next." The labor historian Philip Foner supplied more detailed explanatory notes: "The labor songs included in this album are among the finest and most famous in the literature of the American working class."[27]

Although Seeger now had few chances to appear at a labor meeting or rally, the new album was an opportunity for his voice to reach some union members. *Sing Out!* editor Irwin Silber welcomed its release, while expressing his preference for the original recordings, long unavailable. He pointed out that the "Almanacs sang their songs on picket-lines and at the center of union struggles," while in contrast the Song Swappers, unnamed on the album but actually composed of Erik Darling, Mary Travers, and Tom Geraci, "have learned their songs from records and hootenannies and other singers." Still, he wishfully concluded that the "album as a whole is exciting and important. Our thanks go to Folkways for filling an awfully big gap on the record shelves of union halls all over the country."[28]

Sing Out! had emerged in 1950 from the ashes of People's Songs and, and while struggling through the decade, it printed dozens of labor and occupational songs and articles. For example, in the same issue as Silber's review appeared the reprint of Margaret Larkin's 1929 article on Ella May Wiggins, along with her songs "Chief Aderholt" and "Mill Mother's Lament." There was also a brief review of Paul Clayton's Stinson album *Whaling Songs and Ballads*. Silber had also edited *Lift Every Voice! The Second People's Song Book* in 1953, which included a brief section on the "Commonwealth of Toil: Labor Songs," beginning with "Commonwealth of Toil," then "I Ride An Old Paint."[29]

Seeger followed *Talking Union* a year later with the impressive Folkways album *American Industrial Ballads*. The songs were arranged in rough chronological order, beginning with "Peg and Awl" (1801), "The Blind Fiddler" (1850), "The Buffalo Skinners" (1873), and on into the twentieth century. In his lengthy notes, Irwin Silber explained that more "than half of them have been composed since 1920. . . . Three occupations dominate the song selection in this album: Coal mining; textile; farming. This is no accident or caprice. These three pursuits likewise dominate the great body of industrial folk song which exists in our country." Among the more recent selections were "Seven Cent Cotton and Forty Cent Meat" (1929) "Beans, Bacon and Gravy" (1931), "Pittsburgh Town" (1941), and ending with "Sixty Per Cent" (1948-49).[30]

While there was only a vestige of a singing labor movement during the 1950s, as well as little assistance from the radical left in promoting work songs, there were, nonetheless, other odd examples here and there. *The Pajama Game*, a musical based on Richard Bissell's novel *7-1/2 Cents*, opened on Broadway in May 1954 and ran for 1,063 performances. The story revolved around a union dispute over wages at the Sleep-Tite Pajama Factory, with labor issues mixed in with various romantic twists and turns; in the end everything was resolved, as the workers got their hourly increase of 7½ cents. The popularity of *The Pajama Game* reflected not so much labor union support, but rather the sparkling musical numbers and interesting plot lines.

While many unions turned their attention to other fronts, a small number did publish songbooks in the 1950s. The *CIO Song Book* appeared from the union's Department of Education and Research in 1951, while the Pacific Coast Office of the ILGWU printed *Let's All Sing* during the decade, and the Westcoast Workers Vacation School issued their *Militant Songbook* in 1954. The union also backed two albums, *We Work—We Sing* by the ILGWU Local 91 Chorus, and *My Name is Mary Brown* from the union's Northeast Department, during the decade. In Chicago the UPWA thought it necessary to distribute *Sing A Union Song* to its members in 1955, as did the Textile Workers of America its *TWUA Songs* in 1951, the same year that the United Rubber Workers's *URW Song Book* appeared. Sometime during the decade the United Steelworkers (USWA) circulated the *Steelworkers' Song Book*, and in 1962 the UAW produced *Songs For Labor*. Whether or not music was much in evidence at union meetings or on picket lines, some of the newer industrial unions at least gave lip service to the idea.[31]

Songs about work, rather than about labor unions, were also a small part of country music at the time. Merle Travis's "Sixteen Tons" became a hit for Tennessee Ernie Ford in 1956, while Travis's other work songs, such as "Dark As A Dungeon" and "Nine Pound Hammer," helped establish his reputation. There were also a few small label recordings issued, such as Bill Carter's "By the Sweat of My Brow" (Republic 7126-F) in 1956, the Wright Brothers "Island Creek Mine Fire" (Golden Leaf 45-106A) in 1960, and Jimmy Simpson's "Oilfield Blues" (Republic 7065-45) in 1953.[32]

The folklorist and anthropologist John Greenway published *American Folksongs of Protest* in 1953, the first major study setting work songs into their historical contexts. He devoted chapters to "Negro Songs of Protest," "The Songs of the Textile Workers," "The Songs of the Miners," "The Migratory Workers," "Songs of the Farmers," "A Labor Miscellany," concluding with "The Song-Makers" (Ella May Wiggins, Aunt Molly Jackson, Woody Guthrie, and Joe Glazer). Including a thorough discography and bibliography, the book quickly became influential among scholars and students. Greenway agreed with Glazer that "99 percent of American industrial workers do not sing labor protest songs except during strikes," and that "Most songs of this nature come from the rural South." Two years later Greenway recorded eighteen labor songs for the Riverside album *American Industrial Folksongs*, including "There Is Power In A Union," "Hard Times In The Mill," "Dark As A Dungeon," Woody Guthrie's "Ludlow Massacre," Aunt Molly Jackson's "Hard Times In Coleman's Mines," and Joe Glazer's "Too Old To Work." "The songs on this record are a selection from several thousand songs of protest," Greenway explained. "In making such a selection, the primary factor considered was to achieve a representative collection of modern American protest singing." Simultaneously, Riverside released Greenway's *The Great American Bum and other Hobo and Migratory Workers' Songs*. "This recording chronicles the growth and gathering of these *grapes of wrath*, from the boisterousness of the hobo to the bitterness of the migrant," Greenway clarified in his notes. "For despite their fundamental differences the hobo and the migrant had one thing in common—their singing." He included "The Great American Bum," "Hobo Bill's Last Ride," and "Hard Travelin'" among the nineteen offerings.[33]

During the 1950s scholars continued to compile books on cowboy, whaling, and other occupational songs, many of which were also published in *Sing Out!* Numerous records appeared, including those by the musician/collector Paul Clayton. Born in New Bedford, Massachusetts, in 1933, he learned whaling songs as a teenager before heading south to attend the University of Virginia. He recorded numerous albums from the mid-1950s into the 1960s, including *Bay State Ballads* (Folkways Records FA 2106), *Foc'sle Songs and Shanties* (Folkways Records FA 2429), *Timber-r-r!* (Riverside Records FLP 12-648), and *Whaling and Sailing Songs From the Days of Moby Dick* (Tradition Records TLP 1005). Clayton was not alone at the time in keeping the traditions alive, but he was more prolific than most. In 1951 Folkways Records issued Sam Eskin's *Sea Shanties and Loggers' Songs* (Folkways FA 2019), as well as *This Land Is My Land: American Work Songs* (Folkways FC 7027) which included recordings of Pete Seeger's "Young Man Who Wouldn't Hoe," Woody Guthrie's "Columbia River," Cisco Houston's "Down In The Mines," and Lead Belly's "Haul Away Joe."[34]

Labor and occupational songs would make even a stronger comeback in the 1960s, as the folk song revival reached a fevered pitch and then settled in for the long haul. While a singing labor movement was not dead, most of the interest in union and occupational songs, both old and new, came from scholars and younger musicians who had little connection with organized labor.

(Endnotes)

1 Ruth Crawford Seeger, *American Folk Songs for Children: In Home, School, and Nursery School* (New York: Doubleday & Company, 1948).

2 David Bonner, *Revolutionizing Children's Records: The Young People's Records and Children's Record Guild Series, 1946-1977* (Lanham, MD: The Scarecrow Press, 2008), 207, 213.

3 Beatrice Landeck, *Songs To Grow On: A Collection of American Folk Songs For Children* (N.Y.: Edward B. Marks Music Corporation, 1950), 69; Beatrice Landeck, *More Songs to Grow On: A New Collection of Folk Songs For Children* (N.Y.: Edward B. Marks Music Corporation, 1954).

4 Tom Scott, *Sing Of America* (N.Y.: Thomas Y. Crowell Company, 1947); Margaret B. Boni, *Fireside Book of Folk Songs* (N.Y.: Simon and Schuster, 1947), 129. Also in 1947, John and Alan Lomax published *Folk Song U.S.A.* (N.Y.: Duell, Sloan and Pearce, 1947), with a large number of work songs pulled from their previous compilations.

5 Dave Marsh and Harold Leventhal, eds., *Pastures of Plenty: A Self Portrait, Woody Guthrie* (N.Y.: HarperCollins Publishers, 1990), 157, an essay by Woody dated March 19, 1946; "People's Songs International Constitution," copy in author's possession; Mike Gold, "Change the World," *Daily Worker*, January 2, 1946.

6 *People's Songs*, vol. 1, no. 1 (February 1946), 1.

7 Felix Landau, "Talkin' Union And Singin', Too," *Union Voice* (District 65, United Retail and Wholesale Employees of America), 1946; Douglas, "Westinghouse Marchers Show Bitterness, Humor," *Pittsburgh Press*, March 23, 1946; Marsh and Leventhal, eds., *Pastures of Plenty*, 174, an essay by Woody dated March 23, 1946.

8 Felix Landau, "UAW-CIO Leader Tells Union Problems," *People's Songs*, vol. 1, no. 3 (April 1946), 2; Alan Reitman, "PAC Up Your Songs," *People's Songs*, vol. 1, no. 4 (May 1946), 1.

9 "Words and Music—CIO," *CIO News*, February 11, 1946. This was the beginning of its later incarnation. According to the New York City Central Labor Council AFL-CIO website: "The New York City Labor Chorus, with 75 members representing over 20 labor unions and District Councils, was founded in 1991. Our Chorus promotes union solidarity by expressing through song the history and ongoing struggles of workers for economic and social justice. Our dynamic repertoire combines the power and culture of union music with the great gospel, jazz, classical and folk traditions." The original chorus also had 75 members.

10 Frederick Woltman, "Communist Minstrels Set Tunes for PAC,' *World-Telegram*, undated clipping; "UNION RECORD COMPANY ESTABLISHED," press release, undated, copy in author's possession. The songs from *Songs For Political Action*, but not *Roll The Union On*, appear in Ronald Cohen and Dave Samuelson, comps., *Songs for Political Action: Folk Music, Topical Songs and the American Left, 1926-1954*, Bear Family Records BCD 15720, 1996.

11 "Selling Union," *People's Songs*, vol. 3, nos.1 & 2 (Feb. & Mar. 1948), 6.

12 Rolf Cahn, "Detroit Picketline Troubadours," *People's Songs*, vol. 3, no. 5 (June 1948), 2; Alan Lomax to Leonard Bernstein, January 20, 1947, copy in author's possession; "Editorials: People's Songs," *The Christian Science Monitor*, March 4, 1947.

13 The NMU-CIO recordings, as well as those by White and Glazer (except for his CIO Research and Education album), can be found in Cohen and Samuelson, comps., *Songs for Political Action*; "Pete Seeger, Famed As Folk Singer, Star of Challenge Fete," *Challenge*, July 21, 1947.

14 "Bob Claiborn Back Singing Cross-Country Tour," *Daily Worker*, October 1, 1947. All of the Charter Records can be found in Cohen and Samuelson, comps., *Songs for Political Action*.

15 Alfred Frankenstein and Isaac Stern, letter dated March 1, 1946, copy in author's possession; Carl Williams, "Working and Singing in Unison," *People's World*, April 24, 1947; "Songster Jerry Walter: A Culture From the People," *People's World*, July 12, 1948.

16 "Vern Partlow-Singing Organizer," *People's Songs*, Vol. 1, No. 10 (November 1946), 5. These and other FTA songs can be found in Cohen and Samuelson, comps., *Songs for Political Action*.

17 Irwin Silber, "United Songsters Make A Chain," *People's Songs*, vol. 2, no. 10 (November 1947), 2; Craig Smith, *Sing My Whole Life Long: Jenny Vincent's Life in Folk Music and Activism* (Albuquerque: University of New Mexico Press, 2007).

18 "UAW SONGBOOK," *People's Songs*, vol. 2, nos. 6 & 7 (August 1947), 4; Alan Lomax, "Foreword," B. A. Botkin, "Preface," *The People's Song Book* (N.Y.: Boni and Gaer, 1948), 3, 6; Pete [Seeger] to Zilphia [Horton], November 13, 1946, Zilphia Horton letters, Highlander Folk School Collection, Tennessee State Library and Archives, Nashville, TN.; *A People's Songs Wordbook, No. 1* (N.Y.: People's Songs, Inc., 1947); *Amalgamated Song Book* (N.Y.: Education Department, Amalgamated Clothing Workers of America—CIO, *ca.* 1948).

19 "Meeting of National Board of Directors of People's Songs, December 18, 1948," copy in author's possession; Richard A. Reuss with JoAnne C. Reuss, *American Folk Music and Left-Wing Politics, 1927-1957* (Lanham, MD: The Scarecrow Press, 2000), 199-204.

20 Michael Vary, "3,000 Join in Song at the Freedom Festival of UE Union," unidentified clipping; Ronald D. Cohen, *Rainbow Quest: The Folk Music Revival and American Society, 1940-1970* (Amherst: University of Massachusetts Press, 2002), chaps. 2 and 3 for the general story, esp. 86-87.

21 *People's Songs*, vol. 3, no. 8 (Sept. 1948), 8.

22 Wilson J. Warren, Bruce Fehn, and Marianne Robinson, "They Met at the Fair: UPWA and Farmer-Labor Cooperation, 1944-1952," *Labor's Heritage*, vol. 11, no. 2 (Fall 2000/Winter 2001), 26, 29-30.

23 Joe Glazer, *Labor's Troubadour* (Urbana: University of Illinois Press, 2001), 15.

24 Glazer, *Labor's Troubadour*, 31, 47. Years later Glazer published *Textile Songs: Songs From the Mills* (Chevy Chase, MD: Joe Glazer, 1988), but I am not familiar with the booklet he mentions.

25 Glazer, *Labor's Troubadour*, 80; Bill Friedland, "Labor Arts and the First Recorded IWW Album," in Archie Green, David Roediger, Franklin Rosemont, Salvatore Salerno, eds., *The Big Red Songbook* (Chicago: Charles H. Kerr Publishing Co., 2007), 457-462. Joe Glazer, *The Songs of Joe Hill*, Folkways Records FA 2039.

26 Edith Fowke and Joe Glazer, *Songs of Work and Freedom* (Chicago: Labor Education Division, Roosevelt University, 1960), 11; it was reissued by Fowke and Glazer as *Songs of Work and Protest* (N.Y.: Dover Publications, Inc., 1973); Joe Glazer and Charlie Byrd, *Songs of Work and Freedom*, Washington 460, 1960; *CIO Song Book* (Washington, D.C.: CIO Department of Education and Research, 1951).

27 "Introductory Notes by Peter Seeger," and "Notes by Philip S. Foner," *The Original Talking Union with the Almanac Singers & other Union Songs with Pete Seeger and Chorus*, Folkways Records FH 5285, 1955.

28 Irwn Silber, "Record Review," *Sing Out!*, vol. 5, no. 4 (Autumn 1955), 23.

29 The original *The People's Song Book* remained in print during this time.

30 "Industrial Folk Songs (About the Background of the Songs) by Irwin Silber," *American Industrial Ballads*, Folkways Records FH 5251, 1956. Both Seeger's *Talking Union* and *American Industrial Ballads* were among the first albums I obtained in the 1950s, and they had an immeasurable impact on my musical and political life.

31 *We Work—We Sing*, N.Y. Cloak Joint Board CB772, nd; *My Name is Mary Brown*, Columbia TV15219.

32 On Travis see chapter 3, and Hedy West, "Merle Travis on Homeground," *Sing Out!*, vol. 25, no. 1 (May/June 1976), 20-26.

33 John Greenway, *American Folksongs of Protest* (Philadelphia: University of Pennsylvania Press, 1953), 303; John Greenway, *American Industrial Folksongs*, Riverside Records RLP 12-607, 1955; John Greenway, *The Great American Bum and other Hobo and Migratory Workers' Songs*, Riverside Records RLP 12-619, 1955.

34 Bob Coltman, *Paul Clayton and the Folksong Revival* (Lanham, MD: The Scarecrow Press, 2008).

Solidarity Forever: Songs for UMWA members on strike against the Pittston Coal Company (Washington, D.C.: UMWA Organizing Department, [1989])

chapter six

Recent Decades

The increasing popularity of folk music through the early years of the 1960s resulted in vast numbers of old and new performers, concerts, festivals, recordings, and other commercial products, spanning a wide variety of musical styles and genres, including labor and occupational songs. "Although the renaissance in folk music—both from the performing and the listening ends—continues to grow, the lines of division among the motley enthusiasts remain sternly drawn," jazz critic Nat Hentoff wrote in early 1962. "On the one hand there is the mass audience which has settled for the hollow high spirits of Harry Belafonte, the Kingston Trio, the Brothers Four, and the Limeliters. Directly opposite in criteria is the minority of specialists which is contemptuous of all but authentic ethnic singers." While Hentoff was none too favorable about the current folk craze, he did try to capture the split between the commercial and traditional sides of the Revival.[1]

Ed Kahn, a young folklorist in Los Angeles, published an article on "The Ballad of Coal Creek" in *Sing Out!* in 1960. "Since Pete Steele's famous recording of 'Coal Creek March' for the Library of Congress in 1938 (AAFS 1703A) there has been a great deal of interest in the various mine disasters at Coal Creek (now Lake City), Tennessee," Kahn began. While Steele thought the song came from a 1911 explosion, based on his own research Kahn traced it to 1891. "The text, and the tune accompanying the sung part of the march, are obviously related to the 'Trouble Down At Homestead' ballad, stemming from a similar incident in Pennsylvania in the same year," he concluded. Scholars had long been interested in labor-related songs, but with the upsurge in performing and recording folk music, the fascination intensified. Thus a song from 1891, recorded by Alan Lomax for the Library of Congress fifty years later, had become part of the repertoire of Pete Seeger and various other performers by the 1960s. Along with "John Henry" and other antique labor songs, "Coal Creek March" had entered the cultural mainstream.[2]

The following issue of *Sing Out!* published Pete Seeger's glowing review of Edith Fowke and Joe Glazer's *Songs of Work and Freedom*. "This is one helluva fine book," he began, then concluded: "Union educational departments, if they are concerned that new union members do not sufficiently appreciate the struggles their predecessors went through to gain present day positions, should buy a copy for every single local." This had long been Seeger's dream, now perhaps made possible as the songs and their stories became more accessible, but there remained somewhat of a gap between the labor songs of old and the current labor and political climate. Musicians such as Tom Paxton, Phil Ochs, the Greenbriar Boys, and Buffy Sainte-Marie, however, occasionally performed during labor strikes, such as for the coal miners in Hazard, Kentucky, in early 1965. Basically, however, labor songs had become increasingly part of popular folk music rather than union organizing.[3]

Sing Out! under the editorship of Irwin Silber since the early 1950s, continued to publish occasional articles on labor songs and their lyrics. For example, "Winnsboro Cotton Mill Blues" appeared in late 1960 and "Railroad Bill" a few issues later. Hamish Henderson's piece on the songs of Scottish miners, appearing in November 1964, was a rare example of an interpretive article. The following year, however, Pete Seeger published "Whatever Happened to Singing in the Unions?" After a brief overview of the checkered history of union songs, he sorrowfully concluded: "Today, a few unions still publish songbooks, and a few even have choruses. But an average of only three per cent of American union members attend union meetings, except during crises, and the songbooks are by and large unused. 'Union Maid' is far better known on college campuses than it is in the average union hall."[4]

In 1966 *Sing Out!* published Archie Green's short essay "Dorsey Dixon: Minstrel of the Mills," who had written "Weave Room Blues" in 1932. Along with other traditional musicians newly rediscovered, he appeared at the 1963 Newport Folk Festival, and was recorded by Piedmont Records and the Library of Congress. Two issues later Jim Garland, the sibling of Aunt Molly Jackson and Sara Ogan Gunning, contributed a short autobiographical piece. "I just been setting here reading the April issue of *Sing Out!*, and it occurred to me that just maybe an old timer might venture to say a word or two," he began. "I have sung the fighting union songs of the IWW and other labor org[anization]s." He also performed his composition "I Don't Want Your Millions, Mister" at Newport in 1963, later released on Vanguard's *Newport Broadside: Topical Songs at the Newport Folk Festival, 1963* (Vanguard VRS 9144). While he had been out of the public eye for some decades, he had always kept up his performing.[5]

In 1958, Jerry Silverman published his ground-breaking collection *Folk Blues*, which began with a selection of "Work and Prison Blues" including the song "Hard Times Blues." Two years later Alan Lomax issued the massive *The Folk Songs of North America In The English Language*. He covered numerous work songs under the headings "Workers and Farmers" in the section on the North,

"Hard Times and the Hillbilly" in the section "The Southern Mountains and Backwoods," "Cowboys," "Farmers," and "Railroaders and Hoboes" in the section on the West, and "Work Songs" and "Ballads" in the section "The Negro South." Each song had a lengthy introduction. Concerning "Johnny, Won't You Ramble?" for example, Lomax explained, "From the beginning it was the white man standing in the shade, shouting orders with a club or whip or pistol in his hand—while out in the sun the blacks sweated with the raw stuff of wealth, cursing under their breath, but singing at the tops of their voices. Thus work songs flowered richly in the South. Every new job brought a fresh style with a special rhythm. Without these songs the South, as we know it, would never have come into being." Three decades later Lomax crafted his prize-winning *The Land Where The Blues Began*, where he described how the harsh lives and work experiences of African Americans in the Mississippi Delta had influenced the music they created.[6]

When the Lomax, Guthrie, and Seeger compilation *Hard Hitting Songs for Hard-Hit People* appeared in 1967, after waiting twenty-five years for a publisher, it was only one of many such folk song collections available, but surely one of the richest. On the other hand, many of the earlier books and folios dealing with ballads from lumberjacks, miners, cowboys, sailors, and other manual occupations were now long out-of-print, available only in libraries, along with most of the labor union songbooks.[7]

By the 1960s it was, therefore, easy to come across numerous published work-related songs from throughout the country's history. Moreover, there were an increasing number of accessible recordings. For example, some albums were connected with labor unions. The United Auto Workers (UAW) sponsored *Songs for a Better Tomorrow* in 1963, with Ronnie Gilbert (a member of the Weavers), the Tarriers, and the Irish musician Tommy Makem performing established labor songs such as "Joe Hill," "Solidarity Forever," "We Shall Not Be Moved," and "Sit Down." The following year the union produced the more ambitious *This Land Is Your Land: Songs*

Of Social Justice, with a wide variety of songs and performers. A few, such as Tennessee Ernie Ford's rendition of "Sixteen Tons" and the Weavers's version of "Drill, Ye Tarriers, Drill," directly spoke of the hardships suffered by working men and women, while the majority had a wider social reach, such as Leon Bibb's "Another Man Done Gone," Billie Holliday's "Strange Fruit," and Peter, Paul and Mary's "Blowin' In The Wind." About the same time the UAW issued an album of songs by Joe Lise, titled *It's The UAW All The Way*.[8]

A few union-related films also featured musical soundtracks. The Amalgamated Clothing Workers of America's seminal documentary *The Inheritance*, produced in 1964 by Harold Mayer, with a memorable script written by Millard Lampell, included performances by Tom Paxton, Pete Seeger, and Judy Collins. While there was no accompanying album, some of the lyrics were printed in a booklet, also titled *The Inheritance*, which was issued by the union. But Mayer's film *Movin' On*, a history of the United Transportation Union, did have a related album, with music by the New Lost City Ramblers and Bonnie Dobson.[9]

Joe Glazer remained the most prolific of the labor songsters. In 1970 he founded Collector Records as a manageable outlet for his recordings. He had already issued *Songs of Coal* in 1964, recorded at a United Mine Workers of America (UMWA) convention, on the Sound Studios label; an album for the American Newspaper Guild, *The Golden Presses*; as well as *AFSCME Sings with Joe Glazer* (1968) and *Singing about Our Union* (1969) for the American Federation of State, County, and Municipal Employees (AFSCME) union. In 1971 he released the first AFSCME album as the Collector title *Joe Glazer Sings Labor Songs*, and he was now off and running. Over the next few decades he would continue to appear at numerous labor functions and follow with an album, mostly issued by Collector, including *Joe Glazer Live at Vail* for the Central Pension Fund of the Operating Engineers International Union (1973), *Down in a Coal Mine* (1974), *Songs of Steel and Struggle—the Story of the Steelworkers of America* (1975), *Textile Voices—Songs and Stories of the Mills* (1975), *Songs for Woodworkers* (1977), and *Service Employees International Sings with Joe Glazer* (1980). The American Federation of Teachers (AFT AFL-CIO) sponsored *We've Only Just Begun: A Century of Labor Song* (1982). Glazer spanned labor's history, from "Hard Times in the Mill," "John Henry," and "Union Maid" to "Farm Workers' Song." As union president Albert Shanker noted on the album: "The songs are performed in a warm and lively style with excellent musical accompaniment and should make it easier for teachers to accent and develop important labor themes." While unions had a dwindling interest in publishing songbooks, Glazer had a hand in *Textile Voices; Songs From the Mills and Songs for AFSCME*. "I know that the mills will not be made of marble here on earth," he confessed in his autobiography. "I know that machines will not be made of gold. Workers will become tired and grow old. But I hope that through the years I have helped, through my songs, to make life a bit better for others. I have been called a 'musical agitator for all good causes,' and I hope to continue in that role." He died at home in September 2006.[10]

While hardly as prolific as Glazer, Hazel Dickens also had a productive career as a labor performer and songwriter. Born in Mercer County, West Virginia, in 1935, she moved to Baltimore in 1954, where she launched her musical career. She soon met Mike Seeger, son of musicologists Charles and Ruth Crawford Seeger, who introduced her to performing in public. A bit later she teamed up with Alice Gerrard, and their first album for Folkways Records, *Who's That Knocking?*, appeared in 1965, which included "Coal Miner's Blues." Their initial album for Rounder Records, *Strange Creek Singers*, was released in 1972, two years after the company's founding in Cambridge, Massachusetts. Four years later Dickens moved to Washington, D.C., where she increased her output of original women's and labor songs. "Hazel Dickens's compelling voice and eloquent songs first reached a large American public in the soundtrack of *Harlan County, USA*, a 1976 Academy Award-winning documentary film that told of a protracted and dramatic strike in the eastern Kentucky coalfields," historian Bill Malone has written in the introduction to *Working Girl Blues: The Life & Music of Hazel Dickens*. She performed her composition "They'll Never Keep Us Down" following the film's opening in New York, then accompanied the film to Harlan County, Kentucky. She was soon doing benefits for striking miners in Stearns, Kentucky. She had already written "Black Lung" in 1969, in honor of her brother Thurman who died of the disease.[11]

Hazel Dickens continuing performing, composing, and recording through the end of the twentieth century and into the next. She appeared on the soundtrack for the film *Matewan* in 1980, and for numerous albums issued by Rounder, including *Hard-Hitting Songs for Hard Hit People* (1980); *They'll Never Keep Us Down: Women's Coal Mining Songs* (1984), including her "Coal Mining Women" and " Coal Miner's Grave"; *By the Sweat of My Brow* (1984); and *It's Hard to Tell the Singer from the Song* (1986). Not all of her songs were directly about miners and other workers, for example, her 1980 song commemorating labor composers Sarah Ogan Gunning, Nimrod Workman, and Florence Reece, "Freedom's Disciple (Working-Class Heroes)." She was well represented in Rounder's *Coal Mining Women* album with her songs "Coal Mining Women," "The Yablonski Murder," and "Mannington Mine Disaster." As Bill Malone observed in 2008, "Hazel's commitment to social justice has not been dampened by her successes, nor has her conviction that music should be put to the service of working people's welfare."[12]

While Dickens mostly focused on the trials and tribulations of coal miners and working women, others were exploring additional facets of labor songs, of which there appeared to be no limit. Mike Seeger, often performing with the New Lost City Ramblers, Hazel Dickens, and various others, issued the Folkways album *Tipple, Loom & Rail: Songs of the Industrialization of the South* in 1966. He included "A Factory Girl" from the nineteenth century, and the more recent "Coal Creek Troubles," "Harlan County Blues," "Cotton Mill Colic," and "The Virginian Strike of '23." Detailed liner notes by Archie Green documented each song's origins. "The unique feature of *Tipple, Loom & Rail* is its concentration on songs of the three industries symbolized by this title," Green explained. "Excluded are logging, rafting, sawmilling, and woodworking, although many mountain hunters and trappers first worked 'for gain' in their native forests. . . . Naturally, some of these numbers are indigenous union songs, for many Southern workers could, and did, look beyond the mill's barbed-wire fence or the company town's store to a new way of life."[13]

In addition to the valuable Seeger album, Archie Green, a most prolific researcher and creative writer, contributed detailed notes to numerous other albums. For example, in 1964 he recorded and wrote the notes for the Folk-Legacy Records album *Sarah Ogan Gunning: "Girl of Constant Sorrow,"* issued in 1965. "Like other folksingers, her repertoire encompasses a variety of emotions: anger at needless poverty and exploitation, affirmation of self-help as a way of life, pleasure in love, solace in religion, peace in death," concludes his description of her life. In the notes to Glazer's *Songs of Steel and Struggle*, distributed at the United Steelworkers of America (USWA) 1978 convention, Green writes: "To listen to a single LP with 15 songs is but to lift the lid of a treasure chest of folklore. Steel ballads and folklore go back more than a century in North America. Behind the heritage left to today's unionists by the proud craftsmen in the Sons of Vulcan is a timeless span of magic and power inherent in the shaping of iron out of the earth itself. Can we hear Vulcan and Loki roar when we now open our eyes and ears to the creative traditions of steelworkers and listen to *Songs of Steel and Struggle*?" The somewhat unusual selections included "I Lie in the American Land" in Slovak and "The Miner's Ballad" in Spanish.[14]

Green also did the notes for the Rounder compilation *Hard Times*, an anthology of commercial blues recordings from 1916 to 1952. It included Barbecue Bob's "We Sure Got Hard Times," Pinewood Tom's (Josh White) "Silicosis Is Killing Me," and Smokey Hoggs's "Unemployment Blues." "My response to this anthology has been to view it as basically a commentary on job exploitation and unemployment," he explained. "Others may wish to stress the element of personal lament or internal despair. Although I have never tried to force blues into the mold of conscious protest, I have long felt that work blues inferred positive socio-political statements. . . . Does the bluesman have to spell out a political belief in industrial democracy to make his song socially significant?" Rounder issued somewhat of a companion album about the same time, *Poor Man, Rich Man: American Country Songs of Protest*, with detailed liner notes by Mark Wilson, the company's resident old-time music expert. Beginning with Dave McCarn's 1930 recording of "Poor Man, Rich Man (Cotton Mill Colic, No. 2)," it included the Hart Brothers's "A Miner's Prayer" (no date), Fiddlin' John Carson's "The Farmer Is The Man That Feeds Them All" (1923), Green Bailey's "Shut Up In Coal Creek" (1929), and even Gene Autry's "The Death Of Mother Jones" (1931). "The diverse, salty and unprompted songs heard here reflect the struggle for reasonable working conditions in a manner more engaging and convincing than many more didactic pieces," Wilson wrote. "I think no one remotely sympathetic to the working man and woman can fail to be moved by these performances, not through pity but from admiration for that rare blend of humor, goodwill and self-affirmation which continues to mark our best country songs today."[15]

In the late 1970s, about the time *Hard Times* and *Poor Man, Rich Man* appeared, June Appal Recordings in Whitesburg, Kentucky, released *Brown Lung Cotton Mill Blues*. These were new songs by Si Kahn, "Cotton Mill Blues" and "Aragon Mill," and Charlotte Brody, "Boxes of Bobbins," as well as new versions of the older "Babies in the Mill," "Winnsboro Cotton Mill Blues," and "Hard Times Cotton Mill Girls." Combining old and new compositions, the album was issued to raise awareness and benefit the Carolina Brown Lung Association.[16]

In 1985, Pete Seeger and Bob Reiser published a powerful book of work songs, *Carry It On! A History in Song and Picture of the*

Working Men and Women of America. A committee had been formed to commemorate the 1886 Haymarket Square uprising in Chicago, and its members selected the dozens of songs to be published in order to "inspire a deeper love for the hardworking people of past generations and encourage future generations not to run way from problems, but to dig in and try to solve them." Organized chronologically, beginning with the Revolutionary War era and ending with recent compositions, there were helpful notes, as well as numerous period quotes and illustrations, along with the verses for the four score songs. This was a team effort, designed to "encourage people to put on musical programs, occasions for people of all ages to get together and listen to music that has reached around the world, touching friends and fellow working people on every continent and island." But there was no mention of singing on the picket line or during a union meeting. Many had previously been published, but those more recent were a strong indication that work songs were still alive and well, such as Dolly Parton's "9 to 5," Paul McKenna's "The Union Buster," Tom Juravich's "Rise Again," and Lorre Wyatt's "Somos El Barco/We Are the Boat." Flying Fish Records quickly released two companion albums, *Carry It On: Songs of America's Working People* and *Songs of the Working People: From the American Revolution to the Civil War.* The former featured Pete Seeger, Jane Sapp, and Si Kahn doing "Talking Union," "Carry It On," "Soup Song" and much more. The latter had all fresh recordings by Seeger, Ronnie Gilbert, Odetta, Alan Lomax, Chet Washington, Earl Robinson and others of such standards as "Bennington Rifles," "Buffalo Skinners," "John Henry," "No Irish Need Apply," "Follow the Drinkin' Gourd," and "Farmer is the One."[17]

By the 1980s there were various performers, male and female, singing and recording work songs. Johnny Paycheck (aka Donald Lytle) had a hit in 1978 with David Alan Coe's country-style "Take This Job and Shove It," more-or-less an anti-work song. "The contrast between 'Take This Job and Shove It' and 'Which Side Are

You On?' touches large differences in meaning between folk and popular expression," Archie Green has explained. "One began its journey literally in a mountain miner's cabin; the other, in an ultra-modern recording studio. . . . We deal here with large polarities: we/they, insider/outsider, marginal/mainstream." The community organizer Si Kahn proved to be a prolific performer and composer, beginning with his June Appal album *New Wood* in 1975, with his signature song "Aragon Mill." Flying Fish followed with *Home* in 1979, which included "Spinning Mills of Home" and "Union In My Soul." It was succeeded by *Doing My Job* with "Black Gold," "Doing My Job," and "Five Days a Week." Kahn also contributed his own (with Charlotte Brody) "Paper Heart" to the Smithsonian/Folkways compilation *Don't Mourn—Organize!: Songs of Labor Songwriter Joe Hill*, a grouping of older and newer recordings. Larry Penn, a truck driver in Milwaukee, composed and recorded numerous songs about truckers and other workers. His 1980 album for Collector, *Workin' For A Livin'*, included "East Chicago Run," "Overtime," and "Duffy's Truck." He also appeared at a Labor Concert in Kenosha, Wisconsin, in 1986, sponsored by UAW Local 180, along with Pete Seeger, Joe Glazer, and Kim and Reggie Harris. Penn's "Nobody Cares About That" appeared on the subsequent Collector album *Labor Concert 1986*. Magpie recorded mostly older songs in *Working My Life Away* for Collector, which also issued Bobbie McGee's *Bread and Raises: Songs for Working Women*, sponsored by the Coalition of Labor Union Women, AFL-CIO.[18]

Bruce "U. Utah" Phillips (1935-2008) was another late century pro-labor musician and storyteller. Born in Cleveland, Ohio, he was long a member of the IWW and a creative voice for workers' rights. While a prolific performer, having produced numerous records, much of his output only tangentially touched upon labor issues, except for his album *We Have Fed You all A Thousand Years*, songs of the IWW. It included "Dump the Bosses Off Your Back," "Mr. Block," "Casey Jones—The Union Scab," and other wobbly hits, ending with "Solidarity Forever" and "There is Power In A Union."

Charlie King, a generation younger than Phillips, added his own body of protest songs. His 1979 album *Somebody's Story* included the compositions "The Dancing Boilerman," "Taft-Hartley," and "Our Life Is More Than Our Work."[19]

While fewer labor strikes seemed to produce topical songs, a small number managed to use music to promote worker energy and solidarity. For one, the Brewery Workers Local no. 366 in Colorado had a few songs accompanying their late 1970s strike against the Coors company. The union issued a small 45 rpm including "The Ballad of Joe Coors" / "Coors Brewery." Tom Juravich released a recording of his "Trying to Break My Union," about the United Auto Workers' Local 430 strike against Sterling Radiator Plant in Massachusetts in 1981-1982. Juravich followed with the album *Rising Again* for the United Auto Workers. The United Mine Workers of America (UMWA) published a small songbook during their strike against the Pittston Coal Company in 1989. It included "Down At The Picketline," "We've Been Working For Pittston," and "The Picket Boogie," as well as "We Shall Not Be Moved." About the same time the union also published *Which Side Are You On?: Our Songs, Our Struggle, Our Union*. Dedicated to Florence Reece, it included thirteen old and newer songs, such as "Which Side Are You On," "Rise Again," and "Hey, Mr. Massey." The clerical and technical workers at Yale University, on strike against the university in 1984, issued *Local 34 Songbook*, with fourteen songs, including "We Are Local 34," "Ain't Gonna Let Nobody," "Arbitration, Binding Arbitration," and "We're Not at Work Today."[20]

A few other unions adhered to the belief that songs could continue to play some role in organizing workers. In addition to Joe Glazer's output, the Amalgamated Clothing and Textile Workers Union (ACTWU) produced the expansive *The ACTWU Song-Book*, which spanned the musical repertoire from "Casey Jones" to Bob Dylan's "Blowin' In The Wind." The AFL-CIO's Department of Education issued the 10th edition of the *AFL-CIO Song Book* in 1974, and the larger *Songs for Labor* in 1983. The latter began with "Bread and

Roses" and ended with the Almanac Singers's "Union Train." Late in the century Joe Uehlein produced a rich compilation, *The Labor Heritage Songbook*, for the Labor Heritage Foundation in Washington, D.C. "We sing to organize, educate, activate and motivate," he wrote in the foreword, "and just to have fun. . . . Whether it's a picket line, boycott rally, educational function, monthly union meeting, picnic, or organizing meeting, these songs will help you along the way." The songs were old and new, the latter including Si Kahn's "Aragon Mill," Charlie King's "The Dancing Boilerman," Fred Small's "Fifty-Nine Cents," Tom Juravich's "Putting the Blame On Me," and Willie Sordill's "Please Tip Your Waitress." The Labor Heritage Foundation also published a series of small satirical songbooks by Julie McCall, including *Camo Carols*. The United Auto Workers and the Union Label and Service Trades Department of the AFL-CIO also released updated songbooks.[21]

Broadside magazine, published from 1962-1988, included a few labor-connected songs, particularly regarding migrant workers. Many of the songs that appeared in the magazine during the 1960s were reprinted in the three volumes of collected *Broadside* songs, such as "El Picket Sign" (1967) and "The Migrant's Song" (1965) in volume 2, as well as Malvina Reynolds's "Blood on the Grapes" (1968) in volume 3. Recordings of these and other migrant workers songs, such as "Welcome, Welcome Emigrante" and "Contra La Por (Against Fear)," appeared in the Smithsonian Folkways CD collection *The Best of Broadside*. This set also included Matt McGinn's "If It Wasn't For The Union," David Cohen's "More Good Men Going Down" (about coal miners), and two by Sis Cunningham, "Sundown" and "My Oklahoma Home (It Blowed Away)."[22]

In late 1966 *Sing Out!* magazine published editor Irwin Silber's article "La Huelga: Songs of The Delano Grape Strike." "Last spring the movement was dramatically projected into the American consciousness by an incredible 250-mile march to Sacramento organized by the strikers," he began. "The march was more than a line of walkers. It was a combination fiesta, religious pilgrimage, labor struggle and race demonstration." Following an interview with Luis Valdez, director of Le Teatro Campesino, Silber concluded: "America has not heard such militant workers' songs since the 1930's when Harlan County miners adapted their mountain traditions to the urgency of strike and union. Like all folk songs, the songs of *La Huelga* come from the people." A few songbooks followed, such as the United Farm Workers's *Canciones/Songs*, the Texas AFL-CIO's *Songbook/Canciones*, and the anonymously published *Boycott Now*, which included "Joe Hill," "Bracero," and Woody Guthrie's "Deportee." There were also various albums, such as *Las Voces de Los Campesinos* (1978) with Francisco Garcia and Pablo and Juanita Saludado; *Viva La Causa: Songs and Sounds from the Delano Strike* (1966), with Los Huelguistas De Delano and El Teatro Campesino; *Si Se Puede* (1976); and El Teatro Campesino's *Huelga En General!* (*ca*. 1975). The strikes and boycotts organized by the farm workers stretched through the century and into the next, although music would play a progressively less vital role. Initially, however, the songs helped to motivate and invigorate, as they had done for a long time.[23]

Conclusion

By the first decade of the twenty-first century labor unions had effectively abandoned music as an organizing tactic. Not that they have ever depended primarily on songs to promote their goals, but surely during the height of the 1930s and into the following decades, when labor unions reached a large segment of the working class, music seemed to play some role. Music continued to have organizing power into the 1960s and '70s, particularly among miners, migrant farm workers, and a few other constituencies. As for the singer-songwriters, labor songs would continue as part of their performances and political commitments, but in a minor fashion. Older occupational songs would live on, however, as one aspect of traditional songs that would persist in songbooks and artists repertoires. Modern technology, including CDs and Internet streaming, has made available virtually all twentieth century recordings of labor/occupational songs. Numerous songbooks, old and new, are also readily accessible.

While labor songs have generally faded from view, music still plays a vital role in spurring some groups of workers to take action to improve their working conditions. In recent years, the social historian George Lipsitz has argued, "because consumption plays such a central part in the activities of everyday life in today's society, the products of popular culture often become focal points for the expressions of desires suppressed in other spheres—desires for connections to others, for meaningful work, for a culture not based on lies." That is, contemporary workers have the same needs and goals as their working-class ancestors. Lipsitz focuses on minority groups, such as Mexican Americans in the Southwest, where banda music has quickly emerged. "In the wake of the banda boom, low-wage immigrant Mexican workers and their allies have mobilized themselves politically as well as culturally," he has argued. "Nonunion janitors, maids, garment workers, and restaurant employees have taken direct action to secure improvements in wages and working conditions." Other racial and ethnic minorities have had their own musical identities, as workers' indigenous cultures and their musical tastes have proliferated. Workers' music has had a long, vibrant, and continuing history, now into the twenty-first century. There is little promise that singing at work has much, if any, future, but music on a picket line or at a union meeting has continuing need and promise, and labor songs will long remain part of popular culture.[24]

(Endnotes)

1 Nat Hentoff, "Folk Finds a Voice," *The Reporter*, vol. 26, no. 1 (January 4, 1962), 39. For background information, Ronald D. Cohen, *Rainbow Quest: The Folk Music Revival and American Society, 1940-1970* (Amherst: University of Massachusetts Press, 2002), chaps. 6-8. For the increasing spate of recordings see, Richard A. Reuss, *Songs of American Labor, Industrialization and the Urban Work Experience: A Discography* (Ann Arbor: Labor Studies Center, Institute of Labor and Industrial Relations, The University of Michigan, 1983); Phyllis J. Jones, *Every Monday Morning: A Discography of American Labor Songs in the Conservatory Library of Oberlin College* (Oberlin: Oberlin College Library, 1993).

2 Ed Kahn, "The Ballad of Coal Creek," *Sing Out!*, vol. 10, no. 1 (April-May 1960), 18; Neil V. Rosenberg, " 'An Icy Mountain Brook': Revival, Aesthetics, and the 'Coal Creek March,'" Archie Green, ed., *Songs About Work: Essays in Occupational Culture for Richard A. Reuss* (Bloomington: Indiana University, Special Publications of the Folklore Institute No. 3, 1993), 163-183.

3 Pete Seeger, "Songs of Work and Freedom," *Sing Out!*, vol. 10, no. 2 (Summer 1960), 26-27; Michael Schumacher, *There But for Fortune: The Life of Phil Ochs* (N.Y.: Hyperion, 1996), 72-74.

4 Pete Seeger, "Whatever Happened to Singing in the Unions," *Sing Out!*, vol., 15, no. 2 (May 1965), 31.

5 Archie Green, "Dorsey Dixon: Minstrel of the Mills," *Sing Out!*, vol. 16, no. 3 (July 1966), 10-12; Jim Garland, "it seems to me . . . Some handwrought comments on life, hard work, and song-making," *Sing Out*!, vol. 16, no. 5 (Oct./Nov. 1966), 10; Julia S. Ardery, ed., *Welcome the Traveler Home: Jim Garland's Story of the Kentucky Mountains* (Lexington: University Press of Kentucky, 1983).

6 Jerry Silverman, *Folk Blues* (N.Y.: Macmillan Company, 1958); Alan Lomax, *The Folk Songs of North American In The English Language* (N.Y.: Doubleday & Company, 1960), 514.

7 In 1970, Tom Glazer published *Songs of Peace, Freedom, and Protest* (N.Y.: David McKay Company, 1970), which includes a smattering of older labor songs.

8 *Songs for a Better Tomorrow*, UAW Education Department, 1963; *This Land Is Your Land: Songs Of Social Justice*, UAW Education Department, 1964; Joe Lisi, *It's The UAW All The Way*, Lem Productions ESS-1185.

9 *The Inheritance* (N.Y.: Amalgamated Clothing Workers of America, AFL-CIO, CLC, 1964); *Movin' On*, United Transportation Union, AFL-CIO, HMP-69.

10 *Joe Glazer Sings Labor Songs*, Collector Records 1918, 1971; Joe Glazer, ed., *Textile Voices: Songs From the Mills* (Chevy Chase, MD: Joe Glazer, 1988); Joe Glazer, *Songs for AFSCME* (Washington, D.C.: American Federation of State, County, and Municipal

Employees, AFL-CIO, 1978); *We've Only Just Begun: A Century of Labor Song*, Collector Records 1934, 1982; Joe Glazer, *Labor's Troubadour* (Urbana: University of Illinois Press, 2001), 283.

11 Hazel Dickens and Bill C. Malone, *Working Girl Blues: The Life and Music of Hazel Dickens* (Urbana: University of Illinois Press, 2008), 1. For Rounder's history see, Michael Scully, *The Never-Ending Revival: Rounder Records and the Folk Alliance* (Urbana: University of Illinois Press, 2008).

12 Dickens and Malone, *Working Girl Blues*, 24.

13 Archie Green, "Tipple Loom & Rail notes," *Tipple, Loom & Rail: Songs of the Industrialization of the South*, Folkways Records FH5273, 1966.

14 *Sarah Ogan Gunning: "Girl of Constant Sorrow,"* Folk-Legacy Records FSA-26, 1965; *Songs of Steel and Struggle: The Story of the Steelworkers*, United Steelworkers of America, 1978 (originally Collector Records 1975). In the early 1970s Rounder Records issued some of Alan Lomax's 1939 Library of Congress recordings of Aunt Molly Jackson, with booklet notes by John Greenway; *Aunt Molly Jackson: Library of Congress Recordings*, Rounder Records 1002. On the lives of Sarah Ogan Gunning and Aunt Molly Jackson consult Shelly Romalis, *Pistol Packin' Mama: Aunt Molly Jackson and the Politics of Folksong* (Urbana: University of Illinois Press, 1999).

15 *Hard Times*, Rounder Records 4007; *Poor Man, Rich Man: American Country Songs Of Protest*, Rounder Records 1026.

16 *Brown Lung Cotton Mill Blues*, June Appal 006, 1976.

17 Pete Seeger and Bob Reiser, *Carry It On! A History in Song and Picture of the Working Men and Women of America* (N.Y.: Simon and Schuster, 1985), 254; *Carry It On: Songs of America's Working People,* Flying Fish Records FF70104, 1987; *Songs of the Working People: From the American Revolution to the Civil War*, Flying Fish Records FF483, 1988.

18 Archie Green, "Afterword," Reuss, *Songs of American Labor*, 103; Si Kahn, *New Wood*, June Appal JA002, 1975; Si Kahn, *Home*, Flying Fish Records FF207, 1979; Si Kahn, *Doing My Job*, Flying Fish Records 221, 1982; *Don't Mourn—Organize!: Songs of Labor Songwriter Joe Hill*, Smithsonian/Folkways Records SF 40026, 1990; Ronnie Gilbert, *Ronnie Gilbert on Mother Jones: Face to Face with the Most Dangerous Woman in America* (Berkeley: Conari Press, 1993); Larry Penn, *Workin' For A Livin'*, Collector Records 1931, 1980; *Labor Concert 1986*, Collector Records [1987]; Magpie, *Working My Life Away*, Collector Records 1936, 1982; Bobbie McGee, *Bread and Roses: Songs for Working Women*, Collector Records 1933, 1981; Dick Wright, *Sing a Labor Song*, a Main Street record.

19 *We Have Fed You all A Thousand Years*, Philo Records 1076, 1984. He also contributed "Joe Hill's Last Will" to the Smithsonian/Folkways collection *Don't Mourn, Organize!*; Charlie King, *Somebody's Story*, Rainbow Snake Records RSR 002. For a compilation of Phillips's recorded output, *Starlight On The Rails: A Songbook*, AK Press AKAO41CD, 2005.

20 *Coors Brewery Strike Songs*, Dare to Struggle Records DTS 001, 1977; Tom Juravich, *Rising Again*, UAW002, 1982; *Solidarity Forever: Songs for UMWA members on strike against the Pittston Coal Company* (Washington, D.C.: UMWA Organizing Department, n.d.); *Which Side Are You On?: Our Songs, Our Struggle, Our Union* (Washington, D.C.: United Mine Workers of America, n.d.); *Local 34 Songbook* (New Haven: Yale University, Local 34, 1984).

21 *The ACTWU Song-Book* (N.Y.: ACTWU, n.d.); *AFL-CIO Song Book* (Washington, D.C.: AFL-CIO Department of Education, 1974); *Songs for Labor* (AFL-CIO Department of Education, 1983); *The Labor Heritage Songbook* (Washington, D.C.: Labor Heritage Foundation, n.d.), 3; Julie McCall, *Camo Carols* (Washington, D.C.: Labor Heritage Foundation, 1989); McCall, *Songs Of Christmas Sneer* (Washington, D.C.: Labor Heritage Foundation, n.d.); McCall, *Christmas Carols for the War Zone* (Washington, D.C.: Labor Heritage Foundation, 1994).

22 Agnes Cunningham, *Broadside, Volume 2* (N.Y.: Oak Publications, 1968, 39, 65; A. Cuningham and A. Friesen, eds., *Broadside, Vol. III* (N.Y.: Oak Publications, 1970), 22; Jeff Place and Ronald D. Cohen, producers, *The Best of Broadside, 1962-1988: Anthems of the American Underground from the Pages of Broadside Magazine*, Smithsonian Folkways Recordings SFW CD 40130, 2000.

23 Irwin Silber, "La Huelga: Songs of The Delano Grape Strike," *Sing Out!*, vol. 16, no. 5 (November 1966), 4, 6; *Canciones/Songs* (np: UFW, n.d.); *Songbook/Canciones* (Austin: Education Department, Texas AFL-CIO, n.d.); *Boycott Now* (no publishing information); *Las Voces de Los Campesinos*, FMSC-1, 1978; *Viva La Causa: Songs and Sounds from the Delano Strike*, Thunderbird Records TR00001, 1966; *Si Se Puede*, Pan American Records PA101, 1976; *Huelga En General!*, El Centro Campesino Cultural TC1352, ca. 1975.

24 George Lipsitz, *Footsteps in the Dark: The Hidden Histories of Popular Music* (Minneapolis: University of Minnesota Press, 2007), xv, 74. The Labor Heritage Foundation, www.laborheritage.org, sells a wide variety of music CDs, for example by the Seattle Labor Chorus, NYC Labor Chorus, and Steel Choir of Bethlehem, PA, including many in Spanish. There is also the recent CD release *When Miners March: The Battle of Blair Mountain*, Mountainwhispers, 2008, which includes new recordings of songs about the 1921 United Mine Workers of America strike in Logan County, West Virginia; and Tom Breiding, *The Unbroken Circle: Songs of the West Virginia Coalfields*, AmeriSon 0807, 2008.

CIO Song Book (Washington, D.C.: CIO Department of Education and Research, 1951)

Index

Index

I

N

O

P

T

Y

Z

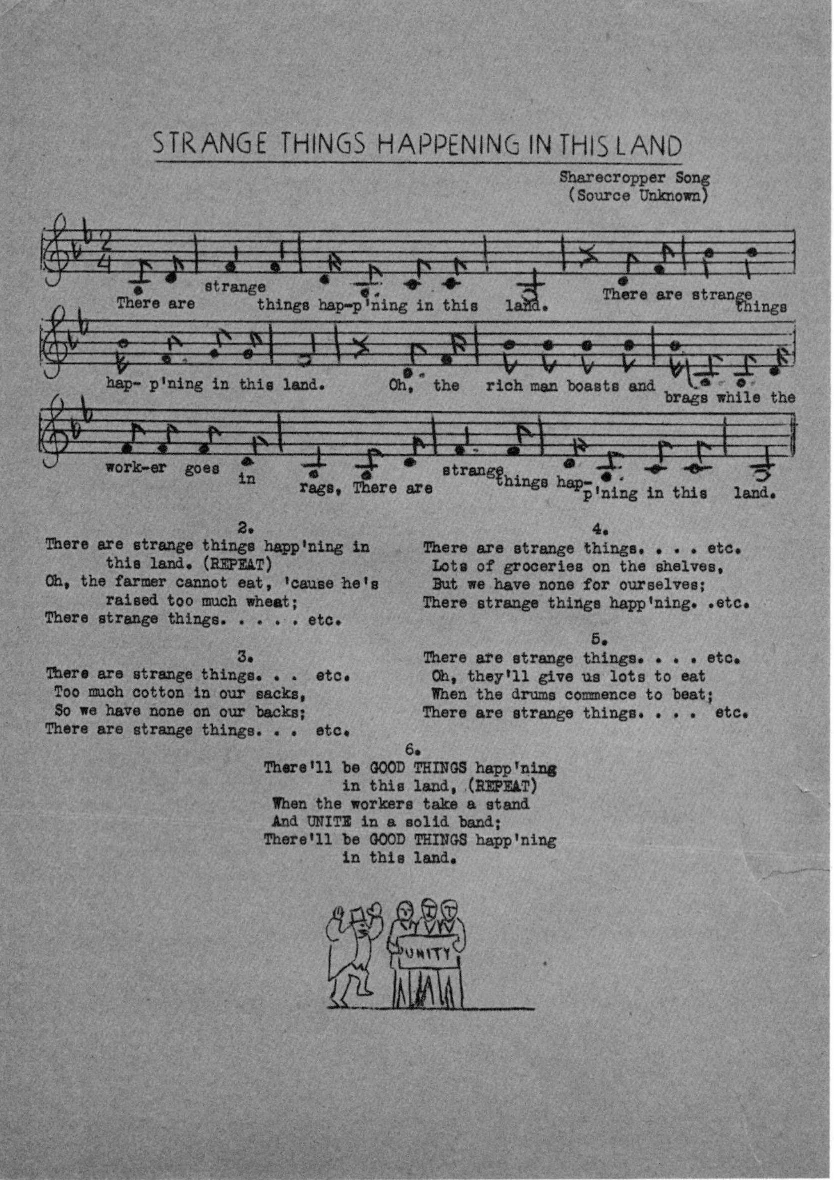

"Strange Things Happening In This Land," sheet music, 1948.

U.S. LABOR SONGBOOKS:
Bibliography, 20th Century

Note on selection procedure: I have tried to include all songbooks that I know about issued in the U.S. in the 20th century. I am defining labor songs to mean songs that basically refer to physical rather than mental work, that is work done by brawn rather than the brain. Some of these songbooks have been published by various labor unions, local and national, although many have not, particularly those dealing with cowboys, miners, lumberjacks, sailors, and other such employments. Many have been published commercially, while others appeared as mimeographed booklets, of various lengths, that would have had local, and probably limited, circulation. Some of these songbooks were connected with leftwing political parties, but are only included if they contain mostly work or union related songs. Leftwing songbooksthat were more politically focused have been excluded.

1 *The ACTWU Songbook*. N.Y.: ACTWU, nd 58 pp. (one version) and 68 pp. (second version). No music. (1) (first version) and (3)

2 AFL-CIO Department of Education. *Songs For Labor*. Washington, D.C.: AFL-CIO Publication No. 56, 1983. 56 pp. Includes music. (1)

3 *AFL-CIO Song Book*. Washington, D.C.: Department of Education, AFL-CIO, ca. 1956 (10th edition 1974). No music. (1)

4 Allan, Anne. *Sing America*. N.Y.: Workers Bookshop, ca. 1943. 62 pp. Includes music. (1)

5 Alloy, Evelyn. *Working Women's Music: The Songs and Struggles of Women in the Cotton Mills, Textile Plants and Needle Trades*. New England Free Press, 1976. 44 pps. Includes music. (1)

6 Almanac Singers. *Songs of the Almanac Singers, Book 1*. N.Y.: Bob Miller, 1942. 15 pps. Includes music. (1)

7 Almanac Singers. *Talking Union: 8 Union Songs of the Almanac Singers*. New York: New Theatre League, 1941. 8 pp. Includes music. (2)

8 *Amalgamated Song Book*. N.Y.: Amalgamated Clothing Workers of America-CIO, nd (1948). 31 pp. No music. (1) And other editions. (7)

9 Auville, Ray and Lida. *Songs of The American Worker*. Cleveland: John Reed Club, 1934. 5 pp. Includes music. (7)

10 Barry, Phillips. *Maine Woods Songster*. Cambridge: Powell Printing Company, 1939. 102 pp.

11 Beck, Earl Clifton. *Songs of the Michigan Lumberjacks*. Ann Arbor: University of Michigan Press, 1942. 296 pp. No music. (1)

12 Bogorad, Miriam et al. *Songs For America: American Ballad, Folk Songs, Marching Songs, Songs of Other Lands*. N.Y.: Workers Library Publishers, 1939. 64 pp. Includes music. (1)

13 *Boycott Now. ca.* 1960s. 12 pp. No music. (1)

14 Berkowitze, Edith, comp. *Song Book*. Np and nd ILGWU? 54 pp. (7)

15 *Brookwood Chautauqua Songs: A Singing Army Is a Winning Army.* Katonah, N.Y.: Brookwood Labor Publications, nd (ca. 1937). 23 pp. No music. (1) (There is also *Brookwood Chautaqua Song,* Np and nd 8 pp. No music. [3])

16 *Canciones: UFW Songs.* Np: El Taller Grafico, nd 12 pp. No music. In English and Spanish. (1)

17 *CIO Song Book.* Washington, DC: C.I.O. Dept. of Education and Research, 1951. 31 pp. No music. (1)

18 *CIO Songs.* Birmingham, Al: Birmingham Industrial Union Council, nd (1930s). 31 pp. No music. (1)

19 Colcord, Joanna C. *Roll and Go: Songs of American Sailormen.* Indianapolis: Bobbs-Merrill, 1924. 118 pp. Includes music. (1)

20 *Commonwealth Labor Hymnal.* Mena, Arkansas: Commonwealth College, 1938 [1940]. No music. (1)

21 *Commonwealth Labor Songs: A Collection of Old and New Songs For the Use of Labor Unions.* Mena, Arkansas: Commonwealth College, 1938. 10pp. No music. (1)

22 Cunningham, Agnes. *Six Labor Songs.* Mena, Arkansas: Commonwealth College, nd 8 pp. Includes music. (1)

23 Dickens, Hazel and Bill C. Malone, *Working Girl Blues: The Life and Music of Hazel Dickens.* Urbana: University of Illinois Press, 2008. 102 pp. No music. (1)

24 *District 65 Song Book.* Np: District 65 Distributing Workers of America, nd "Songs Reprinted From District 65's 1941 and 1952 Song Books." 22 pp. No music. (3)

25 *Dixie Union Songs.* Atlanta, Georgia: ILGWU, nd (4) and (7)

26 Doerflinger, William. *Shantymen and Shantyboys: Songs of the Sailor and Lumberman.* N.Y.: Macmillan Company, 1951. 374 pp. Includes music. (1)

27 Eckstorm, Fannie Hardy and Mary Winslow Smyth. *Minstrelsy of Maine: Folk-Songs and Ballads of the Woods and the Coast.* Boston: Houghton Mifflin Co., 1927. 390 pp. No music. (1)

28 Education Department, Texas AFL-CIO. *Songbook/Canciones.* Austin: Education Department, Texas AFL-CIO, ca. 1990. 20 pp. No music. (1)

29 *The Eastern Shuffle: Songs For the Eastern Picketline.* Washington, D.C.: Labor Heritage Foundation, nd 21 pp.

30 *Everybody Sings.* N.Y.: Educational Dept. ILGWU, 1942. 48 pp. No music.* And other editions. (7)

31 *Farmers Union Songs.* Jamestown, Np: Farmers' Educational and Cooperative Union of America, nd (5)

32 *Farmers Union Songs: Sung by the Williams Sisters Harmony Trio of Endicott, Nebraska at National and State Farmers Union Conventions and Local Meetings.* Fairbury, Nebraska: Np and nd. 11 pp. No music. (1)

33 Fife, Austin and Alta, eds. *Ballads of the Great West.* Palo Alto: American West Publishing Company, 1970. 272 pp. No music. (1)

34 Fife, Austin and Alta, eds. *Cowboy and Western Songs: A Comprehensive Anthology.* N.Y.: Bramhall House, 1982. 372 pp. Includes music. (1)

35 Finger, Charles J. *Sailor Chanties and Cowboy Songs.* Little Blue Book No. 301. Girard, Kansas: Haldeman-Julius Company, 1923. 64 pp. No music. (1)

36 *Finkelpuss Song Book.* Np: United Office & Professional Workers of America, 1938. 4 pp. No music. (3)

37 Foner, Philip S. *American Labor Songs of the Nineteenth Century.* Urbana: Univ. of Illinois Press, 1975. 356 pp. No music. (1)

38 Fowke, Edith and Joe Glazer. *Songs of Work and Freedom.* Chicago: Roosevelt University Press, 1960. 208 pp. Includes music. Republished as Fowke and Glazer, *Songs of Work and Protest.* N.Y.: Dover Publications, 1973. (1)

39 Friedman, Samuel H. *Rebel Song Book.* N.Y.: Rand School Press, 1935. 92 pp. Includes music. (1)

40 Frothingham, Robert, ed. *Songs of the Sea and Sailors' Shanties.* Boston: Houghton Mifflin, 1924.

41 Garon, Paul and Gene Tomko. *What's the Use of Walking if There's a Freight Train Going Your Way?: Black Hoboes & Their Songs.* Chicago: Charles H. Kerr, 2006. 288 pp. No music. (1)

42 Gelbart, Michael. *Let's Sing.* N.Y.: Education Department, Workmen's Circle, 1937-38. In Yiddish. (3)

43 Gellert, Lawrence. *"Me And My Captain": Chain Gang, Negro Songs of Protest.* N.Y.: Hours Press, 1939. 32 pp. Includes music. (1)

44 Gellert, Lawrence. *Negro Songs of Protest.* N.Y.: American Music League, 1936. 47 pp. Includes music. (1)

45 Geoghegan, J.B. *Down In a Coal Mine.* Philadelphia: Lee & Walker, nd (1)

46 Glazer, Joe. *Adapting Labor Songs For Every Occasion.* Prepared for the Labor Heritage Foundation, ca. 1995. 11 pp. No music. (1)

47 Glazer, Joe and Charlie King. *Carry It On: Historical Labor Music Song Swap.* 20th Annual Great Labor Arts Exchange, June 27-30, 1998. Includes music. (1)

48 Glazer, Joe. *Songs for AFSCME.* Washington, D.C.: American Federation of State, County and Municipal Employees, AFL-CIO, 1978, 64 pp. Includes music. (1)

49 Glazer, Joe. *Textile Voices: Songs From the Mills.* Chevy Chase, MD: Joe Glazer, 1988. 51 pp. Includes music. (1)

50 Goodenough, Caroline L. *Melodies of the People.* Des Moines, IA: Caroline L. Goodenough, nd [ca. 1920]. 32 pp.

51 Goodin, Virginia. *Sounds of the Lake and the Forest: Michigan Folk Songs.* Ann Arbor: Ann Arbor Press, 1960.

52 Gray, Roland Palmer. *Songs and Ballads of the Maine Lumberjacks.* Cambridge: Harvard University Press, 1924. 191 pp. No music. (1)

53 Green, Archie et al, eds. *The Big Red Songbook.* Chicago: Charles H. Kerr Publishing Co., 2007. 538 pp. No music. (1)

54 Greenway, John. *American Folksongs of Protest.* Philadelphia: Univ. of Pennsylvania Press, 1953. 348 pp. Many songs, a few with music, as well as text. (1)

55 Guthrie, Woody. *Three Songs For Centralia.* N.Y.: People's Songs, Inc., 1947. 4 pp. Includes music. (1)

56 Harlow, Frederick Pease. *Chanteying Aboard American Ships.* Mystic, CT: Mystic Seaport Museum, 2004 (original ed. 1962). 250 pp. Includes music. (1)

57 Harris, Rose, ed. *Sing, Juniors, Sing.* [NY]: International Workers Order, Junior Section, ca. 1930s. 56 pp. Includes music.

58 Helfman, Max, ed. *Gezang un Kamf* (Repertoire for Chorus). N.Y.: Jewish Workers Musical Alliance, 1938. #6. 116 pp. Yiddish and Hebrew.

59 Helfman, Max, ed. *Gezang un Kamf* (A Book of Contemporary Choruses). N.Y.: Jewish Music Alliance, 1940. #8. 94 pp. Yiddish and Hebrew.

60 *The History of the ILGWU In Song and Poem: A Sequence of Narrative, Group Singing and Poetry Reading.* N.Y.: Educational Dept., ILGWU, 1957. (7)

61 *The Hobo In Song and Poetry*. Cincinnati: V.C. Anderson, nd 24 pp. No music. (1)

62 *Hobo: Songs, Poems, Ballads, Recitations, Etc.* Cincinnati: Hobo-College Press Committee, nd 16 pp. No music. (3)

63 Hoffman, Alice M. *Sing a Song of Unsung Heroes and Heroines: Stories and Songs of Pennsylvania Labor Pioneers*. [State College]: Dept. of Labor Studies, Pennsylvania State University, 1986. 71 pp. No music. (1)

64 Horton, Zilphia. *Labor Songs*. N.Y.: Textile Workers Union of America, 1939. 64 pp. No music. (1)

65 Hudson Shore Labor School. *Lift Every Voice and Sing*. Np: Hudson Shore Labor School, 1941. (7)

66 *Hudson Labor School Song Book*. Np and nd, 1939. Mimeo. 53 pp. Includes music. (3)

67 Hugill, Stan. *Shanties and Sailors' Songs*. N.Y.: Praeger Publishers, 1969. 243 pp. Includes music. (1)

68 Hullfish, William. *The Canaller's Songbook*. York, PA: The American Canal and Transportation Center, 1984. 88 pp. Includes music (1)

69) Huntington, Gale. *Songs the Whalemen Sang*. Barre, MA: Barre Publishing Company, 1964. 331 pp. Includes music. (1)

70 *ICW Song Book*. Akron, OH: Research & Education Dept., International Chemical Workers Union, AFL-CIO, CLC, nd (7)

71 *I.W.O. Lodge 551: Songs For Victory*. Np and nd 5 pp. No music (1)

72 *Industrial Department Song Book*. Philadelphia: Y.W.C.A., nd. (7)

73 Industrial Workers of the World. *I.W.W. Songs: To Fan the Flames of Discontent* (*Songs of the Workers* inside title). Cleveland: I.W.W. Publishing Bureau, December 1914, Joe Hill Edition. 60 pp. No music; same, Chicago: Industrial Workers of the World, 1956. 29th ed. 64 pp. No music. (1) (These are two of many editions, first published in 1909 in Spokane, Washington.) For almost all early editions. (7)

74 Ives, Edward D. *Larry Gorman: The Man Who Made the Songs*. Bloomington: Indiana University Press, 1964. 225 pp. Includes music. (1)

75 Jackson, Bruce, ed. *Wake Up Dead Man: Hard Labor and Southern Blues*. Athens: University of Georgia Press, 1999 (original ed. 1972). 326 pp. Includes music. (1)

76 *Keep the Union Singing: UAW Song Book*. Detroit: UAW Education Department, 1979. 19 pp. No music. (1)

77 Kerr, Charles H. *Socialist Songs*. Chicago: Charles H. Kerr, ca. 1910 [orig.pub. 1899]. 30 pp. No music. (1)

78 Kerr, Charles H. *Socialist Songs With Music*. Chicago: Charles H. Kerr, 1902. Fourth ed. 46 pp. Includes music. (1)

79 Korson, George. *Black Rock: Mining Folklore of the Pennsylvania Dutch*. Baltimore: Johns Hopkins Press, 1960. 452 pp. Includes music. (1)

80 Korson, George. *Coal Dust On the Fiddle: Songs and Stories of the Bituminous Industry*. Philadelphia: University of Pennsylvania Press, 1943. 460 pp. No music. (1)

81 Korson, George. *Minstrels of the Mine Patch*. Philadelphia: University of Pennsylvania Press, 1938. 332 pp. Some music. (1)

82 Korson, George, ed. *Pennsylvania Songs and Legends*. Baltimore: The Johns Hopkins Press, 1949. 474 pp. Includes music. (1)

83 Korson, George. *Songs and Ballads of the Anthracite Miner*. N.Y.: Frederick H. Hitchcock/Grafton Press, 1927. 196 pp. (1)

84 Kurtz, Louis. *Songs of the Fighting Farmers*. Farmers' National Conference, Chicago, Nov. 15-18,

1933. No music.

85 Labor Heritage Foundation. *The Labor Heritage Songbook.* Washington, D.C.: Labor Heritage Foundation, nd 79 pp. Includes music. (1)

86 *Labor Sings.* N.Y.: Educational Dept., ILGWU, 1940. 28 pp. No music. (3)

87 *Labor Sings: Presented to Delegates at the Fortieth Anniversary Convention, International Ladies' Garment Workers Union, by the ILGWU Locals of New York City, May 27-June 7, 1940.* N.Y.: Educational Dept., International Ladies' Garment Workers' Union, 1940. (7) (Perhaps same as previous listing.)

88 *Labor Sings With the United Labor Party.* Np: Educational Dept., United Labor Party of America, nd (7)

89 *Labor Songs For All Occasions.* Madison: Univ. of Wisconsin Songbooks For Summer Sessions, 1938, 1940.

90 Larkin, Margaret. *Singing Cowboys: A Book of Western Songs.* N.Y.: Alfred A. Knopf, 1931. 196 pp. Includes music. (1)

91 Lee, Katie. *Ten Thousand Goddam Cattle: A History of the American Cowboy In Song, Story and Verse.* Flagstaff, AZ: Northland Press, 1976. Albuquerque, NM: University of New Mexico Press, 3rd printing rev., 1985. 257 pp. No music. (1)

92 LeMon, Melvin and George Korson. *The Miner Sings: A Collection of Folk-Songs and Ballads of the Anthracite Miner.* N.Y.: J. Fischer & Bro., 1936. Includes music. (1)

93 *Let the People Sing.* Madison: Univ. of Wisconsin Summer School for Workers, 1941. (4)

94 *Let's All Sing.* L.A.: Education Dept., Pacific Coast Office, ILGWU, 1950s. (7)

95 *Let's Sing!* N.Y.: Educational Dept., International Ladies' Garment Workers' Union, nd (late 1930s). 32 pp. No music. (1)

96 *Let's Sing.* Monteagle, TN: Highlander Folk School, 1937. (4)

97 *Let's Sing.* Np: UAW, 1962. (7)

98 *Let's Sing.* Np: Industrial Department, nd Mimeo. 47 pp. No music. (1)

99 *L.I.D. Songs.* N.Y.: League For Industrial Democracy, 1923 + 1925. 4 pp. No music. (3)

100 Liebich, Rudolph. *March of the Workers and Other Songs.* Chicago: Young Workers League of America, ca. 1925. 68 pp. Includes music. Large format. (3) And see below under title.

101 Liebich, Rudolph. *Proletarian Song Book of Lyrics From the Operetta The Last Revolution by Michael Gold & J. Ramirez.* Chicago: Local Chicago Workers Party of America, nd (7)

102 Lingenfelter, Richard and Richard Dwyer, eds. *Songs of the American West.* Berkeley: University of California Press, 1968. 595 pp. Includes music.

103 *Local 34 Songbook.* New Haven: Yale University, Local 34, 1984. 16 pp.

104 Logsdon, Guy, ed. *"The Whorehouse Bells Were Ringing" and Other Songs Cowboys Sing.* Urbana: University of Illinois Press, 1989. 388 pp. Includes music. (1)

105 Lomax, Alan, Pete Seeger and Woody Guthrie. *Hard Hitting Songs For Hard-Hit People.* N.Y.: Oak Publications, 1967. 368 pp. Includes music. (1)

106 Lomax, John. *Cowboy Songs and Other Frontier Ballads.* N.Y.: Sturgis Walton, 1917. 414 pp. Includes music. (1) (Originally published in 1910)

107 Lomax, John and Alan. *Cowboy Songs and Other Frontier Ballads.* N.Y.: Macmillan Company, 1938, expanded and enlarged. 431 pp. Includes music. (1)

108 McCall, Julie. *Christmas Carols for the War Zone.* Washington, D.C.: Labor Heritage Foundation,

1994. 16 pp.

109 McCall, Julie. *Como Carols*. Washington, D.C.: Labor Heritage Foundation, 1989. 18 pp. No music. Illustrations by Mike Konopacki. (1)

110 McCall, Julie. *Songs Of Christmas Sneer, Or How Marc Grinch Stole Christmas*. Pittsburgh: United Steelworkers of America, AFL-CIO/CLC, ca. 1991. 16 pp. No music. Illustrations by Mike Konopacki. (1)

111 *Madison Hotel: Songs for Christmas Cheer*. Np and nd 18 pp.

112 *Maine Stands United; Rieve and His Administration: Convention Songs*. Portland, ME: Bryant Press, 1952, 16 pp. No music. (1)

113 *March and Sing*. N.Y.: American Music League, 1937. 16 pp. No music, with one exception. (1)

114 *The March of the Workers and Other Songs*. Chicago: Young Workers League of America, ca. 1925. 48 pp. No music. (1) (Another edition has 62 pp. and music. [5])

115 Marks, Gerald and Milton Pascal. *Sing a Labor Song*. N.Y.: Gerald Marks Music, Inc., ca. 1950. 18 pp. Includes music. (3)

116 Meeropol, Anne, ed. *Sing With the Union*. [N.Y.]: New York State Federation of Teachers Unions, nd but ca. 1940. 32 pp. No music. (2)

117 Milburn, George. *The Hobo's Hornbook: Repertory for a Gutter Jongleur*. N.Y.: Ives Washburn, 1930. 295 pp. Includes some music. (1)

118 *Militant Songbook*. L.A.: Westcoast Workers Vacation School, 1954. (7)

119 Morgan, Elizabeth. *Socialist and Labor Songs of the 1930s*. Chicago: Charles H. Kerr, 1997. 82 pp. Includes music. (1)

120 Moyer, Harvey P. *Songs of Socialism*. Chicago: Co-Operative Printing Co., 1911 [orig. pub. 1905]. 97 pp. Includes music. (1)

121 Murdock, Lee. *Lake Rhymes: Folk Songs of the Great Lakes Region*. Np: Depot Recording Publications, 2004, 146 pp.

122 *National Farmers' Union Annual Convention* program. Kankakee, IL: National Farmer's Union, November 19-20, 1935. Includes 6 pp. of songs. No music. (1)

123 *New Songs for Butte Mining Camp*. Butte, Montana: Century Printing Co., ca. 1920. No music. (7)

124 Odum, Howard W. and Guy B. Johnson. *The Negro and His Songs: A Study of Typical Negro Songs in the South*. Chapel Hill: University of North Carolina Press, 1925. 306 pp. No music. (1)

125 Odum, Howard W. and Guy B. Johnson. *Negro Workaday Songs*. Chapel Hill: University of North Carolina Press, 1926. 278 pp. No music. (1)

126 Ohrlin, Glenn. *The Hell-Bound Train: A Cowboy Songbook*. Urbana: University of Illinois Press, 1973. 290 pp. Includes music. (1)

127 *Palkkaorjain Lauluja* (Wage Slave Songbook). Duluth, Minn.: Workers Society Publishing Co., 1925. (7)

128 Patterson, Charles. *Paint Creek Miner: Famous Labor Songs from Appalachia*. Huntington, WV: Appalachia Movement Press, 1970. 20 pp. No music. (1)

129 *The Pavement Trail: A Collection of Poetry & Prose From the Allis-Chalmers Picket Lines*. West Allis, WI: Local 248, United Automobile Workers of America, CIO, nd 30 pp. Includes a few songs but no music. (3)

130 *Pennsylvania Folk Songs and Ballads For School Camp and Playground*. Lewisburg: Pennsylvania Folk Festival, 1937. 13 pp. Includes music. (1)

131 *Peoples Sing: 100 International Ghetto, Resistance, Negro, Labor, Folk, Youth Songs*. N.Y.: Peoples

Sing, Pub., 1950. 72 pp. No music. Half in Yiddish. (1)

132 Peoples Songs. *Sing*! N.Y.: Workers Bookshop, 1947. 64 pp. No music. (1)

133 *Picket Line Songs*. Andalusia, Alabama: Local #489-A.C.W.A., 1946. (4)

134 Potamkin, Harry Alan. *Pioneer Song Book: Songs For Workers' and Farmers' Children*. N.Y.: New Pioneer Publishing Co., 1933. 30 pp. Includes music. (2)

135 *Proletaarilauluja Songbook*. Duluth: Np, 1918.

136 Proletarian Notes, *Let's Sing*. 12 pp. No music. (1)

137 *Red Song Book*. N.Y.: Workers Library Publishers, 1932. 32 pp. Includes music. (1)

138 Richards, Bob. *The Miner's Song*. N.Y.: Quality Music, ca. 1947. (7)

139 Rickaby, Franz, ed. *Ballads and Songs of the Shanty-Boy*. Cambridge: Harvard University Press, 1926. 244 pp. Includes music. (1)

140 Robinson, Earl. *America Sings*. N.Y.: Workers Bookshop, ca. 1939. 62 pp. No music. (1)

141 *"Roll the Union On": Songs for UAW Members*. Detroit: UAW Education Department, nd 24 pps.

142 Schaefer, Jacob, ed. *Gezang un Kamf*. N.Y.: Jewish Workers Musical Alliance, 1935. #3. 66 pp. Yiddish and Hebrew.

143 Schaefer, Jacob, ed. *Gezang un Kamf*. N.Y.: Jewish Workers Musical Alliance, 1936. #4. 72 pp. Yiddish and Hebrew.

144 Schaefer, Jacob, comp. *Mit Gezang Tzum Kamf* (Songs for Voice and Piano). N.Y: International Workers Order, 1932. 100 pp. Yiddish and Hebrew with four in English. Includes music. (1)

145 Schaefer, Jacob. *22 Selected Songs of Jacob Schaefer--Ich Heer A Kol*. Foreword by Chaim Suller. 1st ed. 1952. N. Y.: Jewish Music Alliance, 1952. 176 pp. Yiddish and English. (1)

146 *The School For Workers Song Book*. Madison: The University of Wisconsin School for Workers, nd 40 pp. No music. (1)

147 Seeger, Pete and Bob Reiser. *Carry It On: A History In Songs and Picture of the Working Men and Women of America*. N.Y.: Simon and Schuster, 1985. 256 pp. Includes music. (1)

148 Shay, Frank. *Iron Men and Wooden Ships*. N.Y.: Doubleday, Page, & Co., 1924. 154 pp.

149 Shoemaker, Henry W. *North Pennsylvania Minstrelsy*. Altoona, PA: Altoona Tribune Company, 1919. 158 pp. No music. (1)

150 Siegmeister, Elie. *Work & Sing: A Collection of the Songs That Built America*. N.Y.: William R. Scott, Inc., 1944. 96 pp. Includes music. (1)

151 *Sing*. Np: Educational Department, United Oil and Petroleum Workers of America, nd (4)

152 *Sing!*. N.Y.: Workers Party and Young Peoples Socialist League, nd 19 pp. No music. (1)

153 *Sing: Labor and Socialist Songs*. Los Angeles: Workers Party, Los Angeles Section, 1945. 18 pp. No music. (1)

154 *Sing A Labor Song*. N.Y.: Gerald Marks Music, Inc. 1950. (4)

155 *Sing Amalgamated*. Chicago: The Amalgamated Meet Cutters and Butcher Workmen of N.A., Dept. of Research and Education, nd 49 pp. (7)

156) *Sing, Amalgamated: A Book of Songs for Picket Lines, Meetings, Parties, and Other Union Occasions*. N.Y.: Amalgamated Clothing Workers of America, 1940. 20 pp. No music. (1)

157 *Sing, America: Song Book of the United Rubber Workers of America*. Akron, Ohio: Dept. of Education and Research, United Rubber Workers of America, nd (4)

158 *Sing! UAW-CIO Songs.* Detroit: Education Dept., UAW, nd 4 pp. No music. (2)

159 *Sing A Union Song.* Chicago: United Packinghouse Workers of America-CIO, 1955. 38 pp. No music. (7)

160 *Sing For Victory.* N.Y.: International Workers Order, 1942.

161 *Sing Out Brother.* Monteagle, Tenn.: Highlander Folk School, ca. 1946. 55 pp. Includes music. (1)

162 *Sing While You Fight.* N.Y.: Recreation Dept. of Wholesale & Warehouse Employees Local 65, U.R.W.E.A., CIO, nd [1942]. 48 pp. No music. (3)

163 *Singing Farmers: A Songbook of the Farmers Educational and Cooperative Union of America.* Denver: National Farmers Union, 1947.

164 Siringo, Charles. *The Song Companion of a Lone Star Cowboy: Old Favorite Cow-Camp Songs.* Santa Fe, N.M.: C.A. Siringo, 1919 (reprinted 1974).

165 *Solidarity Forever: Songs for UMWA members on strike against the Pittston Coal Company.* Washington, D.C.: UMWA Organizing Department, ca. 1989. 18 pp. No music. (1)

166 *Song and Struggle.* N.Y.: Jewish Workers Musical Alliance, 1938.

167 *Song Book.* Washington, D.C.: Communications Workers of America, CIO, nd. (7)

168 *Song Book.* Seattle: Pacific Coast School for Workers, 1938 (see 183 for later edition).

169 *Song Book.* Washington, D.C.: Union Label and Services Trades Department, AFL-CIO, nd 48 pp. Includes music.

170 *Song Book.* Np: UOPWA-CIO, nd Mimeo. 16 pp. No music. (1)

171 *Song Book.* Np: Abraham Lincoln School (UOPWA-CIO), nd 32 pp. No music. (1)

172 *Song Book For Workers.* N.Y.: Red Star Publicity Service, 1932. 13 pp. No music. (1)

173 *Song Book of the ILGWU.* L.A.: Educational Dept., International Garment Workers' Union, 195-? (7)

174 *Songs.* Katonah: Brookwood Labor College, nd (7)

175 *Songs.* N.Y.: Textile Workers Organizing Committee of the CIO, nd 8 pp. No music. (1)

176 *Songs: Knowledge Is Power.* N.Y.: Educational Dept., ILGWU, nd 4 pp. Music. (1)

177 *Songs About Labor.* Monteagle, TN: Highlander Folk School, nd (4)

178 *Songs and Class Struggle.* N.Y.: Red Star Publicity Service, nd 22 pp. No music. (3)

179 *Songs: First International Congress of Working Women.* Washington, D.C. October 1919. Chicago: National Women's Trade Union League of America, 1919. 15 pp. No music. (3)

180 *Songs For Action.* N.Y.: Amalgamated Clothing & Textile Workers Union, 1977. 48 pp.

181 *Songs For Labor.* Np: Education Dept., UAW, 1962. (7)

182 *Songs For Labor.* Np: Research and Education Dept., Oil Workers Intl. Union-CIO, nd (late 1940s). 19 pp. No music. (1)

183 *Songs For Labor.* Forth Worth, Texas: Oil Workers International Union, 1942. (This could be an earlier printing of #182.)

184 *Songs For May Day.* Chicago: Chicago May Day Committee, 1957. (7)

185 *Songs For Rebel Workers.* Chicago: Chicago General Membership Branch, Industrial Workers of the World, (1976?). (7)

186 *Songs For Seamen.* N.Y.: National Maritime Union, CIO, 1947. 10 pp. No music. (1)

187 *Songs For Victory*. 3rd edition of *Sing While You Fight*. N.Y.: Recreation Dept. of Wholesale & Warehouse Workers Union, Local 65, URWDSEA, CIO, 1942. 48 pp.

188 *Songs for Workers*. Monteagle, TN: Highlander Folk School, 1939. (4)

189 *Songs for Workers*. Reading, PA: United Workers' Federation, nd (7)

190 *Songs of Field and Factory*. Monteagle, TN: Highlander Folk School, 1940. (4) and (5)

191 *Songs of Freedom: Famous Labor Songs from Appalachia, Part II*. Huntington, WV: Appalachia Movement Press, nd 17 pp. Includes music. (1)

192 *Songs [of] Labor, Folk, War*. Monteagle, TN: Highlander Folk School, 1943. 54 pp. (4)

193 *Songs of Struggle*. N.Y.: Workers Bookshop, nd 28 pp. (2)

194 *Songs of Struggle*. N.Y.: Workers Bookshop, late 1930s. 60 pp. No music. Half in English, half in Yiddish. (1)

195 *Songs of the Class Struggle...In Memory of Ella May Wiggins & Steve Katovis*. Np: Workers' International Relief, 1929. 16 pp.

196 *Songs of the People*. N.Y.: Workers Library Publishers, 1937. 64 pp. Includes music. (1)

197 *Songs of the Soil*. Monteagle, TN: Highlander Folk School, nd (4)

198 *Songs of the Southern Mills*. Mineral Bluff, Georgia: Cut Cane Associates, 1972. (7)

199 *Songs of the Southern School for Workers*. Asheville, NC: Southern School for Workers, 1940. (4) and (7)

200 *Songs of the Southern Summer School*. Monteagle, TN: Highlander Folk School, 1938. (4) and other copies (7)

201 *Songs of Work*. Pittsfield, MA: Shaker Village Work Camp, 1954. 40 pp. Includes music. (3)

202 *Songs Our Union Taught Us*. N.Y.: Educational Dept. ILGWU, [1938?]. 26 pp. Includes music. (1)

203 Songs to Fight By. Washington, D.C.: United Federal Workers of America, 2nd Constitutional Convention, [1942]. No music. (2)

204 *Southern School for Union Women, Songbook*. Lexington: Center for Labor Education and Research, University of Kentucky, 1982. (7)

205 Stavis, Barrie and Frank Harmon [aka Fred Hellerman]. *The Songs of Joe Hill*. N.Y.: People's Artists, 1955 [reprinted N.Y.: Oak Publications, 1960]. 46 pp. Includes music. (1)

206 *Steelworkers' Song Book*. Pittsburgh: Dept. of Education, United Steelworkers of America, 1950s. 34 pp. (1)

207 Stevens, John. *Songs of Labor*. Huntington, Arkansas: Herald Publishing Co., nd (1930s). 36 pp. No music. (3)

208 *Song Book*. Memphis, TN: Educational Dept., Southern Tenant Farmers' Union *STFU*, nd (4)

209 *Strike Songs*. Prepared by ILGWU Training Institute. Np: The Institute, 1951. (7)

210 Tallmadge, James and Emily. *Labor Songs: Labor Songs Dedicated to the Knights of Labor*. Chicago, 1886.

211 *Taxi Rank & File Coalition Songbook, 3rd Edition*. N.Y.: Taxi Rank & File Coalition, 1974. (1)

212 *Texas AFL-CIO, Education Department Songbook*. Austin: Texas AFL-CIO, nd (7)

213 Thomas, Philip J. *Songs of the Pacific Northwest*. Saanichton, B.C.: Hancock House Publishers Ltd., 1979. 176 pp. Includes music. (1)

214 Thorp, N. Howard "Jack." *Songs of the Cowboys*. Estancia, N.M.: News Print Shop, 1908. Reprinted and enlarged, Boston: Houghton Mifflin Co., 1921. 184 pp. No music. (1)

215 Tinsley, Jim Bob. *He Was Singin' This Song: A Collection of Forty-eight Traditional Songs of the American Cowboy, with Words, Music, Pictures, and Stories*. Orlando: University Presses of Florida, 1981. 255 pp. Includes music. (1)

216 *TWUA Songs*. N.Y.: Textile Workers Union of America Education Dept., 1951. 32 pp. No music. (3) And other editions. (7)

217 *TWUA-CIO Songs: For Union Hall and Picket Line*. N.Y.: Education Dept., Textile Workers Union of America, CIO, 1947. (7)

218 *UAW-CIO Sings*. Detroit: UAW-CIO Education Dept., [1943]. 60 pp. Includes music. (1)

219 *UAW CIO Union Songs*. Detroit: UAW-CIO Education Dept., 194-? (7)

220 *URW Song Book*. Akron, OH: Education Dept., United Rubber, Cork, Linoleum and Plastic Workers of America, AFL-CIO, 1951. 39 pp. No music. Also other editions. (7)

221 *Uusi Työväen Laulukirja*. Hancockissa, Michigan: Työmiehen Kustannusyhtiön, 1910. 132 pp. And a different version: *Uusi Työväen Laulukirja (A New Songbook for Workers)*. Superior, Wisconsin: Työmies Kustannusyhtiön kustannuksella, 1915. 190 pp. No music. (1)

222 *Victory Songs of Labor*. N.Y.: Young People's Socialist League, nd 16 pp. No music. (3)

223 *Victory Verses For Young Americans*. N.Y.: Young American Volunteer's Service—International Workers Order, ca. 1943. 24 pp. Includes some music. (1)

224 *Vihan Vassamia*. Duluth, MN: Workers Socialist Pub. Co., ca. 1919. (7)

225 Vincent, Elmore. *Elmore Vincent's Lumber Jack Songs*. Chicago: M. M. Cole Publishing Co., 1932. 64 pp. Includes music. (1)

226 Walton, Ivan. *Windjammers: Songs of the Great lakes Sailors*. Detroit: Wayne State University Press, 2002. 267 pp.

227 Wassermann, Caroline, comp. *Song Book of the Pacific Coast School for Workers*. Berkeley: Pacific Coast School for Workers, 3rd ed., 1939. 32 pp. No music. (1)

228 West, Don. *Songs for Kentucky Workers*. Lexington: Kentucky Workers Alliance, 1936. (Originally mimeographed, then published as *Songs for Southern Workers*, see below.)

229 West, Don. *Songs for Southern Workers*. Lexington: Kentucky Workers Alliance, 1937. [23 pp.] Republished: Huntington, WV: Appalachian Movement Press, 1973. No music. (1)

230 Wheeler, Mary. *Roustabout Songs: A Collection of Ohio River Valley Songs*. N.Y.: Remick Music Corp., 1939. 48 pp. Includes music. (2)

231 Wheeler, Mary. *Steamboatin' Days: Folk Songs of the River Packet Era*. Baton Rouge: Louisiana State University Press, 1944. 121 pp. Includes music (1)

232 *Which Side Are You On? Our Songs, Our Struggles, Our Union*. Washington,D.C.: United Mine Workers of America, 1980s. 17 pp. (7)

233 White, John I. *Git Along, Little Dogies: Songs and Songmakers of the American West*. Urbana: University of Illinois Press, 1975. 221 pp. Includes music. (1)

234 Williams, J.A. *The Revolution In Song and Story*. Sawtelle, CA: By the Editor and Compiler, nd 46 pp. No music. (3)

235 Wilson, Harry R. *Singing Farmers: A Songbook of the Farmers Educational and Cooperative Union of America*. Denver: National Farmers Union, ca. 1947. (7)

236 Workers Party & Labor Action. *May Day Songbook: Fifth Anniversary*. ca. 1945, 2 pp. (1)

237 *Workers' Song Book, 1*. N.Y.: Workers Music League, 1934. 32 pp. Includes music. (1)

238 *Workers Song Book, 2.* N.Y.: Workers Music League, 1935. 48 pp. Includes music. (1)

239 *Workers Songs.* Nashville, TN: Textile Workers Organizing Committee, nd (4)

240 *Workers' Songs.* Monteagle, TN: Highlander Folk School, 1935. (4)

241 *Workers' Songs.* Katonah: Brookwood Labor College, 1934.

242 *Workers Songs.* S.F.: Friends of the Soviet Union, nd 24 pp. No music. (1)

243 *YCLA Song Book.* N.Y.: Young Circle League (Youth Section of Workmen's Circle), nd 30 pp. No music. (3)

244 *Yiddish Songs of Work and Struggle.* N.Y.: Jewish Students' Bund Production, 1972.

245 *The YPSL Sings.* N.Y.: Young People's Socialist League, nd (7)

246 *Y.P.S.L. Song Book.* N.Y.: Cultural Circle, N.Y.Y.P.S.L., ca. late 1930s. 22 pp. No music. (1)

247 Young People's Socialist League. *Socialist Songs For Young and Old.* N.Y.: Young People's Socialist League, ca. 1910. 15 pp. No music. (1)

248 *Young People's Socialist League Song Book.* N.Y.: Young People's Socialist League, nd 24 pp. No music. (1)

249 Young People's Socialist League. *Songs of Solidarity and Struggle: 11th National Convention.* [N.Y.]: YPSL, nd (7)

250 Young Pioneers of America. *Pioneer Songs and Cheers.* New York: National Pioneer Buro, 1930. 9 pp. No music. (6)

SOURCES:

Denisoff, R. Serge. *Songs of Protest, War & Peace: A Bibliography & Discography*. Santa Barbara, Calif.: ABC-Clio, 1973.

Reuss, Richard A. "American Folklore and Left-Wing Politics: 1927-1957." Unpub. PhD diss., Indiana University, 1971.

We would like to thank the following for their assistance: Charlie Maiorana, Clark "Bucky" Halker, Archie Green, Gail Malmgreen, Andrew Lee, Hillel Arnold, Irwin Silber, Paul Mishler, Steve Weiss, Saul Schniderman, Bill Friedland, and others.

For earlier labor songs see Philip S. Foner, *American Labor Songs of the Nineteenth Century* (Urbana: University of Illinois Press, 1975), and Clark D. Halker, *For Democracy, Workers, and God: Labor Song-Poems and Labor Protest, 1865-95* (Urbana: University of Illinois Press, 1991), both of which include helpful bibliographies.

(1) Cohen has original

(2) Cohen has copy

(3) Held by Tamiment Library, Bobst Library, New York University

(4) Held by Zilphia Horton Folk Music Collection, Manuscript Division, Tennessee State Library and Archives Nashville, TN

(5) Held by Irwin Silber, and now in the Southern Folklife Collection, University of North Carolina-Chapel Hill

(6) Held by Paul Mishler

(7) Held by Archie Green collection, Rare Book Collection, University of North Carolina-Chapel Hill